About the Author

At just sixteen years old, everyone's life is just beginning, but not for John, it was ending! There is however a fifty/fifty chance that his whole right leg would be amputated. This fateful decision starts the journey few have undertaken, but how does it impact his family, friends, work, and the rest of his life, holistically transitioning from being able-bodied to disabled?

They Want to Amputate

John Paffett

They Want to Amputate

Olympia Publishers
London

www.olympiapublishers.com
OLYMPIA PAPERBACK EDITION

A CIP catalogue record for this title is
available from the British Library.

ISBN: 978-1-80074-512-4

First Published in 2023

Olympia Publishers
Tallis House
2 Tallis Street
London
EC4Y 0AB

Printed in Great Britain

Dedication

This book is dedicated to my beautiful wife, Brenda, for prompting me many times to write this book but like many a good husband, I just would not listen!

Acknowledgements

Thank you to my family, for your help and support along life's road, reminding me of all the love we shared and continue to.

Introduction

I thought I was getting better, the wound had healed, even though the painful spasms were there and getting worse. Mum and Dad had been to the hospital to see the consultant to discuss me; they looked terribly upset upon their return as they entered our small living room and said those haunting words to me, 'They want to amputate your leg, John'.

I was brought up in a loving home with my brother, Arthur, and my sister, Margaret. We were relatively poor but there was a lot of fun and laughter. I had a great childhood but at eleven years of age, the first pain in my groin started with no clear diagnosis given. Over the next four years, as the pain continued to get worse, there was uncertainty and no clear diagnosis. At fifteen I had a biopsy, which did not find anything amiss and led to the consultant saying that I was just trying to get off from school as there was nothing wrong with me. At sixteen the tumour appeared, they operated and tried to remove it but could not get rid of it entirely. I was given four to six months to live and my parents were told that I was inoperable. Three weeks later, I was examined by two different consultants, who had reviewed my case and my parents were told by that there was a fifty-fifty chance of success if I had my leg amputated. The decision was eventually left for me to make; life was sweet, death unknown – so I chose amputation.

The cancer was so far spread in my leg they had to

perform a hemipelvectomy, which involved the removal of the whole right leg and part of the hip bone. It is the rarest of lower extremity amputations and I was told at the time there were only two cases like mine a year in the whole of England. My journey through life was now going to be far different, far more difficult and challenging than it might otherwise have been. Sometimes, you must smile in the face of adversity because I had to learn to walk again, manage pain and manage to have a disability with the stigma that entailed at the time for someone so young.

I met Ann when I was nineteen, who fully accepted my disability, and I married her just over a year later. We waited six years before starting a family and had three lovely children. It was a wonderful time of our lives, hectic but rewarding. After having four related engineering jobs by the age of twenty-seven, I eventually found one I really enjoyed at John Brown Engineering, staying there for most of my working life.

Walking was both difficult and painful, but I persevered and managed to develop my own gait and way of walking, as limiting as it was. During the many hospital maintenance visits to get my artificial leg repaired I met many characters from all walks of life. In the waiting room for numerous hours, I had the opportunity to talk to many people with similar problems and their stories unfolded along with the problems they had but, in most cases, their stoic approach to life shone through with the indomitable human spirit inside all of us.

If I wanted to have a career progression in the company I had joined, then I needed to visit construction sites and spend time there during this latter phase of a project. This entailed being away from home for some time, but it was necessary. Many visits entailed a lot of walking for me and stretched me to my physical limits, but this was balanced with the unique experiences gained, the people I met and the places I travelled to around the world.

Ann developed breast cancer at thirty-seven years of age and the traumatic events of this progressive illness for the whole family, which we all went through, left their indelible mark following her untimely death at the relatively young age of forty-four. Ann's death was just eleven days short of our Silver Wedding Anniversary and a truly devastating event along life's road, which we all keep adjusting to every day. It broke my heart.

I later met Brenda who brought new meaning and love into my life from those dark days. We married six years later and despite what I had previously thought, you can fall in love again no matter what age you are. Her sense of humour, kindness, loyalty, fun and spirit of adventure is a perfect fit as we enter the autumn of our lives, walking hand in hand, growing young together.

Chapter 1:
Early Carefree Days

I am a Portsmuthian or known locally as a Pompey boy, born and bred in a local area known as Buckland. I live in the far south of England in a city called Portsmouth and can trace my family origins back to 1759, so far, I might add.

I was born in St. Mary's Hospital in 1950 and was part of the post-war baby-boomer generation, as they now call it. I had a loving family and was the middle child, having a younger sister, Margaret and an older brother, Arthur.

My parents were hard-working but relatively poor. My dad worked in the Civil Service and Mum kept the house, which was the norm post-war. They lived and stayed in the same terraced house they moved into just before my birth until they died more than sixty years later. A small house but filled with so much enduring love and happy memories and with a few sad ones too.

As was the way then, the man of the house worked and the wife stayed at home, so ours was no different, but the irony was that my dad worked for the Ministry of Pensions Artificial Limb Service, which was formed in 1948. He was a Clerical Officer there and stayed in that position all his working life although, he had the potential to do much better, the war experiences proved a burden on him. I can only imagine the experience of being captured in North Africa at Tobruk in

Libya and spending three and a half years in several German Prisoner of War Camps, which must have taken its psychological toll. He always said it was a dreadful experience that words can't describe, and he did not want the added responsibility of promotion at work because he had a younger brother John, who had a mental breakdown at twenty-one and died of Tuberculosis (TB) at twenty-three years of age.

At four years old, I went to primary school, about one hundred yards up the road from where I lived, before moving into the junior part of the school until I was eleven years old. They were good, carefree years playing with friends and my siblings. We played on the bombsites or played in the street with all the neighbourhood children. I well remember playing marbles in the gutter and coming across the occasional horse manure, but it never stopped us!

My mother was a Salvationist and went to the local Salvation Army, known as Portsmouth North. It seemed natural for all the children to follow suit, so myself, Arthur and Margaret also attended there. We had previously gone to a local Baptist church, but the Salvation Army seemed so much livelier and fun by comparison.

With my mother playing the piano and organ for the Songsters and Singing Company it was inevitable that we all joined the Singing Company or choir as they call it in churches. Before long, Arthur and I were in the Junior Band too and it was great fun. Margaret did not have the same inclination to play an instrument so she joined the Timbrels instead, where tambourines were swirled around to the beat of the band music.

I started to have piano lessons when I was eight years old and played the second cornet in the band whilst Arthur played the baritone. I suppose there were around twelve to fifteen in the band at the time and we played quite well. I have always enjoyed music and still occasionally play the piano.

I was hoping to follow in my mother's footsteps and play the piano like her as she was quite gifted, but I plodded away until I was fourteen and gave up when girls seemed a better hobby! However, I did play the piano for the Singing Company on occasion and played for my mother singing when she sang solos. We also played 'four hands' piano where she played the bass, and I played the treble. Years later, we occasionally played together when we visited there, virtually every Saturday for a nice roast dinner my mother was famous for. It was a routine to go there for dinner at twelve thirty, have a chat and often Arthur and Margaret used to pop in as well, before going to watch the Pompey football match with my dad.

There were lots of fun afternoons and evenings on either side of the sermon around the Salvation Army Hall and one memory is of the Paffett Group, which was pre-Beatles. Arthur played the baritone, Margaret the tambourine, myself the cornet and my Mum on the piano. We never got discovered as it was before the X-Factor, but we had some fun doing it.

We had lots of happy times in our early childhood, proving you do not need money to enjoy yourselves. We always had grazing, scabs and cuts on our legs and knees from antics at old bomb sites or just messing around on the road playing marbles. There were hardly any cars on our road and the only time we went in one was at Christmas time, returning from our granddad's in Ivy Street, Southsea. Arthur and I used to play a lot in the small garden we had, pulling our sister's plaits, throwing darts at the shed door so she could not get out, or playing hopscotch.

My parents were determined that all their children should be able to swim so we regularly went swimming in the sea and eventually had lessons at the local Victoria Swimming Baths where, after a few lessons, we proudly got a certificate proving we could swim one length of the baths. What an achievement!

Being the middle child, I remember having hand-me-down clothes from Arthur once he outgrew them. We never threw anything away, so it was a natural process for me to have his hand-me-downs.

We never had a television when we were young, but I remember going to Mrs Page's, a neighbour's house, who lived three doors away. I was about seven years old, and she was the first in our street to have a television. We were asked if we wanted to see a children's programme called 'Bill and Ben, The Flowerpot Men', so we jumped at that and ran to the house. I clearly remember about twelve children seated, cross-legged on the floor, in the small room all watching our first television show, which seemed marvellous at the time.

Eventually, a few years later my parents rented a television so, as a family, we could all watch and enjoy it. I remember watching 'Sunday Night at the London Palladium' together, which was a family entertainment show full of various acts. One time, Margaret and I had to go to bed halfway through the show as it was getting late, but we did not go straight to sleep that night. I could smell cooking, so Margaret and I crept down the stairs and opened the door into the middle room expecting to see Arthur and my parents still watching the television. They were all surprised to see us both, and we too were surprised to see them all tucking into a small piece of steak each, with bread and butter. It was a treat for my parents, and Arthur, being the eldest, was being spoilt that night.

There used to be lots of outings with the Salvation Army, either visiting other Corps or just fun days out during the summer. The fun days were just that, visiting many places, like Lyndhurst in the New Forest, beaches or travelling to Petersfield, which nowadays is less than thirty minutes away but back then seemed a long journey via the coach. Those coaches smelt terribly of diesel, and we all suffered from motion sickness. We were always sick on those journeys.

I remember vividly one trip to Petersfield when I was about nine years old and took part in a race on The Heath. There were about seventy children of all ages running in this hundred -yard race and I enjoyed running so I was determined to do well. When the flag went up, I ran and immediately fell over. Those new school sandals were a bit big and no good for running in! As luck would have it, the organiser blew his whistle as it was a false start, so I immediately kicked off my shoes and joined the lineup once more. The white flag was raised, and I ran as fast as I could, and I came in first. The prize was a whopping two and sixpence, which was a huge sum for me as I was then getting three pence per week pocket money.

We had what was called a 'Runabout Ticket' in the summer, which lasted a week and the whole family went away each day on the train to any destination within a twenty-five -mile radius of Portsmouth. We went to Hayling Island, Bognor Regis, Littlehampton, Petersfield, Winchester and a few other locations. If we walked from our house to the train station, we were treated to an iced ring doughnut, which was delicious. Occasionally, we would take a friend with us for the day, which was a treat for them as not many children where we lived ever went away on holiday, even for a day. We fostered a girl, called Nora, at this time and we got on well with her and she, of course, joined us on our travels. As things became easier financially, we went to Butlins Holiday Camp at Bognor Regis and Minehead, which seemed lovely to be waited upon.

In junior school, I was in both the cricket team and football team. I loved the physical side of sports, although I was quite average at both games, I did enjoy them. I remember going with my father by bicycle to the matches and playing the games with him cheering me on. He first took me and Arthur to Fratton Park when I was just seven years old. Little did I know that I would be going there with him for another fifty-eight years. My dad and I were Pompey season ticket holders, and I went with him for all those years until at ninety-six he could not make the stairs anymore to the South Stand of the stadium. Such wonderful memories I have of the occasional away games we went to and of course, being there when Pompey won the FA Cup in 2008.

We all had bicycles and often went out together for rides over Portsdown Hill and into the countryside. When you live in a very densely populated city like Portsmouth, it is sheer pleasure to escape the city smells and noises, replacing them with some serenity and the sweet countryside odour and freshness.

We were always out somewhere, whether it was just in the street or at the local parks, often with Arthur and his friends playing football or cricket. My earliest recollection of pain when kicking a football was when I was eleven years old in the old school yard. It was a short, sharp pain in my groin area, which I flinched at but ignored. Little did I know this pain was going to intermittently be there for the next five years before that fateful day of amputation.

Chapter 2:
The Pain Begins

I first thought the pain was a one-off as everyone gets, but the sharp, shooting pain returned about a month later. The pain was emanating from my lymph node in my right groin which was very slightly enlarged. I just carried on hoping it would go away but it did not. Visiting our family GP, he said it was probably growing pains.

In my last year at junior school, we had to take the eleven-plus examination, which was always taken in the last year of primary education. This academic selection decided whether you would go to a secondary, technical or grammar school. Arthur had already passed and was going to a technical school and being the middle child, my turn was next.

As children, all of us had the blue-lined writing books of the day, with all the tables on the back page and we spent endless hours doing our tables with my dad. I do believe all the effort was not wasted because I became proficient at numeracy, and I am sure this helped pass my eleven-plus exam and going on to grammar school.

My father was particularly adept with numbers and even stunned the local waiters in a Cyprus restaurant when all the family were holidaying there for my parent's sixtieth wedding anniversary. He was ninety years old and I mentioned to one that he knew up to his twenty-five times table. He said he did not believe it and so we had a few tests. He was amazed and called another waiter over and again he had a few tests and they confirmed it with their calculators. Soon there were four waiters asking him multiplication questions and checking with their calculators and Dad just loved doing it with that beaming smile of his.

I had a choice of the Northern or Southern Grammar Schools to choose from and as a former English Prime Minister, James Callaghan, had gone to the Northern Grammar School, I decided to go there. I was duly kitted out with the blazer, cap and satchel bag plus short trousers, as long trousers could only be worn in the second year. The special present from my parents for passing the eleven-plus exam was a brand-new Coventry Eagle bicycle, for which they had saved, to enable me to cycle to school. I was a fussy eater and did not like school dinners. As we had one hour and twenty-five minutes for the lunch break, I used to cycle home for dinner every day with the occasional twinge of pain. On the way back to school after dinner, my friend Terry and I used to always visit the girls' school to talk to them.

I enjoyed the sport at school, apart from the first year playing rugby. I even managed to become captain of the basketball team. I was always right-handed and right-footed, but I did notice when playing football, that I was kicking more with my left foot than my right. As time went on, I seemed to be asking my mother to write more notes excusing me from my P.E. lessons (Physical Education). This and the shooting pains were the first signs that all was not well.

After talking with my parents about the occasional pain in my groin, they decided to take me to the family doctor. He thought it might be a strain and gave me some obnoxious blue-black ointment to rub in. After rubbing this ointment in for a few weeks the pains returned, and I noticed the period of time between the pains re-occurring was getting less and less. We went back to the doctor who referred me to an orthopaedic consultant.

My first visit as a twelve-year-old to the Royal Hospital in Portsmouth was somewhat daunting as doctors were, in those days, held in high esteem and consultants were of god-like status. After a long wait, my name was called, and I had to lie down on a trolley waiting for the consultant to appear. In strode this white-coated, brusque, stern-looking man whose face would have cracked with even half a smile. His military bearing was there for all to see, and I believe he was previously a major in the Army. He started examining me and pushed my lymph node hard; the excruciating pain made me cry out. Ignoring my pain, he continued prodding and probing and told my parents it was nothing to worry about, but he would see me in three months' time.

I went back to school and continued my education, but the pain did not go away. I could walk for miles and enjoyed cycling, running and swimming, but I noticed from the age of thirteen that I started walking with a barely perceivable limp, which I suppose compensated for the increasing pain I was experiencing. Children can be cruel whilst developing and learning their social skills, and at grammar school, it was no exception. When cruel jibes are made and you are sensitive to it, it can hurt. I remember it still, more than fifty years later. It was a minor thing to my school friends but still hurt me somewhat. One of the boys said to all our friends 'Look, who is this walking?' and he walked away with an exaggerated limp. They all laughed, and I smiled, but inside I knew then I was different from the norm.

I had a cousin called Maurice, who was a district nurse and when I was younger, whilst he went on his rounds visiting the local sick people, he used to give me some money to buy a big bag of sweets, to eat while I waited in the car. One day, I was riding my bicycle with a school friend and, being near Maurice's, we called in. My leg was hurting, and I did not want to do P.E., so I thought, with him being a nurse, it would have some authority if he wrote a note to excuse me from lessons. Unfortunately, he just laughed and said he could not. It was a good try anyway.

My leg continued to cause me more discomfort, so we duly went back to the consultant after three months and I provided the note to my schoolmaster, written by my mother, that I had another hospital appointment. After twelve months and four visits to the consultant, he came forward with his diagnosis that there was nothing wrong with me and that I was trying to get off school! He also said, on another occasion to my parents, not to waste his time, which did not go down well at all.

It was 1964, the year I was to stop going to the Salvation Army and they had a fancy-dress competition. It was to be judged by the two owners of a string of local cafés, who were good Christians and conducted the meeting. The prize, though, was ten shillings; about the same amount I earned for doing a weekly paper round, so it was certainly worth winning. I talked it through with my mother and between us, we came up with Miss World 1964. I wore my mother's swimming costume with her high heels, and we made a sash with '1964' on and a small gold crown. There were a lot of entries and we all had to parade around the hall, up a few steps to the platform and past the two judges. As I passed one of the judges, he pinched my bottom, and everybody laughed. I laughed too, it was all good fun and then the winners were announced. Third place, second place and finally the winner was… John. Wow! My claim to fame that I would use many times in the future. When you are at meetings and want to break the ice, you have to say something about yourself that no one knows. Not many have been 1964 Miss World winners!

During this time of my life, I had a couple of paper rounds to earn extra pocket money and many Saturday jobs. These included washing up in a local restaurant for eight hours on a Saturday, peeling and chipping potatoes in a fish and chip shop, working in a grocery shop, and humping sacks of potatoes around and crates of fruit. One job was in a café, helping to build a patio at the back of the shop, I was only fourteen but I had to move large slabs around and I struggled with my leg a little. I remember the owner asking me if I had a friend who could also help, so I got a close friend to help too. That day we worked together and got some good work done then, at the end of the day, he paid me and said he no longer needed me and got my friend to help him from then on. It taught me a lesson in life I would carry through my working career: always treat somebody the way you would want to be treated. If he had explained to me why, I would have accepted it, but to me, at fourteen it was a cut-throat decision.

I did enjoy riding my bicycle and one day in late autumn, returning home from my paper round not far from home, I clearly remember a shooting, searing pain in my groin so bad I had to stop because it had brought tears to my eyes. I guess at that moment I knew there was something seriously wrong. I mentioned it to my parents, and they arranged another appointment several weeks later with the consultant who, again, said there was nothing wrong.

My right leg was getting thinner than my left leg and slightly numb in places. I was fifteen years old by this time and clearly remember standing in the small living room at home thinking to myself would they be able to cut my leg off so high to get rid of the pain. It was my earliest recollection of the potential loss of my leg.

Chapter 3: My Operations

It was in my third year at school, getting ready for the mock O Levels, when, in early December 1965, I had my regular three-monthly appointment with the consultant. The pain was still there and getting worse and when he pushed hard on my lymph gland I literally screamed out in pain. He must have thought, after nearly three years, there must be something wrong and decided an investigation was necessary.

I went into the Portsmouth Royal Hospital in the third week of January 1966 for a biopsy. The ward I was in had several interesting characters and one in particular springs to mind. It was the beginning of the 'Flower Power' era where many were trying drugs and there was a young man, around twenty years old with long black hair lying in a bed next to me. We got to talking and I asked him what had happened to him, as he was in a plaster cast having broken many parts of his body. I immediately thought it was a car accident he had been involved in, but no, he had taken LSD, thought he was a butterfly and decided he could fly out of his bedroom window! What a shame!

There were also two Portsmouth footballers, John McClelland and Frank Haydock, a few beds away from me, and being a Pompey supporter, I thought it was great being able to chat with them. A male nurse arrived saying he needed to shave me down below for my operation and I thought, 'Oh no' but there was no choice. To this day I don't know why, but the strange thing was he dry shaved me using talcum powder rather than a lather. I remember it pulling the hair and really hurting. Ouch!

Hospital wards were run very efficiently in those days and the ward sister on the Harold Pink Ward was called Sister Bacon. She was small in stature but a force to be reckoned with in keeping the nursing staff working efficiently, second only to the matron. She had a reputation for this, and you could see the nurses' reactions as she approached them. To me, as a patient, she was very kind and I remember I was receiving an injection from a male nurse into my right thigh muscle, which was wasting and painful. He tried to inject it, but it was so painful I cried out. She immediately came along and consoled me and proceeded to inject me herself, without too much pain. She was very caring toward the patient but also a strict disciplinarian.

The next day I was operated on, and they must have had a good rummage around where the pain was coming from in my groin, judging from the scar it produced. It healed quickly and I was left with a six-inch-long by half-an-inch-wide scar in my groin. It was quite ugly, but they found nothing and could not explain what the problem was. The consultant almost did not believe me but could not understand why the pain remained there.

Life just carried on and I eventually went back to my schooling, but the shooting pains continued. Even more worryingly, my right leg seemed to be gradually wasting away, more and more.

By the summertime, I do remember my right leg being

overly sensitive and the top of my thigh was a little bit numb. There also appeared small blackheads all over the thigh, despite me intensely washing myself. When I measured my leg around the thigh muscle, it was one and a half inches smaller than my left thigh. It was wasting away and getting worse.

At grammar school, in my third year, I managed to come top of my class, so went up to a higher group. The following year, I did well again, and again was moved to a higher group, but then I had to do the exams. It turned out I had not done very well at school in my O Levels, due, in part, to the time off for medical appointments and the occasional pain I was getting, but it was also down to me not applying myself.

I left school at sixteen and had several job offers but joined The Southern Gas Board and became an Apprentice Gas Fitter. The job was somewhat physical, and I remember struggling at times with my leg, which often caused me pain. I was also getting day release to go to college, but I had been employed just five months when I noticed a swelling starting to appear on my right leg, about eight inches above and to the left of my knee. There was little medical awareness of unusual swellings appearing at that time and I thought I must have knocked it somehow. I did not think it was anything to worry about because it was not in my right groin, where all the pain was occasionally emanating from, and the scar from the biopsy had healed well.

The swelling got larger as we approached Christmas, but it just felt soft and never hurt at all when I pushed it, so I just thought it strange it was not disappearing. I decided to mention it to my parents and a visit was arranged to the family doctor, who immediately arranged for an appointment with the orthopaedic consultant a week later. After examining me he said he needed to operate. I would have really liked to have seen his thoughts at this time, given his earlier accusations of me wasting his time and trying to get off school. It is strange to say, but I had a sense of self-satisfaction thinking 'There you are, I told you there was something wrong and now you can see it too'. Quite perverse, really, considering the outcome!

I had imagined they would just remove the swelling and that would be it. I had no idea of the seriousness of this operation.

Chapter 4: It's Cancer

I was in the Harold Pink Ward of The Royal Hospital in Portsmouth for three weeks in total and unbeknown to me, my parents had been given the devastating news that I had four to six months to live and that I was inoperable. I knew nothing of this and was reading my college books in preparation for a gas fitting exam in a few months' time. I know I was amazed at how many visitors I was getting, especially from work. They also had a collection from the people I worked with at the Southern Gas Board depot in Rudmore, Portsmouth, which was a tremendous amount of money; equivalent to about eight times my weekly apprenticeship wage. They knew, but I did not know, that I would not be going back and were very generous indeed.

They operated the next day and during the operation, there was massive blood loss as they tried to remove the malignant cancerous tumour. They managed to remove the tumour but not the fibroids, so the cancerous cells just continued their uncontrolled division into the thirty-five billion cells of my body. I was put in the intensive care ward with blood and dextrose drips and had my own room.

We had no phone then and the police came to my parent's house in the early hours of the morning after the operation, as the medical staff thought I was going to die. The police told my parents they were needed immediately at the hospital. They were told the tumour was so deeply embedded that I was inoperable and that they had tried to sew me up but could not, completely.

It was at this time I had an out-of-body experience, which I vividly recall. I left my body and floated to the ceiling on the opposite side of the room to the door. I saw my parents entering and, on the wall, just by the door was a clock which showed it was 4:05 am. Then I did not remember anything else until my parents came to see me later the same day in the evening. They told me they had come to see me early in the morning and they were flabbergasted when I said, 'I know because it was 4:05 am'. I also told them who was in the room at the time, but they could not understand this as they said I was asleep in bed.

My parents were called in to see the consultant who had said there was nothing wrong with me and that I was just trying to get off school, to be told I was inoperable. My mother welled up with tears, only to be told by this heartless person, who did not know the meaning of compassion, 'Pull yourself together, you don't want the boy to see you upset'.

There were tears shed by my mother, I am told because she was trying to feed me up as the weight was dropping off and I just had no appetite, coupled with extreme pain. Arthur recalls I was sometimes rude to her, rejecting the food, and my mother later said to me she had little money at that time, so it must have hurt her. I hold my hands up to that. It is so true when they say you hurt the ones you love.

Looking back to my time as a young teenager you only see life through your eyes, not through others, so I never really understood or even thought about the impact on individuals or the family unit. I was pushing boundaries to see how far I could go or get away with things just like many young teenagers of today do. I suppose it was part of growing up because at that time I had no responsibilities and just wanted to enjoy myself.

From Arthur's perspective, he says, looking back, it was clear to him our parents had realised the seriousness of my illness long before and this had caused a major shift in their attitude toward their children. I had become a priority with them trying to give me anything I wanted.

The impact on the family can reverberate for a long time, many years, in fact. Arthur was, by then, nineteen, and our parents must have felt able to leave him to his own devices. He said he does not think he ever got their affection and concern back again completely. He always felt he remained last in their concerns or praise, relative to me, as they never expected me to be able to live a 'normal' life. This, he said, resulted in any of my achievements being magnified in their eyes.

My family visited me a lot in the hospital and Arthur brought his girlfriend along one day. I knew Lyn (and her sister Janet) well, so it was nice to see them, and she had brought me a bag of plums, which I loved. Unfortunately, when she arrived, she casually swung the bag towards me and let go, whereupon it landed right on the area they had operated on. As I cried out in pain, the nurses ran over to me and pulled the curtains around my bed. Lyn was beside herself for unintentionally hurting me.

Lyn and Arthur went on to marry and celebrated their golden wedding anniversary in 2019, which was lovely. I have reminded Lyn, for over fifty years, of the pain she caused me by throwing those plums at me and milked it relentlessly as brothers-in-law do! At sixteen, I was not aware of the family trauma it must have caused, but looking back, having my own family of two boys and a girl, like my parents, I can only begin to imagine the shock and impact it had on the family unit. When your child hurts, then so do you. I remember Arthur saying to me once, that he could not believe in God as he would not allow this to happen to me!

After two weeks in the hospital, I had a visit from two oncology specialists: Miss Cade and Dr McEwan. They wanted to examine me internally, which I suppose was to see if cancer had spread to my internal organs. They did their examination and left to confer, and a few weeks later spoke to my parents about options. There were two: firstly, it was to amputate the whole of my right leg or secondly do nothing and I die. My parents, whilst remembering the era they lived in, had a lot of faith in the family doctors and valued their input in arriving at their decision. Two doctors conferred at the surgery they went to, and they were unanimous that if it were their son, they would not let him go through an amputation, as the likelihood was cancer would either go to his lungs or travel across to the other leg. My parents went home with heavy hearts, knowing they were seeing the consultants the following day.

The decision had been made. My parents walked into the consultant's office and said they did not want me to go through an amputation as the cancer was likely to spread anyway. The response from Miss Cade was to really lay that decision on their doorstep stating they, and they alone were denying their son the chance of life. My mother recalled the meeting to me, saying it was so upsetting and many tears flowed but Miss Cade was right; how could they deny their son a chance. When asked for her view of success, she said it was fifty-fifty. My parents must have trudged home so upset after that meeting, quite distraught knowing the conversation they were to have with me.

Meanwhile, I had been discharged from the hospital after three weeks and had a wound about the size of a ten-pence piece in my groin by my lymph node. It was dressed every day and I asked my cousin Maurice, the district nurse if he would do it, which he kindly did. The wound was not healing, but very slowly it seemed to me to be closing, so the dressings continued to be required.

With all this happening and being so young, I never really considered the impact it was having on the family unit. Arthur recently recalled how our father spoke to him in his bedroom about me needing to have my leg amputated. He explained that they had been told it was a choice between having the leg off or dying. While he was aware of the seriousness of my condition, he did not think, before, that it had truly registered with him there was a possibility of my death. He did not remember showing much emotion himself at the time, but he was upset and shed a few tears when he was on his own.

That fateful day, I will remember until I die, was the day my parents had to go and see the consultants at the hospital. I thought I was slowly improving, even though the wound was still open about six weeks after the operation. I decided to get some coal and firewood and make the fire in the living room, and this would show them I was slowly getting better. They came through the door, both looking visibly upset and said they needed to talk to me following their hospital visit. Mum looked at me with tears rolling down her cheeks and said slowly, 'They want to amputate your leg'. It was such a statement and was akin to having an electric shock through my whole being. It was awful, plain awful. I burst into tears, and they hugged me and hugged me. How it must have hurt them both to tell their child that devastating, traumatic and life-changing news. They said it was not their decision to make but mine and if I did not have my leg amputated, I had four to six months to live. After just two or three days since recovering from this shocking news, I accepted my fate, although, those six words said to me have resonated in my head for the past fifty-odd years. Death I did not know and, at sixteen, life was sweet. What was the point of keeping something that was slowly killing you? With the decision made, I did not realise how long I would have to wait before my next major operation.

To avoid cancer from spreading and contain it, I was to have six weeks of radiotherapy at St Mary's Hospital. I needed an ambulance five days a week for six weeks to transport me for treatment. I met many interesting people who lived locally and whom I talked to. One character called Ron, we picked up after me and I remember he was smoking outside his terraced house when we arrived. He was helped into the ambulance because his right leg was missing below the knee, and we talked all the way to the hospital. He said he had hardening of the arteries because of his smoking habit, the blood was not getting to the extremities of his right leg and gangrene had started to appear, so they had to amputate. I liked Ron but could not understand why he continued to smoke given his terrible legacy of it. The reason I remember him is because two years later when I was at the Artificial Limb and Appliance Centre for an appointment, I bumped into him again. This time he was in a wheelchair with both legs off. He was smiling but looked a very yellow colour; quite unwell. I spoke with him, and he said he was still smoking and just could not give it up. There were circulatory problems on his right stump, and they were talking about amputating above the knee. I never saw Ron again.

The radiotherapy machines were huge, and my first visit entailed using marker pens to target the exact place the high-energy ionizing beams were to hit to kill the cancerous cells and halt the spread. It is used before surgery to shrink a tumour, so it can be easier to remove, but in my case, it was to slow the spread of cancerous cells in my body.

It was always warm in the radiotherapy department and the radiotherapists all wore white buttoned-up dresses with a V-neck at the top. One lasting memory is that after the daily treatment, I always had my dressing changed. The radiotherapist doing this was only about five years older than me and attractive. We had good banter between us, and at sixteen you are impressionable when there is a young lady bending over to apply the new dressing in your groin area, and you are looking straight down her cleavage. What gentlemanly restraint I had to show for a sixteen-year-old, but with the hormones flowing it was a masterclass of self-control on my part.

I finished my course of radiotherapy but was getting weaker and the wound was not healing. I was rapidly losing weight and, at the time, weighed just over six stone. I remember my mum washing my back in the front downstairs room of our house, where my bed was, as I could not climb the stairs. She had tears in her eyes, as she said my spine was almost coming through the skin.

When it came to eating, I had no appetite and did not enjoy food at all, especially after one or two mouthfuls. All my favourite meals would be cooked, to encourage me to eat, but cancer had a death grip on me. My mother was a strong woman, who had joined the ATS (Auxiliary Territorial Services) at the start of the war and had gone to Stevenage in Hertfordshire, where they were making bombs. She always kept her feelings under control, and I learned later, through Margaret, that she sometimes had to leave the front room, where I lay, to shed her tears in another room. How sad and traumatic it must have been to see your young child slowly ebbing away.

The neighbours, being post-war, were a close-knit community and looked after each other. We had a key on a string, behind the letterbox of the front door, to get in, and, with a couple of knocks on the wall, we would often go next door for a cup of tea or coffee. It does not happen like that nowadays, but it was very safe because everybody looked out for each other. I do not ever recall any burglaries in our area, because nobody had anything of value to take, in a relatively poor area of the city.

When the neighbours heard of my illness, a Mrs Collins of Balliol Road, just around the corner from us, called on my mum and offered to collect donations in the neighbourhood to raise money for any treatment that could help me. This was prompted by a recent article in one of the national newspapers, with the headline, 'Cure Found for Cancer'. This gave us all such hope, but when mum and dad took the article to the cancer consultant, he told them there was no truth in the article, which was a bitter blow to them. Such eye-catching newspaper headlines still happen today. Another lovely neighbour, who owned the corner shop, even offered to have her leg amputated, if it could be given to me! I guess in hindsight it would look somewhat strange having a woman's leg sewn onto me, who was eight inches shorter than me, but what a lovely, generous, kind offer to make.

I worked at the Southern Gas Board with an old-time gas fitter, Harold, who took me under his wing, to work with and learn from. He was quite a character and a staunch trade unionist. He would tell me stories of his encounters, as a union representative, with the management, and how he always won against them. The following week he would repeat it all again to me! Harold came to visit me every week for the whole nine months I was off work, and always brought me fruit and a box of chocolates. On a few occasions, I was doing too poorly or in pain to see him, but he would always return the next week. He was a good, kind man and when I was well again, I regularly visited him and his wife, which continued throughout their lives.

Later in life, after his wife passed away, we invited Harold to spend Christmas Day with us and the two children we had at the time. His one and only son had tragically died in his forties from a heart attack, and they had no grandchildren, so it would have been Christmas on his own. I still have the picture of him, sitting in one of our lounge chairs, with the two children sitting on both knees, and Harold sporting a beaming smile. He really enjoyed himself that Christmas, as did we.

There were also a couple of my grammar school masters, who visited me regularly. The English master, whom I really did not like, had poor conversational skills, and he would often just stare at me, without saying anything and I even resorted to pretending to be asleep at times. In the end, my mother had to tell him not to visit. The other master, an ex-squadron leader, also called Harold, taught Technical Drawing, which I had really enjoyed, as he was a good teacher and taught me a lot. He often visited me, and one day, when he found out I was joining the Southern Gas Board's Distribution Drawing Office, gave me his son's leather-bound compass set. This was of huge sentimental value to him, because his son tragically died young, so I really appreciated it.

I did visit Harold regularly when I was well, but one day, he had a bandage on his head and told me he was having treatment for a brain tumour. Sadly, the treatment was unsuccessful, and he passed away, but I have fond memories of a good teacher as well as a kind and generous man.

My mother was in the Salvation Army and, although I had stopped going there when I was around fourteen, I knew all the people there. There were also affiliations with other churches, and I was told that I was included in many of their prayers. A few days before I was due to go to Westminster Hospital for my amputation, the Salvation Army band came to play and pray outside the house. It was lovely and showed how caring and supportive they were, as each band member came into the front room where I was bed-ridden, shook my hand and wished me luck. I vividly remember some of those people, young and old, with tears in their eyes. It was very moving for everyone.

I had a few girlfriends along the way, but I do remember Kathy, one of my first loves, who went to Lyndhurst Road Girls School. My friend, Terry, and I used to see the girls of a lunchtime, and I went out with her a few times. She often wore red, knee-length PVC boots with her mini skirt, which I thought was most becoming. She came to visit me, about six weeks before I went to London for my operation. I was in my bed, quite poorly and it must have been a sight to see me, having lost so much weight, but she never spoke about it. We laughed, talked a lot and played some old forty-fives and then, after about an hour, said it was soon time for her to go. It was lovely to see her, but my mother later said she cried her eyes out once she had left the front room, as she was so shocked by my condition. I never saw her again.

I was unaware of the impact this was having on Arthur and Margaret. When told of the latest developments, Arthur would quietly walk away to the bathroom or his bedroom and stay there for a while. It must have been difficult for him and everyone. Margaret would tell a school friend what was happening but not the teachers and they never asked her why she was sometimes crying. It was only later that Mum told Margaret she had gone to the school and told them because it could impact her exams at the time.

At this time, Margaret had to write an essay at school on the subject 'There's never smoke without fire'. She wrote about my tumour and all the events associated with it, likening my pain to the smoke and cancer to the fire'. Following this, the teacher praised her for the essay and told the class 'that Margaret has had to grow up early'. That was all that was ever said to her.

Chapter 5:
The Amputation

I was to have the operation to amputate my leg at Westminster Hospital in London by Professor Lee in June 1967. To get there, I had a volunteer driver who would take me in her car and claim any mileage expenses incurred. The driver was a Miss James and she reminded me of a school headmistress who took charge of the girl's hockey team. She was very kind and considerate though and drove very well to get me through the London traffic. I remember arriving at the hospital and seeing the nurses looking so smart, with their white hats and navy capes over white uniform with a red cross on their front.

It was early June on a Sunday, a very warm and sunny day, as I entered the hospital. Inside the ward entrance on both sides were single rooms with curtains pulled across, and alongside one of these was the ward sisters' office. This opened up to eight beds going around the room. It was quite a small ward and the patients there were friendly and said 'Hello' as I arrived. Next to me, there was a nineteen-year-old lad, who had severed some arteries in his arm, through an accident while working as a window glazer. A bit further on, there was a very polite, older German dentist, who had serious abdominal problems. Directly opposite me, there was a retired army major, who smiled and waved to me. I settled into my bed and remembered looking out of the window at the skyline.

I counted fourteen large cranes, and it is probably the same today, as they are always building or demolishing things in London.

I was to be in this hospital for ten days, occasionally going in and out of the ward for tests, the operation itself and to use the toilets. I went past those two curtained-off rooms a few times and it shocked me terribly. During visiting times, the curtains were closed, but otherwise, they were opened. In one room, there was a poor fellow who had throat cancer, and I learned he had endured nine major operations and countless minor ones; he looked grim. He was making strange noises to the nurses, and I could not make out what he was saying, but he had been there so long, that the nurses could understand him. In the opposite room, there was a middle-aged man who had cancer of the jaw, and in those early pioneering days of skin grafting, they were trying to graft skin back to his jaw. He had skin splayed out around his jaw, which narrowed down to around two inches in diameter and connected to a splayed area on top of his shoulder, to try to graft skin back onto his jaw. They had both been in hospital for many months. I had never seen anything like this, and it left a lasting impression, making me think how fortunate I was to only lose my leg.

It was Monday, the fifth of June, and I was going down to the operating theatre to have my leg amputated to save my life. The night before was a sleepless one, just feeling my leg for the last time but always thinking to myself, 'What was the point of keeping something that was killing me?' It had to be done. I believe the operation lasted less than three hours and I was soon back in the ward. I remember coming to my senses and feeling with my hands to see if my leg was gone, and sure enough, it was no longer there. It was a huge relief, with all the traumatic build-up to the operation. It did feel odd, because if I shut my eyes, I could still feel my leg, and fifty years later this remains so. In particular, the parts that moved the most, like my toes, my ankle and my knee, still feel as if they are there. I remember telling my mother that when she came to my bedside, I had one foot in the grave, which I thought was funny anyway. She did not laugh.

They had performed what they term a right hind quarter or a hemipelvectomy. It is one of the most demanding and invasive orthopaedic surgical procedures you can have and consists of removing the whole of the right leg and half of the pelvis.

I was, in some ways, quite fortunate, because my tumour was a soft tissue sarcoma rather than a bone tumour, in which survival rates are far less, and there was a greater than fifty per cent chance of complications.

A recent survey, undertaken over thirteen years, on thirty-five patients, who underwent the hemipelvectomy operation, showed the mean survival rate was only thirty-three months. Bearing in mind, that my operation was forty years earlier I think Lady Luck was smiling over me, especially, as, in the survey, only four per cent. of patients were able to walk with a prosthesis.

My mum and dad stayed in Richmond with a family friend and travelled across London to see me every day. This family friend, who was a single parent, knew me well, as I had stayed in Richmond with them for a week when I was twelve. I got on well with her son, Tim, and daughter, Judy.

My parents were able to stay there overnight, but not during the day, which must have been difficult. During these times, particularly in the mornings when they could not be in the hospital, they just sat in the local park. It must have added to their difficulties. It was also exacerbated by the manager, to whom my dad reported, at the Artificial Limb and Appliance Centre, only allowing him a week off work on compassionate grounds. I know this distressed him a lot and caused a lot of anguish having to leave my mum on her own, in London, during this family crisis.

The first few days were not too bad, as the anaesthetic was still in me and slowly dissipating, but then the first phantom pains started, and they were very painful. They were very sharp, shooting nerve pains, which only lasted a few seconds but when they started, they would invariably come back like clockwork, every minute, so I was tensing myself for the next pain onslaught. A few of us on the ward were given liquid morphine, or 'jungle juice', as we and the nurses called it. The nurses were great and all quite young, so they brightened the day. My parents visited me every day, but some days were worse for me than others. Sometimes, I would be asleep, or after a few minutes I would say, 'Thanks for visiting, but you can go now'. Looking back, it was not nice, but I never meant to hurt them, it was just that I was so weak, weary and in pain that I did not want to talk to anyone; it was such an effort. They always understood, and, like any parent, their love was simply unconditional.

I could sit in the chair next to the bed after a few days, and it was nice to get out of bed for a few hours. I still had blood and dextrose drips in either arm, as well as the catheter, but it was nice to see a few visitors while sitting there. The blood drip was taken out the next day, so things were slowly improving.

After returning home and back to work, my dad joined us

at the weekend with my mum, who came to see me too, which was lovely. My parents, at the time, had little money, so this must have been quite a financial burden for them, but they, like any parent, would do anything for their children given the circumstances.

Around this time, Arthur had bought his first car, a grey Ford Classic. He drove up to Westminster Hospital with Lyn and Margaret to see me. It was always good to see them, and until you are separated from your siblings, you do not realise how much you miss them, as they are a big part of your everyday life. It was their first visit, and I knew they were coming to see me, so I met them in a wheelchair outside the ward. They were not expecting me to be there, and they weren't expecting to see their brother in a wheelchair with his leg missing. It was a shock to them all, which I did not realise at the time.

I had spent many, many hours before and after losing my leg, trying to remember if I had knocked or cut it somehow, to cause cancer. I have yet to come up with anything that would have caused it, to my knowledge. Maybe now, in hindsight, I could have been born with it and the cells just happened to start mutating when I was ten years old. I think it will remain one of life's mysteries.

The German Dentist had his surgery, too, for bowel cancer, and was told shortly after the operation he needed to pass wind, to show things were working correctly internally. Nothing was secret in small wards like that, as all discussions with relatives or the doctors could be heard, even behind pulled curtains. One evening he did manage to pass wind; he immediately apologised and was acutely embarrassed, but we all cheered and made light of it. He had a big smile then.

The Major opposite me would often talk to my mother and me. I suppose it was unusual for a sixteen-year-old, frail lad having his leg amputated, to be in a ward surrounded by all types of different ailments. He was discharged after a week and the very next day I had a huge wicker basket of fruit delivered to me in the ward. What a kind, generous gesture it was, and I have never forgotten it.

Two days after the operation the surgeon, Professor Lee, came to the ward doing his rounds, with his entourage of about ten junior medical staff, which was part of their training, followed by a ward nurse. He examined me and said the operation had gone well. I thanked him and immediately burst into tears. The stress and trauma had finally caught up with me. I have often looked back on that moment and felt it strange to thank someone for giving you a life-changing amputation, but he did save my life.

I do remember, that after three days, they removed the urinary catheter inserted during the operation. A young nurse came along and told me what she was going to do. She said there would be a slightly uncomfortable pain, but it would not take long to do. The nurse held onto my penis and started pulling the tube out, which was inserted almost twelve inches into the bladder. As a sixteen-year-old, whose hormones were bubbling away, I can only describe the experience as extremely, exquisitely erotic and, therefore, extremely embarrassing until the full length had been withdrawn. I am sure I saw a slight smirk on the nurse's face though, as she left.

During this period of my hospital stay, it was time to get me moving and out of bed. I do remember getting out and hopping a short distance. I have never, in all my life, experienced anything as fantastic as that moment because I felt so incredibly light. It was almost as if I could fly, or the earth's gravity had changed, and I could almost float. It is difficult to describe but imagine suddenly losing a seventh of your body weight because that is what your whole leg weighs. It was absolutely amazing, but sadly the feeling only lasted for twenty-four hours before I must have adjusted to it. What an elation it was, never to be forgotten.

The physiotherapist arrived at my bedside the next day, to have a conversation about crutches and walking with them. She would later show me how to use stairs safely with them, which was not easy. For the next task, she said, 'I want you to put your sock on your leg'. I thought that would be easy and she sat me down on the side of my bed. With that, she went around the bed to the other side and said go ahead. I thought, 'How strange', and put my sock on and immediately rolled completely over into her waiting arms. We both laughed and I realised this was the beginning of me learning to rebalance my body without my right leg, as my whole centre of gravity had changed.

I also had a visitor whilst there, Captain Rivers from the Salvation Army. He was previously the officer at the local Salvation Army Hall I used to attend, which my mother and sister still did. Both he and his wife were lovely, genuine, Christian folk and he had now been promoted to the commissioner, stationed in London. It was a lovely surprise for me, when he arrived and straight away, he asked me how I was. I threw the bedclothes off and said, 'It's gone'. The look on his face was of sheer shock because he didn't know I had undergone the amputation. I met him a few years ago and he still recalls that instance of complete shock but can laugh about it now.

Toward the end of my stay in Westminster Hospital, I was talking to my mum one day, and asked, if I could be taken outside to the park, which was alongside it. I could see these grounds from my fifth floor ward windows. It was a hot, June day, and, with the ward sister's permission, I was pushed in a wheelchair to the big, outside world. It was wonderful to be outside again, and my mum was pushing me along the pathways of the garden, which had beautiful flowerbeds all around. We stopped by some benches, and I could hear all the birds singing and chirping away. The lasting impression of that visit to the park, though, was seeing the glorious colours of the flowers. It somehow seemed so vivid, almost surreal, or perhaps it was just me appreciating the simple, natural beauty around me. What I did not appreciate, though, was the stares I was getting from people in the park, looking at a sixteen-year-old in a wheelchair, with one leg!

The trip to the park was a lesson in life for me. I believe the modern terminology for this is 'mindfulness', but I have been doing this all my life. When I am having a great time or appreciating what I see, I step back and enjoy the moment to enhance it even more, or I just thank God for my good health. How often do we all look back and say, 'How nice such and such was', or wish we were well again during an illness, rather than enjoying the moment more so at the time?

When anyone loses a limb or a sense, the body compensates. Losing my leg certainly improved my awareness of balance and its importance. I needed to familiarise myself with a new centre of gravity for my body, adjust to it and react accordingly. It does not sound much of a problem, but it is and a lot of it is done subconsciously. I was able to hop around indoors and hop up the stairs using my arms, as it was much quicker than one or two steps at a time if I did not wear a limb.

The other aspect of amputees most people are not aware of is how you use your arms far more, not only for balance, but for getting out of a chair or bed, so upper body strength is important. I now needed to build my strength up and nourish my body. I remember joking with my family, one of the earliest 'benefits' of losing my leg was not having to cut so many toenails. It was gallows humour really.

Chapter 6: Leaving Hospital

I said goodbye to the lovely nurses on the ward and will always remember the trip back from Westminster Hospital. I had been there for ten days and had an ambulance take me to Waterloo Station, with a chaperone for the journey. From the ambulance, I had a wheelchair take me to the train. It seemed to me, that everyone was staring at this young boy with his dressing gown on over his pyjamas, in a wheelchair. It was the first time I felt embarrassed and different. I did not like it at all. We arrived at the door to the train carriage, and I was told the whole section was reserved for us. I looked in, and a stranger was sitting there looking out of the window at me, but worse than that was the paper notice taped on the inside of the window, which read, 'RESERVED FOR CRIPPLE'. Three words cut me like a knife and made the reality of my disability so apparent. The chap sitting opposite me would not vacate the compartment, and just nonchalantly sat there for most of the journey back to Portsmouth, getting off at Havant, just ten miles from my destination. It was uncomfortable and thoughtless of him, leaving a lasting impression on me. I arrived, after what seemed a long journey of only an hour and a half, at Fratton Station in Portsmouth. From there, an ambulance took me to C3 Ward in St. Mary's Hospital, where all the cancer patients were put.

It was nice to be in my home city of Portsmouth, and so much easier for my family and visitors. The staff were nice to me on the ward, probably because I was the youngest there and I had my own room and, therefore, some privacy. I never did see another patient there, as most were in the latter stages of dying, hence the individual rooms. I was a fussy eater and did not particularly like hospital food, but almost straight away I had regained my appetite with an interest in food, at last. My mother would cook me my favourite foods, such as cottage pie or a roast dinner, plate them up, wrap them to keep warm and bring them to me in the hospital. I really enjoyed those meals.

A lump at the base of my spine was causing me some discomfort, and my mother, unbeknown to me, asked to see the consultant. She asked him, 'Has cancer returned?', but he gave her no comfort and just said 'It would be tragic if it has'. Margaret recalls walking home from the hospital after this meeting, and my mother crying all the way home. How difficult, as a parent, that must have been.

At this point, I had either been in bed, or just sitting around, for over two weeks, which had taken its toll on my skin, and I had a bed sore starting to develop, right at the base of my spine. Without the whole of my right leg, I must have weighed just over five stone, so the skin on my body must have been quite taut. The nurses seemed to always be rubbing cream on the bed sore, but it continued hurting a lot. The doctors and nurses thought it was a return of cancer, so decided to closely examine the sore, and then found the obvious reason why it hurt so much. Bed sores are painful on their own, but in the middle of this one, there was a deeply rooted double-headed carbuncle. They decided it needed to come out.

Basically, a carbuncle is a group of boils or an abscess that is usually deeper rooted than a boil. Two nurses were tasked with squeezing this out. Both were mature nurses, and one was of a larger frame, shall we say. They set to business, and it was so very painful, and I can remember the larger nurse holding me tight to her bosom, whilst the other did the extraction. It did hurt and I nearly suffocated as she held me tight, but I am told there is not too much difference between pleasure and pain! It left a nasty scar near my coccyx, which I can still feel to this day.

There are three things that still stick in my mind at that moment in my life, and they all revolve around pain. The first one I mentioned was the phantom pains and the second was associated with the bed sore, but the most excruciating pain of all was the removal of the stitches from my amputation scar.

Neuropathic pain is hard to manage, and it seemed then, as it still seems now, that the nerve endings a few inches on either side of the scar line are supersensitive. There were 26 stitches, starting from behind part of the remaining hip bone, right through to my groin and it was relatively neat stitching. The problem was the wound after surgery was weeping, and this formed a long scab over the whole scar line.

The day came to remove the stitches and to do this, they had to scrape off the scab to get to each stitch. It was probably the most painful experience of my life, and as the consultant surgeon said to me at my bedside during his ward visit, 'The only consolation I can offer is you cannot recall the actual pain, you will remember the pain but not recall it.' In hindsight, I should have been given some anaesthetic or morphine, but it was new territory for everyone.

I phoned my cousin, Maurice, from the hospital a few days later. He was really surprised to hear from me, and we chatted for a few minutes. Then, he asked if there was anything, he could get for me, and I said I would like an ice cream. The next day, the nurse came in smiling and asked me if I wanted ice cream as Maurice had just brought a box of twenty-four ice creams into the ward! He always was very generous, and it was a lovely surprise.

My family continued to visit me every day, and I remember my father calling in to see me at lunchtime because he only worked a few hundred yards away, in the hospital at the Artificial Limb and Appliance Centre. After the highlighted concern of bedsore and carbuncle, I was observed closely to see if there was any reoccurrence of cancer. My father came into the room and greeted me, and asked how I was, so I told him I was concerned that, close to the scar line, five bumps had appeared. He looked at me with such compassion and tears welled in his eyes, then I said, 'I think it's my toes starting to grow back.' I burst out laughing, but I think he was too traumatised to laugh and said, 'Oh son, how can you joke about a thing like this', which made me laugh even more. Humour has certainly helped me cope.

I gradually felt a little stronger, my appetite had come back and after nine days in St. Mary's Hospital, I was discharged to go home by ambulance, which was wonderful. I was going home to be with my family.

Chapter 7: Going Home

I finally arrived home, and as they say, 'There is no place like home.' My mum greeted me with that big smile of hers as I showed my newly found prowess in using crutches to get through the narrow doorway of our terraced house. Looking back, it must have been awful seeing your youngest son returning home, now disabled for life but at least I was alive.

I did try the elbow crutches, but they never supported me as much as the old underarm crutches did. They were well padded and quite old, circa the First World War era, but I could walk quite a distance with them, especially as my upper body strength slowly increased. What I had to learn, though, was negotiating the small rooms of the house, the threshold steps and those difficult winding stairs, a little later. For the time being, I kept the bedroom downstairs until I had recovered a little more.

I was still suffering phantom pains, but they were not too excruciating compared to post-operative time, and I had medium to strong painkillers called, Distalgesic, which is a brand name for Co-proxamol, often used for cancer patients to relieve pain. I would say that post-operative pain is so different to pre-operative pain. I almost embraced the post-operative pain as I knew it would lessen over time, whereas the pre-operative pain was getting worse by the day. It was quite the converse and meant to me I was finally healing.

After a couple of weeks of being home, it was my seventeenth birthday, and I had some nice presents. One present was a new pair of pyjamas, but of course, they had two legs. It seemed dreadful to me to have to cut the whole right leg off, but it served no purpose being there. I tried wearing them for a few weeks, but I found they twisted around my body a lot and were uncomfortable, so to this day I stopped wearing pyjamas to bed anymore.

I was in the living room one day, standing with the crutches by the fireplace and was quite relaxed. As I mentioned before, if you closed your eyes, it really felt as though your amputated leg was still there. It is quite surreal, as most amputees will agree. In one brief moment, I forgot I had lost my leg, put my right leg forward to go to the door, and immediately fell with a crash. No one was in the house, and I had not hurt myself too much, but I have never done it since. It is not just the physical changes you have to adjust to, but also the mindset too.

It was good to see my parents smiling again at times, particularly as I was eating well once again. The highlight for my mother was seeing a little tummy appearing on a very thin, frail body. The row of terraced houses we lived in was surrounded by roads and measured outside approximately one hundred yards by sixty yards. This proved to be a useful walking distance for me, to not only have some independence but also to get used to my crutches and build up my strength. I remember occasionally seeing the neighbours, who would always wave or smile, and once I saw a school friend, who lived around the corner at the end of the road. I thought nothing of it when I saw him and said 'Hello', but the look on his face spoke volumes. He was absolutely shocked, hardly smiled back and kept looking back at me as he walked up the road. I guess no one had mentioned to him what had happened to me before he saw me that day.

I often stood in the doorway using my crutches as support, just to pass the time of day, for a few moments break from the boredom I was encountering. One day, I was there, and two young boys came along, who were about five and eight years old, I would guess. You could see they were brothers, and the eldest said to me, 'Cor! Mister, how did you lose your leg?' to which I replied: 'A huge crocodile came along and bit it off, and it is lying in the gutter somewhere. If you find it and bring it back, I will give you two and sixpence'. They said, 'Really?' and I nodded, and they duly set off walking around the roads, looking for my leg the crocodile had bitten off. It still makes me smile today, thinking about it.

Life and living had changed significantly for me, and I soon realised this when getting in and out of a bath, but you soon adapt. The only help from the council at the time, via social services, was to have hand railings put up along the stairway and landing. The house was built in 1888 and the narrow stairs reflected this. They had quite a turn on them at the top, to get to the landing, and I remember the narrowest step on the turn being only six inches wide, narrowing down to two inches. It was not easy if you were able-bodied, let alone being disabled and using crutches. When I later returned to sleeping upstairs, I found the easiest way to get up and down was to just use my arms, hop up two steps at a time, and then from the top of the stairs, sit on my bottom to get back down again. I think the success of the human species is quickly adapting to change.

I had always enjoyed swimming and decided I felt strong enough to start swimming again. The family went to Arundel, nearly thirty miles away, with its huge castle overlooking the town because it had an outdoor swimming pool. To enable me to go swimming my mother had sewn up the right leg of my swimming trunks and I changed into these, used my crutches to approach the side of the pool and prepared to dive in. The lifeguard looked at me with trepidation, fearing he would need to be straight in after me, but I enjoyed diving and so I went for it. I dived in, but straight away I went forward like a corkscrew, round and round. I had not compensated for only using one leg not two! I soon adjusted to it and the family had some fun, for a welcome change.

I also went swimming with Margaret and some friends, one late summer evening in 1967, just by South Parade Pier on the central south side of Portsmouth. It was pitch black and nobody else but us six was there in and out of the sea. I had a swim, and then Margaret brought me my crutches, to get up the beach to where our clothes were. Just as I started to make my way up the beach, a parked car on the road, running parallel with the beach, put its headlights on to bathe us all in their lights. They may have thought it funny, but I did not want to be seen like that with my crutches, trying, with some difficulty, to get up the shingle bank to where my clothes were. They just left their lights on with no regard for any of us. I never went swimming there again.

I went back for my first check-up after six weeks and all went well. I was not only prodded but poked to check that my vital organs were not enlarged at all and my scar area was healing nicely. I had to return in three months' time now, so things were looking up.

The only issue I had was pain management, as the initial phantom pains were intense. What I do remember, though, is the contrasting feeling you get when you have cancerous pain compared to healing pain. The contrast being: that one gets slowly worse and worse, whereas the other slowly gets better and better. I could live with that, quite literally.

With the healing continuing, I could now look forward to getting an artificial leg and getting back to a degree of normality, or so I thought. When I look back, I had no idea what I had facing me, and in many ways, it was just as well.

Chapter 8:
My First Car

I really wanted an artificial leg as soon as possible, as I was fed up using crutches and being unable to carry anything. I wanted mobility, but I was also getting frustrated not working as it was August, by this point, and I had been off work for seven months.

The Southern Gas Board had continued to pay me my full wages for all the time I was off sick, which was marvellous, and I had saved every penny of it. I remember my mother saying to me, many years later, that she often saw all the money I had saved when she hardly had enough money for food and would sometimes go without herself. I just wish I had bought my mother some flowers or something nice during that time, but young lads do not always think that way.

I was seventeen and had enough money to commence driving lessons. The natural choice of the driving instructor was Rodney, a neighbour who lived five doors away, and who did this for a living, but I needed a car. Another neighbour, Chris, who lived two doors away, worked part-time cleaning cars for a local garage at the weekend and arranged for me to view a car. I liken it to buying a puppy or kitten, where you fall in love and must have one, which was how I felt when I viewed a Ford Anglia 105E for the first time. It had forty-two thousand miles on the clock and was a beautiful maroon colour, I still remember the number plate: DTW 715B.

With the price agreed, the garage said they would service and MOT it. Chris would bring it home for me the following Saturday. I said not to clean it, as I would and polish it too. I could not wait to get it home, but how could I drive a manual car with only one leg? The answer was to have Feeny and Johnson vacuum hand controls for the brake and accelerator pedals and just use my left leg as normal for the clutch. I did get some financial assistance for this conversion, and within another week I had the car back, ready for me to drive. The inner lever, shaped around the steering wheel, was for the accelerator, and the outside one was for the brake, which was vacuum-assisted. I also had a knob on the steering to help me turn the wheel.

My driving lessons could now commence, and I booked twelve lessons in advance, which were intensive over just three weeks. I had a lot of road sense, having been riding my bicycle on the roads for eight years, so to me, it felt quite a natural transition from bike to the car. After a few weeks of lessons, Rodney put me in for my driving test in September of that year. Arthur, who had already passed his test the first time, took me out a few times to help enhance my driving skills or lack thereof. He remembers me driving quite fast, which I must admit, has lasted a lifetime.

My eleventh and twelfth driving lessons were all in one day. I had two lessons driving around Portsmouth, before going straight to the Test Centre for my test. I was nervous but quietly confident in my driving abilities, and duly started my journey with the driving examiner. It went smoothly, apart from the emergency stop, which seemed to rather catch him out and he narrowly missed the front console when I slammed the brakes on after his signal, which was to hit his knee with the clipboard he held. After some Highway Code questions, he said to me, 'I am pleased to say you have passed'. Wow! Freedom!

I remember going home and telling my mum, who was as excited as I was. The first thing, after telling her I had passed, was the ceremonial removal of the L plates, then cutting them in half, which felt wonderful. I drove around the block on my own for the first time, filled with that wonderful sense of elation and freedom that many have when passing their test. I was now mobile.

Chapter 9: My First Artificial Leg

Going back more than fifty years, the ways of learning to walk again seem rather antiquated, and this was the case with my first artificial leg made for me. Every leg is bespoke, and I had what was called a bucket seat, with a hip mechanism to release when I sat down. Attached to the socket joint were four strips of metal, at ninety degrees to each other, going down to the knee joint. A locking mechanism on the side of the knee unlocked it to be able to sit down. From the knee, there were further metal strips for rigidity, going down to a quadrant of wood with rubber matting on, to avoid slippage on the floor. This was called a 'rocker foot' and to me it was hideous! I was so disappointed with it because it looked so false.

To get the shape of me to enable me to sit in the 'bucket seat', I was taken to a separate curtained room in the Artificial Limb and Appliance Centre (ALAC), where I was told to take off all my clothes. I was then handed a piece of muslin cloth to slide over me from the knee of my left leg to just under my neck, to cover my modesty.

The fitter, now called a prosthetist, arrived with a large bowl of hot water and about six roles of Plaster of Paris. I sat in a chair and could see a three-legged stool with a round circular seat fixed on a small square length of wood, with numerous holes drilled through it. This round seat could be raised or lowered, so you sat with your stump on it and a metal pin inserted underneath the stool for the correct height.

Each pack of Plaster of Paris was unwrapped and soaked in lukewarm water for a couple of minutes. They were then unrolled and the start of the wrapping process around me began. It felt nice and warm, to begin with, but then got cool, then cold and solidified. Around the amputated area, which was basically a cut from behind of what remained of the hip bone to my groin, with the cheek of my bottom brought round and sewn up, I had to sit on the stool. This stool was adjusted to the correct height so when I was standing and putting pressure down on it, the Plaster of Paris solidified to that shape. It was this shape my leather socket was made to.

The other reality was I now found it difficult to sit down without wearing a limb because it raised the right side of my bottom to be the same as my left. Even sitting in bed is uncomfortable, and if I am waiting for my limb to be repaired, after a half-hour or so, my back really aches because of the now unnatural position it is in.

All this was a difficult thing for a seventeen-year-old to go through on his own, with no support at all, and I remember thinking at the time, A year ago, I was at the Oasis Club, in North End, Portsmouth with Arthur, listening to the latest pop records, looking out for the girls'. My life was turned upside down and would never be the same again.

The 'rocker foot' was supposed to help with the rolling motion of your foot, to assist as you walked forward. Looking back, it never helped me at all. I was extremely disappointed to be given this, as it showed everyone that I didn't have a leg and many would have thought, 'What on earth is it?'

I had to wait three weeks for this first leg to be made, and finally, in late August, my appointment came through. I sat in the waiting room and waited along with around eight or nine seasoned individuals, who all had artificial legs, all with a story to tell. In those days, there were far more double amputees than nowadays, as a direct result of the World Wars they had been in. They allowed smoking in the waiting room, and I clearly remember several girlie magazines on display, being read by many. How times have changed. After a half an hour wait I was attended to by my fitter, called Frank, and he brought out my first prosthetic leg to start walking on. In the waiting room, they had a set of parallel rails along one side of the room for walking between. These rails were at two heights, with most using the top rail because the lower ones were for the double amputees. I was made to sit in a chair at the end of the rails, to start my walking practice.

I sat in the leg, and it fitted me reasonably well, as it should, being a cast of my new body shape. I had a wide leather belt, about four inches wide, attached to the leather socket from my navel to the centre of my spine, with two straps and buckles. Being new leather it was quite rigid and needed about a month's usage to be more malleable. I also had two shoulder belts, crossed over and attached to the socket both front and back. I felt like a trussed chicken!

To enable me to be more comfortable, I asked for the socket I sat in to be trimmed so it was just under my ribcage, and the edge of the socket slightly rolled over to avoid it rubbing me every step I made.

I had to stand up, hold onto the rails and bear my weight down. It hurt me a lot, so there were many adjustments made, especially in the 'bucket' where I had more soft leather padding put in the seating area. Eventually, it felt a little better;

they wanted me to walk and accordingly gave me two walking sticks. I felt like a ninety-seven-year-old, not a seventeen-year-old, and my mind was in turmoil with this life's adjustment.

I walked the length of the rails and then back again, and more adjustments were made. It was quite exhausting, and all this time I had an audience of eight fellow amputees looking or trying not to look at me, with a couple giving me some encouragement. I told Frank, I could manage with one, not two, walking sticks, so I discarded the walking stick in my right hand. It was progress of sorts, but still a long, long road ahead.

When starting to use an artificial limb for the first time, all the new pressure points on your body take many months to adjust and build up the hardening of those areas. It's a painful but necessary process to do this, and you have to go through the pain barrier. I believe the pain threshold of all amputees is quite high because of what they have to endure.

Frank told me the type of leg I had to wear was quite a strain on the body, in particular, a strain on the heart. He then said something to me, which I have always remembered all my life. He said, 'You would be lucky to reach sixty years of age because of the strain on your heart'. When you are seventeen you do not worry about old age, you just want to live life and have fun, but the statement struck a chord.

I could not wait to get home that day and show my prowess at walking on this new artificial leg. The ambulance finally arrived, and I *walked* into the ambulance this time, instead of using a wheelchair. When we arrived home, I was quite pleased with myself and the progress I had made with having a little mobility, compared to hardly any.

I asked my mum to stand at the door and watch me walk

for the first time since my amputation. She stood there watching me, and I walked about six to eight yards to the corner of the road. I turned around, so proud of what I had achieved, with a big smile on my face. I looked at her, and she had tears rolling down her cheeks. I think she was devastated to see her son like that, and there I was, smiling. I quickly realised what was happening and went to her and cuddled her. My mother never cried in front of me, but this was just too much for her, and the floodgates opened. It was both sad and poignant for both of us, in different ways.

I continued to try to walk by going through the pain barrier to harden the skin around my amputation. I also needed to adjust my body to get the balance right, which is a major thing when starting to walk again. When you are walking on a smooth, flat surface at the ALAC, it is totally different to walking on pavements, which are invariably cambered, or the odd slab is proud of the rest. I always need to be looking ahead to where I am walking to, and on what surface.

Most able-bodied people would not realise there is a difference, but when you are walking with an artificial leg, the leg needs to follow through the stride, which is often only a few millimetres from the ground. If you are too early in the stride, you catch the pavement and trip, with the consequential damage to yourself, depending upon how you land. If you over-stride, the leg can cause you to fall over too. Pavements are all slightly uneven, especially over time when movement occurs. The other aspect, of course, is the camber on pavements and roads, which, dependent on which way you are walking on the camber, can be difficult and you easily trip up. I often cross over to the other side of the road where the pavement's camber is less treacherous to me. I won't begin to mention cobbled pavements, which are a nightmare to walk on, and why, when I walk, I am always looking down to see what is just in front of me.

At the ALAC they do not cater for uneven surfaces or cambers for patients to walk on, which, after all these years, I do not understand why, as it is fundamental to walking outdoors. I know many patients, who have come in for repair or a new leg, go and walk on the hospital grounds, as this is the only way to test their walking ability on uneven ground.

Another aspect of walking with an artificial leg is the heel size of your shoe. Often heel sizes vary on the type or style of shoe, but this has a major impact on walking. Those few millimetres of difference in heel height take some adjustment to the way you must walk. Yet another small, but significant, thing I needed to remember.

I was pushing myself to see how far I could walk, but it was so painful. Even now, I associate walking with pain. After a short distance, you get somewhat out of breath, so you need to breathe after the stride. If I continue walking, I either get a headache, which I put down to blood pressure or the stitch. I carry on after this at my peril because the pain gets so bad you cannot continue walking, and recovery from this can be between a quarter of an hour to several hours, with the need to take painkillers to help ease the discomfort.

Through all these early days, I was slowly learning my limitations and continually had to reset my goals to more realistic ones. The reality of the amputation was gradually dawning on me and the long-term impact it would have on my life.

Chapter 10: Back To Work

It took me some time to get used to the mechanisms for sitting down and standing up. If my hip mechanism was not locked properly and you tried to walk, you fell over. There were also the phantom pains to contend with. At the ALAC, they said it would be five or six months before they made me a leg with a proper foot on, so I was determined to try and walk as best I could. This proved exceedingly difficult with a rigid leg and rocker foot.

I had been off work for nearly ten months and, to get back to some semblance of normality, it was decided that I returned to work, but I could not do my old job. The Southern Gas Board were good, though, and as I had always wanted to be a draughtsman, they made a position available in their Distribution Department. This was to be above the showrooms near the Portsmouth Guildhall on the first floor, and I returned to work in October 1967.

If you have your leg amputated below the knee, you can manage stairs as you always have, and walk almost without anyone knowing your loss. With an amputation above the knee, however, you have more difficulty walking, more so the higher the amputation is, but stairs cause the most problems of all. Since my amputation stairs have been, and always will be, the bane of my life. I really dislike having to use stairs and still do, to this day. I feel as if everyone is staring at me and thinking, 'He is disabled', which I am. I do not want to be disabled but it is a fact of life. I want to be seen by society as within the realms of normality, but I am not. This has been a life-long struggle to manage for me, as I open my thoughts for all to read, but not necessarily understand. Over time, this struggle to accept who I am/my disability has lessened, but still, I find myself unable to fully accept this identity. It is strange, not really logical, but we are all individuals with complex feelings and emotions, and I am no exception.

I decided to buy myself a three-piece suit from a local clothes shop and tailor, called, John Collier. Their sing-along catchphrase was 'John Collier, John Collier, the window to watch', which sounds corny nowadays, but this was in the late 1960s. I opened a monthly account to pay into, and had immediate credit, so I was duly measured up by the bespoke tailors. This was my first tailored suit, and I had no idea what to buy, so I chose a conservative, dark blue, striped cloth. The other trousers I wore were getting marked by the side-locking mechanism, and I was persuaded to have the right leg of the suit trousers lined to avoid damaging it. Having been measured I was told it would take three weeks to make the suit.

I needed a new pair of shoes too, so after being measured for the suit, I went into the shoe shop opposite and started to try on some black, chisel-toed shoes, which were all the rage then. I eventually found a pair I liked and tried them on. This was when I made a fundamental mistake in buying these shoes. I walked with them on and decided to buy them even though the left shoe was quite tight and would need wearing in. I had forgotten the shoe only had to be comfortable for my left foot, not my right, but as I could still feel my right foot, I thought that one fitted fine! You live and learn, and I never made that mistake again.

Eventually, I heard from the tailors that my suit was finished and was asked to come in for a fitting and collection. I went there and they showed me to a small, curtained room with a stool, and left me to try on my suit. I had always changed my trousers in the bedroom, by undoing the two straps around my waist and the shoulder strap, then putting the leg on the bed. I could not bend over enough to enable me to leave my artificial leg on and so put the trousers on. I had to take my leg off. This was no mean feat when sitting on a stool, and I struggled, but eventually put the new trousers on my artificial leg followed by the shoe. I was settled down to put my left leg in the trousers, when in walked the tailor, with no warning. He apologised profusely and walked out, but another embarrassing moment had happened, and I thought to myself, 'Whatever next?' The only consolation of the day was the suit fitted fine.

My new job involved having to walk up two old stone flights of stairs. I really did not like this from the very first day and would often wait until nobody was near before I quickly got up those stairs, two steps at a time, so no one would see me. I would also, at the end of the day, time my descent of the stairs to be on my own. I did not like it if anyone was around at the time and often, they were.

There were only half a dozen people in the office, and they were all nice, especially Sheilagh, who was only eighteen years old. I did take her home a few times in the car, and we went out for a few drinks too, which was good fun. She even wrote a love heart with an arrow through it on my leg, much to the mirth of the fitters.

It was agreed that I would continue my disrupted education to obtain some mechanical engineering qualifications and I enrolled at Highbury Technical College, which is to the north of Portsmouth, on a four-year day release and two evenings a week course. They were very generous to me, and I was glad to further my education.

The offices we had were dated, and we soon moved to Tipner, in Portsmouth, near the firing ranges. The offices were, what you might call, temporary/permanent, but were all clean and new. The best part for me was the parking, which was close by so little walking for me and with the bonus of being on one level, so no stairs.

The Southern Gas Board had a Rifle Club at Tipner, so I decided to join it and regularly went every week. I was firing a .22 rifle, and to be honest I was not that good. I believe the highest I scored on the target was ninety-one. It was fun for a while, but I did have a better idea of fun, and it was not with rifles. At that time, having a car seemed to attract the girls.

I was beginning to understand my newfound limitation in walking, and although I had set my sights on reaching the moon, if I got to the top of the telegraph pole, that would be a success for me. I still needed a walking stick, but I did get rid of one of the shoulder belts, as they were both rubbing my shoulders badly.

I had to go to the college to enrol and took my car, to enable me to park as close as I could to the Enrolment Centre. This was another difficult moment for me, where I was faced with young able-bodied people of my age, all around me. I felt quite alone because there I was, walking amongst them with a walking stick and a lump of wood acting as a foot, which I could not hide. Some people stared whilst others looked at me after I passed, as I could see this in the window reflections. I was embarrassed by it, but it had to be done and I duly enrolled. I can understand children staring, but not adults, and I also accept the curiosity factor, but some people have no sensitivity to anyone else's feelings.

I started college in early November, and one lasting memory was finishing the evening's course, which was in some temporary/permanent classroom, situated in the car park. It was dark, and I got to the end of the corridor and opened the door to a small veranda and the two steps down to the car park, where my car was parked close by. I was still getting used to walking with a stick and managing door thresholds, as well as opening doors. As I walked through the door, my artificial leg caught the threshold and I stumbled and hopped to regain my balance to avoid falling over, but I fell straight into two girls talking on the veranda. They could see, from the stick and the rocker leg, that I was struggling. They supported me, and I remember apologising, explaining I had only recently gotten this leg. 'What a strange thing to say', they must have thought, and I still cringe when I remember that embarrassing episode.

When I look back, it was the first fall I can recall. I normally fall about two or three times a year, sometimes in public, sometimes at home, but nowadays I can mostly smile and laugh about it unless I really hurt myself.

Chapter 11: Early Days of Walking

At last, after a six-month wait, I had an appointment at the ALAC for my first leg with a proper foot on. In those days, to maintain the shape of the leg it was made from aluminium. All you could hear in the waiting room was the banging of hammers on these legs, both shaping and inserting the many rivets they required. The longer the artificial leg was, the more rivets were required. Unfortunately, this also meant, for me, that more rivets would either pop out or creak when they became loose.

I always got to the appointments early, around half eight in the morning, to get a parking space close to the ALAC. The vast majority of the appointments I was there for lasted at least three to four hours, and occasionally longer. There must be a correlation between the time it takes for a repair or fitting, and the height of the leg amputation, I think. The higher the amputation, the longer you are there. My amputation was as high as they could go.

They brought out my new leg with a leather socket to sit in, with new leather belts and buckles. I had to wear this leg in, and get used to new pressure points because no two artificial legs are the same, which meant more pain to go through. I walked in between the rails down the side of the waiting room, where all the other amputees waited, and I noticed straight away that the length of the leg was wrong. They told me to take it off, reviewed the leg length, and took it back to the workshop for adjustment. After half an hour, they came back and although the length was correct, now the socket was digging into me. They needed to stretch the leather in a certain place as it was digging into my ribs. I had to take it off and then they took it to the workshop again. Half an hour later, they returned, and I tried it again, and it was a little better, but the knee alignment was out, so further adjustments were made. This backwards and forwards was typical of the process because each artificial leg is bespoke to the individual, as no two amputations are the same.

I did find the shoulder belt was rubbing me a lot, so I made the momentous decision to not use it anymore. I tightened the two straps around my waist a little more tightly, and from that day, I never wore shoulder straps again. It was a relief and progress of sorts, but I needed to readjust to walking again without the extra support given by the shoulder strap. I adjusted quickly but still needed the walking stick. So far, I had managed to get rid of two shoulder straps and a walking stick, which for me was an improvement.

It took several more visits, over a few months, to fine-tune the fitting of the leg to an acceptable degree of comfort. It should always be remembered that the leg itself will not move or adapt, it is you that must adapt to any repairs, realignment or reconfiguration and this can take several weeks.

I was trying hard to walk so it did not show too much that I had an artificial leg. In my mind's eye, I convinced myself it hardly showed but the reality was different. I remember walking past a shop and seeing my reflection, which immediately brought home to me how much more room for improvement there was. I did not like being watched and would see people staring back at me in the reflection of the window or door. As a teenager, you can be quite reactive and worry more about what others think, but I found, as time passed, this worry mellowed.

The new leg had a locking mechanism on the side of the leg for the knee to lock, to enable walking on uneven ground, which I never really used. I liked the leg to spring naturally back from the stride when walking, but it was hard to walk because all the power to move the leg forward came from my stomach muscles, and it was not a natural motion. I found a unique way to assist my walking, though, which has served me well all my life. I had my hand in my right trouser pocket and put two fingers around the top of the locking mechanism, which I had to push down on when locking the leg. By holding this, I could not only help the leg stride through with less bodily effort, but it also improved the gait. The downside was I did not have a spare hand, as one was holding the walking stick and the other was in my pocket but being able to walk a little easier outweighed this inconvenience.

After six months of my first 'real leg', I was given an appointment for a second leg to be made. By this point, I had put on weight from my previous, meagre six and a half stone, and my socket would need to be adjusted to my new size. I had to go through the rigmarole of having Plaster of Paris wrapped around my body again. From this previous pattern, a new leather socket was made, and three weeks later I had an appointment for the fitting.

I arrived at the ALAC, checked in at reception and went to the waiting room. I normally bought a cup of coffee from the Women's Royal Voluntary Service (WRVS) ladies in the reception area where they sold cakes, buns and sandwiches. They were all volunteers and always friendly and willing to help. Eventually, my new leg was brought out, and a few light-hearted comments were made by some of the other amputees, mainly because there were not very many people with amputations this high and, therefore, artificial legs this large. I showed Frank how I was walking using the handle part of the locking mechanism, and he agreed the walking style was far better than before. I explained that I would never use the lock on the leg, and so asked if they could make me a metal, padded plate I could hold onto, with my fingers in my pocket trousers. It needed to be the same as the top section on the locking mechanism. They were bemused by this request but agreed, as they understood the uniqueness of each artificial leg for proper fitting.

There was a lot of trial and error, but eventually, they designed something suitable for me. I thought each leg was made individually for the patient, which is still true, but I had no idea, at the time, how modularisation would impact and improve the service provided.

Six weeks later, they made my second leg, and it took about three weeks of painful practice to get my body to readjust to the new positioning required. They then took my first leg away to get rid of the locking mechanism and copy the new plate on the side. A few more months later, I had two legs. Any amputee will tell you; that no two legs are the same and you always have your favourite. This, however, went against the ALAC advice, which advised alternating each leg weekly. I tried to do this, but the pain was so bad and the walking so different that I never did it again. I am not unique in this, and there are very few who alternate their legs. The age-old argument with the powers that be is until you have had an amputation you would not understand. Having said that, I do understand the reasoning behind it, but there is such a difference between theory and practice.

I needed to return regularly for repair to my leg because I was continually active on it. Some older people would not be doing what I was doing, and I do not believe it was designed for the rigour I put it through, hence the constant repairs. The relationship you have with the fitter at the ALAC is important and I had a good one with Frank. It would, in fact, last almost thirty years, until he retired. I remember going in one day and walking between the railings in the waiting room, and the familiar 'click, click, click' at every step was resonating around the room and driving me crazy. Frank said, 'I can sort that out, but firstly, do you have any cotton wool?' I told him I did not, to which he replied, 'I was going to ask you to put it in your ears and I guarantee the noise will go away!' We all laughed, and he duly took the leg away for repair. The old jokes are the best.

I was now working, had a car and a life, which had new meaning for me. When you face death at an early age, it gives an increased zest to life, especially visually enjoying life around you, and I was at an age to have some fun! I needed to catch up on some lost time.

Chapter 12: Making Up for Lost Time

I was well and truly in the era of Flower Power and hippies, where the slogan was 'Make love not war' and it seemed everyone was trying new drugs coming onto the market.

One warm, summer day in 1968, I bumped into a neighbour who lived not far away from me. He was my age and I always got on with him, but never really mixed with his circle of friends. He had quite a reputation as someone you would not argue with, and he could fight hard. We were chatting away, and he asked me if I had any fishing gear. He knew I had, and invited me out with his cousin, also the same age, in his twelve-foot bass fishing boat for some night fishing. I had always enjoyed fishing and invariably dug my own bait of ragworm on the mudflats of Rudmore, where the cross-Channel ferry berths are now located, on the west side of Portsmouth.

We set off at about eleven p.m. in the evening and met his cousin, who happened to live in Rudmore. It was a beautiful evening, quite calm and balmy, ideal for some night fishing. I carefully got into the boat, which was not easy for me because I now had to unlock the hip mechanism and lift my leg under the knee to get it into the boat. They both jumped in as easy as pie and pushed the boat into the dark waters. We all fished for about an hour but were not getting many bites, and my two fishermen friends looked quite bored. What happened next was something I never expected to happen! One of them reached into their pocket and asked me if I wanted some 'Black Bombers', which were hard drugs. I said, 'Thanks anyway, but not tonight' because I had a vision of taking these, falling overboard and being in Davy Jones's locker with a readymade anchor attached to me. They both took their drugs, and I had a restless night wondering whether they would have the horrors or blissful ecstasy with this trip. If it was the horrors, then the boat would surely capsize, if bliss, they might decide they were butterflies and take off, like my bedside companion I had previously met in hospital. In the end, they tripped away, lying in the boat, oblivious to everything around them. It was a long night, but uneventful, thank goodness. I never did get my fishing rod and gear back, despite asking, and never went fishing with them again.

My neighbour's path in life was to marry a local girl and have several children, but he was into the drug and enforcement scene. I saw him a few times in the years following our fishing expedition and knew he was getting deeper and deeper into drugs. He went to jail quite a few times and eventually moved into the heavy scene in London. We all have choices in our lives, and he made his, but it was not a route I wanted to take to make up for the lost time. He is dead now.

I was pushing myself to walk and it was eight months since I was first given my artificial leg, so a hard decision was needed regarding the walking stick I used in my left hand. If I did not get rid of it then, I felt it would be with me all my life, and I certainly did not want that. I decided, there and then, to literally throw it away, which I did, and it felt brilliant.

Now that I was walking without any shoulder straps or walking sticks, I needed to have the belt, around the socket I sat in, pulled quite tight. This caused problems with it rubbing against the skin, and despite applying creams to help, the skin takes time to harden. Even then, if you walk a little further than normal it chafes your skin, or if it is particularly hot, the skin marks more easily.

It was important for me to appear to be within the 'normal' range because that is what I had always been. I did not want people looking at me thinking 'He is disabled' if I could avoid it. By ridding myself of the walking stick, it stopped the immediacy of that label. It was a bit naive of me, really, but that is how I dealt with it, emotionally, as a teenager. As soon as I walked, people would know something was wrong, but they did not know I had lost my leg. It is a strange thought process, looking back, but I was in uncharted territory and literally every step was now different for me.

I was working and had a car that was like a magnet, in those days, for girls. I did not earn a lot, but enough to be comfortable and just have fun, as do most eighteen-year-old teenagers today. I had quite a few girlfriends and remember having some plastic mistletoe hanging from the inside car mirror. It always worked because the girls would say 'What is that hanging there?' and so I would do what you should do, under the mistletoe.

One day, I was by the front door of our house, when two girls walked by on the opposite side of the road. One I recognised as Heather, a girl who lived about one hundred yards away on the next block of houses, but not the other attractive, dark-haired girl. I called out to them, and they smiled and then crossed over. We started talking and I found out the attractive girl's name was Ann. I asked if they would like a ride in the car, so off we went around town, just listening to Radio Caroline and having a carefree drive. Later, I dropped Ann off at her house, which was about half a mile from where I lived, and while driving home to drop Heather off, I asked her if she wanted to go out that night. She said 'Yes' and I had a date. I liked Heather and we went for a drink and had some fun, but I did keep thinking about Ann.

A week later, I saw Ann walking on the opposite side of the road, in her trendy three-quarter length maroon leather coat, going to visit Heather. I noticed an immediate attraction to her; she was a little shy, but we started talking. I invited her out for a drink that night and we went on our first date to a pub called The Alpenhorn on Hayling Island, not far from Portsmouth. She sat down in the pub, and I went to get some drinks for us at the bar. I ordered her vodka and lime, and when it arrived, I took it straight to her. I always had to make two journeys for the drinks because I only had one hand free, with my right hand always needed to help move my artificial leg when walking. This is always a problem for me carrying drinks. Not only that, but I used to joke that by ordering a pint for myself, it would be half by the time I carried it to the table with the spillage.

Arthur and Lyn had been saving for a long time and bought their first house locally. They got married in September 1969 and I was his best man. I invited Ann along to the evening reception and she met all the family. We got on well and it was the start of my first serious relationship.

Chapter 13:
Finding My Way In Life

I fell in love easily with Ann, who was nearly a year younger than me and started seeing her every day. It is a wonderful time of your life with all those new-found emotions and feelings, even the knot in your stomach because you just want to be with that person all the time.

Ann worked at a local solicitor's office as a receptionist/ secretary, working from nine a.m. until six p.m. Her father was quite strict and said if she could not get home for dinner at five p.m., then she had to provide for herself. He told her mother not to plate up any food, which caused a lot of angst. This meant that Ann's diet was poor, often just eating a sandwich or having a bag of chips for dinner. It remains difficult to understand why he had this approach to his own daughter, but she was unhappy at home.

We ate out a few times and had some lovely times driving all over the place. My disability was never a problem to her and when we went for an evening drink, she would always go to the bar and carry the drinks back to where we were sat. I did, after about four months, finally get invited for Sunday dinner at her house, as did Ann to my house. Ann had four brothers, David and Mike, who were older, and Robert and Keith, who were younger than her. David and Mike had already left home and joined the RAF. Ann's mother cooked a lovely roast dinner, which everyone enjoyed. I met her father, and the feedback I had from Ann was her dad asking her 'Why would you want to go out with someone who only has one leg?' Not a good start.

Only Robert and Keith were still at home but because Ann was always looking after Keith, who was ten years younger than her, she formed a special bond with him. Keith was born when his father was sixty-two and he did not have the same parental upbringing as I had. Ann was particularly close to her youngest brother Keith, who was eight years old when I first met him. She was like a surrogate mother to him and was always tasked with taking him out; they were close. We used to take Keith out in the car with us and he was a lovely lad, but like many youngest siblings he was a little spoilt. When we went out with my family, Keith would often come along with us. I used to tease him somewhat as we played putting. He would have his favourite golf ball and I would somehow manage to pick it up, much to his chagrin and he would bitterly complain to Ann. It was just a bit of fun, but perhaps not to an eight-year-old.

Margaret had gone to school with Ann and remembers a squabble they had. She reminisced with her and laughed about it and was always close after that. My family made Ann welcome and she quickly integrated into it, with many day trips and celebratory birthday and anniversary meals together. We had been going out together for three months and talked a lot on the phone, even during the day when we were supposedly working, when we decided, with the impetuousness of youth, in November of 1969 to become engaged. There was no proposal, we just spoke about it and wanted to spend the rest of our lives together, so we started looking at rings, eventually finding a lovely ruby ring. This cost me nearly a month's wages but Ann's smile, as she put it on her finger, was worth every penny.

We needed to start saving for the future, but it was difficult when you just want to have a good time. There was no overtime where I worked, so no chance of earning any extra money, but I was learning a lot, which would help me no end in the future.

In the summer of 1970, we went on holiday to Cornwall and hired a caravan for a week, visiting the usual haunts of Tintagel, Truro, Mevagissey and Newquay. It was a lovely, carefree time of our lives and we were in love, talking about the future, and making key decisions. One of those decisions was to find a flat to rent and live together after we got back from the holiday. When we returned home, we looked at a few flats close to where we lived, but then something happened to decide the next course of action.

My mother and sister were in the Salvation Army and some officers of another corps were retiring. They heard in early September, through the grapevine, that the home they had in Telephone Road in Portsmouth was going to be sold and we were offered the first refusal. It was quite mind-blowing as I was coming up to my twentieth birthday and Ann was only eighteen and there we were, thinking about buying our first house. We looked at the house, which was in the 1920s/1930s time warp. It was very dark, but the rooms were a good size and it had three bedrooms. It had potential but was in a bad state of repair.

We were excited about this opportunity and the cost was a whopping one thousand, eight hundred pounds, which sounds small nowadays, but it is all relative to the marketplace at that time and what you earn. We had a little money saved, but my father said he would lend me the balance for a deposit. I paid him back as soon as I could, over the next two years. I knew my parents had little in the way of savings, so that was very generous of them. My father said to us all, he always had enough savings to pay for a new roof but that was it.

We decided to go to the Portsmouth Building Society to enquire about a mortgage and were accepted with our combined wages, subject to the survey. We then made an offer to buy the house at the full asking price. Then the reality of home ownership hit us. The survey had come back with the house needing some roof repair, it also had some damp proofing issues, needed new electrics throughout and the back-garden party wall needed replacing. We got a quote for the work and Arthur offered to do the electrics as he was now a qualified electrician. We presented the one hundred and twenty pounds quote for the additional work to the house owners, who accepted it and lowered the asking price of the house to one thousand, six hundred and eighty pounds. We shook hands, engaged a solicitor and before long we had our first house. Looking back, I was so lucky to be on the property ladder at a young age and it set me up for life, owning my own house.

Things were moving at pace, and we decided to get married in the November of 1970. Not only were we trying to get the house up to a standard to move into, but we were also planning our wedding. They were heady days.

My father would join me most days after work, to help with decorating the house. He was a stalwart father and I owed him a lot for all his hard work. Arthur, too, worked hard at rewiring the house, and my cousin, Ron, who had his own roofing business, did me a special deal by putting a new roof on. We needed to engage a builder for all the other works required, so got three quotes. The quotes were all within ten per cent. of each other and the middle quote was from the son of neighbours we had known all our lives. We decided to take the middle quote, and to this day I regret it. I should have researched his past work.

The work started on the house and then the builder just disappeared for a few days before coming back for a few more days. This went on for several weeks as he was finishing another job. He was a one-man band, a jack-of- all-trades and the work just dragged on and on.

He had knocked the scullery down and covered it in a tarpaulin right at the beginning of winter. We continued decorating the house, but his progress was so slow and there was no way we could move into the house with no back wall and no hot water. It was so frustrating, and we realised we had made a big mistake in using this so-called builder.

Chapter 14: Married Life

I was twenty and Ann nineteen when we got married. Too young, really, but you can be headstrong at that age and the old adage of not being able to put an old head on young shoulders comes to mind. I believe my parents were simply happy to see me happy and settling down.

It was a struggle with money, I needed a car to get around, and to me, it was not a luxury but a necessity. The house, too, needed money thrown at it, and we were getting married too; life was a struggle, but we were in love. We decided to take out a loan to pay for the wedding and reception. It was the only way forward, although my mum and dad did help a little too.

Arrangements were made for us to marry in St. Mary's Church in Portsmouth, where there has been a church for hundreds of years, going back to the eleventh century, possibly as far back as 650 AD. Amusingly, records show that an Ann Paffett got married there in 1775. We had to attend services for three weeks prior to getting married, to hear the Banns read, announcing the intended marriage and an opportunity for any objections. These were the laws of the land. We also had to attend the church for a talk with the vicar. I did not realise how long this church aisle was and I knew I had to walk this with everyone looking at me. My fears were about to haunt me again.

When walking, I am most comfortable at a moderate pace, too slow or too fast is not easy for me. I am happy to hold hands, but my balance is thrown somewhat if they loop their arm through mine. After the marriage ceremony, I had to walk the whole length of a long church aisle, with my new wife's arm in mine. It was challenging and I did not want to trip up and fall over, but fortunately, I managed it. We had our black and white photos taken and one colour reel because colour photos were so expensive. It was a late November wedding at three p.m. and as we came out of the church, on what had been a cloudy, dank, overcast day, the sun shone low in the sky for our photos.

Our honeymoon was three days in the Chichester Motel, about twenty miles from Portsmouth. We went out one day to Longleat Safari Park in Somerset and the next day to the Petticoat Lane market in London, where I bought Ann a leather coat with rabbit fur. We went home after three nights, back to work and were blissfully happy.

My parents kindly let us stay in my old bedroom at home whilst the work was being undertaken by our chosen builder. We only expected a few weeks, but unfortunately, weeks turned into months. We spoke with the builder so many times and were given false promises about his work and completion. He had knocked the back of the house scullery down, which was being replaced with a new single-storey bathroom. It stayed open to the elements for several months during winter with just a tarpaulin on, so the inside of the house was freezing and uninhabitable. He had over-committed himself, worked on his own and was a jack-of- all-trades and master of none.

My mother was born in an era where she did most things for all of us. I just threw my dirty clothes into a corner at night and *hey presto*, I had clean clothes to put on the next day. All the cooking and cleaning were done for me, so it was a carefree existence, but you do not learn much about how to keep a house, pay bills and upkeep your property like that.

I suppose all of us children were spoilt in that sense, but with the trauma of my illness, there was a determination to get and keep me healthy. My mother did most things for us, but one thing she did for me springs to mind, which, to this day, makes me feel guilty. When I took my leg off at night, I needed to change the sock so my mother would do this for me and push the shoe back on. She did this for me every day I lived at home and when I got married, I just expected Ann to carry on and do this chore. After six months of her doing this, there was a rebellion in the air and she finally said, 'There is no reason why you can't do it!' I look back now and cringe at that, and of course, I should have been doing it a long time ago.

There were two advantages to losing your leg. Firstly, I now had only five not ten toenails to keep trimmed, and secondly, I only got through half the socks I used to because I just swapped the clean one on my artificial leg over with the dirty one.

By early spring, the builder had started to build the external wall of the bathroom and we were not impressed with his brickwork at all. The cement between the levels of brickwork ranged from a quarter of an inch (six millimetres) to one and a quarter inches (thirty millimetres) and the concave bow in the wall from top to bottom was one and a half inches (thirty-seven millimetres). It was poor, shoddy work and he had been working on it for several months with completion at only about twenty per cent. We had to do something.

Ann had changed her job a few months back and was now

working for a quantity surveying company. They had about twenty well-qualified quantity surveyors and we wanted an independent report drawn up, so Ann asked someone she worked closely with if he could help. He produced a ten-page report of defects, so we knew we were vindicated over our concerns. It was messy, but we did, in effect, sack the builder. It was a tough start to house ownership and I had to get additional funding from the building society to correct all the problems found. The lesson here was not to use family and friends for any major work.

All the problems delayed us from moving into the house, but my parents were kind enough to let us stay there until enough work was done by another builder, to at least make it habitable, before we could move in there. It was great having our own house and my dad, for many evenings, helped us with wallpapering and painting the whole house.

Independence is a wonderful thing at twenty but with it comes responsibility so we were both on a quick learning curve, and yes, we made a few mistakes, but those are what you learn from. Nearly two years after acquiring the house, we eventually got all the work completed and were able to carpet the whole house. We bought a lot of second-hand furniture to start with, and the only new item we had was a washing machine.

We had nice neighbours on either side of us. On one side was a couple, a little older than us, with two children and on the other side an older lady on her own. I decided that I could paint the back of the house guttering and soffit, so bought a set of ladders and went about painting. Going up the ladder two steps at a time and holding on for grim death at the top was a challenge for me, but one I was determined to meet. The biggest problem for me was moving the ladders when extended. The whole centre of gravity is changed, and you must balance yourself well to walk and move a few steps with them, especially with only one leg. I remember moving them during this painting task, only to lose my balance and the top of the ladder moved quickly toward the neighbour's window. Somehow it bounced off it and settled on her side of the house. It was a lucky escape, but you live and learn.

The old lady never said anything about the ladder, if she saw it at all, but I felt sorry for her because her family never seemed to visit or help her. One day, whilst I was painting the front of the house guttering and soffit, I offered to paint the front of her house too. She was pleased, and it did not take long to apply the undercoat and later gloss. I have found it is always nice to get on with your neighbours, to help them if you can and have always been lucky in that sense.

We were both working but like most young couples, money was tight. By the time we had paid the mortgage, house bills, petrol, food, etc., there was not much left, but we were just about managing. Arthur worked in the Portsmouth Dockyard at that time and having served his apprenticeship there as an electrician, got promoted to the drawing office. He did occasional electrical work on the side, to get the little extras a young family needed. We hatched a plan between us to get more work.

With my drawing office background, I had drawn up the plans for outline planning permission and building controls for my house so had some knowledge. Arthur and I placed an advert in the local paper, called The Portsmouth News, advertising drawing up extension plans, getting all the relevant approvals, as well as any electrical work. We waited for the phone to ring but it never did, nobody phoned so that was the end of that venture.

I later helped Arthur to rewire a house by chiselling out the walls for the first fit sockets, but I took so much skin off my knuckles with misdirected hammer blows, I just knew I wasn't cut out for that vocation, and I know Arthur agreed.

I felt a sense of loyalty to The Southern Gas Board, but there was no future there for me in their drawing office and I decided to look around for another job, with better prospects and more money. I remember my dad was aghast at this because he always wanted security in work hence why he stayed in one job all his working life. He was old enough to remember The Great Depression in the 1930s so it must have left a scar on him. He was also concerned about my disability and how perhaps smaller firms would treat me. I had no such concerns and started looking around for another job and was offered a job as a design draughtsman at a heating, ventilating and air conditioning company called Dunham Bush. It was more money, close to where Ann worked but above all, they said they would pay for my continued education at the Portsmouth Polytech.

I accepted the offer and started my new job in 1971. It was on a large site with the design and sales offices in the front, research and development (R&D) on the side and the large manufacturing/paint shop behind. I could park close to where I worked but to me, the only drawback was the drawing office being up two flights of stairs. I occasionally had to go onto the shop floor, which was noisy, but the consolation was my (at times) creaking leg could not be heard there, but it was quite exhausting for me, walking around it.

My whole mindset was altered to cater for my disability.

I was always looking ahead at the ground I had to walk on, whether it was uneven or cambered. I would look at where I was going and look for the quickest, straightest route. I would even walk a little further if it avoided steps of any kind to maybe find a slope to go up. I was always mindful of people looking at me and wondering what they thought. It was constant and when you are young you worry more about what others think than later in life, but still to this day, it continues to haunt me somewhat. It has mellowed a little as the years have gone by, but not much.

One other aspect is how much I drink! The more you drink the more you need to visit the toilet. This means more walking, which means more pain. I, therefore, am mindful wherever I go, of how much I drink. I have mostly limited my drinking at work to avoid using the toilets too much. Another example is going to watch a Portsmouth football game, where I stop drinking six hours before I go to the game. In this way, I do not have to navigate stairs and people at half-time. It works for me.

Another aspect of walking, for me, is keeping the same stride and pace to minimise the pain I have walking. I use more energy walking slowly, but it is about effort and balance. I do not like walking with a lot of people because your pace is invariably altering a lot as you move to avoid bumping into one another. I used to do it unbeknown to me and never gave it a second thought, but now it is totally different, and I avoid crowds where possible.

With the type of amputation I have and the socket I need to sit in, there are always two large straps across my lower stomach connected to the belt around my waist. To walk with this, you must control your breathing pattern such that when the artificial foot touches the ground you then must breathe in. It is exceedingly difficult walking any other way and before long I was doing it without thinking, but it all changes when you eat! It is extremely uncomfortable to walk on a full stomach and if I need to, I can only manage a very short walk. On a half-full stomach, it is much more manageable and the straps, which apply pressure to your stomach are not too painful.

It has been a learning process, which could be described as almost symbiotic between my artificial leg and my body. Adjustments are needed every day depending on whether it's body pain, balance or the artificial leg dynamics. Life, to me, is about change, with little being constant, and it is how you adjust to the change which defines you.

Chapter 15:
Planning for the Future

I was now only going for a medical check-up every six months and apart from a few odd shooting pains, which were like the cancer pains, I felt fit and healthy. I was learning a lot at work and Ann was chopping and changing her jobs quite a bit. She never stayed long at her jobs because I think boredom quickly set in. Ann even worked as a wages clerk at Dunham Bush, where I worked, for about a year.

I enjoyed playing darts with Arthur and Margaret in the back garden when I was young, so I decided to join the Dunham Bush Darts Team, which played in the Inter-Firms League. There were matches around the pubs of Portsmouth every Friday and Ann used to come with me for the games. I was soon voted in as captain of the team, which was not because I was a good player, but I did learn later being captain was a poisoned chalice.

It is strange to imagine, but in the team, there was a lot of back-biting particularly as I was the only team member in the office; the rest were on the shop floor. If you changed the team and they won, then you were doing a good job, if they lost, then a new captain was needed. If you did not play certain individuals, they would stir up the mob and anarchy was afoot.

One game I played in, is etched into my memory. Not because of the way we played or who we played but down to one individual's throwaway remark. I was about fifth on the list to play and as a team, we were winning. I went to the oche, which is the toe line behind which the player stands, and this individual said to the one I was playing, 'Don't worry, you should beat him, he is a cripple.' There were a few sniggers, but what an insensitive comment to make! It brought back to me the note in the train window when I was at Waterloo Station travelling back from Westminster Hospital, after my amputation, which read 'Reserved for Cripple'. I lost the game, we lost the match, so my days as captain were numbered and my enthusiasm for it had waned.

I was able to pass, with a Credit, my mechanical engineering exams, so continued at the Portsmouth Polytech for two more years. It was there I met a number of interesting people in their early twenties. One was small in stature and had long curly hair but did not walk well. Over the coming months, I got to talk to him and learnt he suffered from acute arthritis. I had never seen this before in someone so young, and he did seem angry about it. As the first year went on, his walking became more of a shuffle, and he was struggling with his mobility. I did admire his tenacity and the way he continued despite his difficulty in walking. He never completed the second year as arthritis took a terrible toll on him, which was so tragic in someone so young. At times, I feel you must reflect on how fortunate you are compared to some others.

In the final year, we formed groups of four students and had a thesis to produce. We decided on a coin-counting machine and duly contacted many companies, such as De La Rue, for information to aid our research. It was fun and helped not only to get a detailed insight into the mechanics required for these machines but also helped us to work as a team, which is so important in your working life.

I remember one of our team members a few years later, opening his own coffee shop with a range of coffee beans and cake delicacies. Maybe it was the position of the shop for his customers was not right or he was too far ahead of his time, but it never succeeded. I always wondered what his next venture was.

We had lived in our house for nearly four years and inflation was so rampant it averaged over 7% for the decade. This was good and bad for me because wages never kept pace with inflation. House prices were soaring, but then so were the mortgage repayments. I had a valuation on my house and in the four years since I bought it for £1,680, having spent a further £1400 on it the valuation had risen to £8,250. Ann and I started looking around for another property in Portsmouth, when, out of the blue, the estate agent said there was a bungalow we might be interested in, in Horndean, which is a small village about eleven miles north of Portsmouth. We arranged to view the semi-detached two-bedroom bungalow, which straight away interested me, being all on one level and with no stairs to climb. It had been modernised throughout and had a large back garden and thirty-square foot front garden. We made the mistake of letting our hearts rule our heads and plunged into making an offer there and then. It was foolish and without foresight, but you live and learn.

Our house in Portsmouth sold quickly for £8100 and we bought at £10,350. It was a roller coaster event and we moved quickly into our next property. There were lots of pros in buying the property as everything had been modernised, the garden was huge compared to our previous one and we could be in the countryside in under three minutes. The cons were that it was right alongside a dual carriageway, so noise was an issue, and we both worked in Portsmouth so were travelling around thirty thousand miles a year. The biggest issue was starting a family because the second bedroom was used as a dining room, and I did not think it was worth building bedrooms in the attic.

I have always enjoyed gardening and when I moved to Horndean, the back garden was a challenge. It was sixty feet by thirty feet wide and on either side was a privet hedge that had been there for many years. It was between twelve and fifteen feet high and about four feet wide. I intended to cut it down to a manageable six feet high and make it two feet wide. Under normal circumstances, it is quite a task, but looking back it was compounded by the only tools I had being handsaw and secateurs. It took ages to do and a few blisters too, but eventually, it looked good. The front garden hedge I made into a box hedge about two feet high, so that too made a difference.

We had not been there long, when a couple of Gypsies knocked on the door and said they had some spare tarmac and would be able to tarmac my front drive over the concrete base for about a week's wages, at the time. I said I wanted to alter the shape of the driveway slightly and asked them to put a base down before they laid the tarmac. We shook hands on it and off they went. I knew the risks of dealing with Gypsies so I said I would not hand any money over until the job was finished.

A few days later, whilst we were at work, they came along, laid the driveway and we were both delighted with it. It looked good and made such a difference. They came back the next evening, I duly paid them, and we shook hands on a job well done. About two weeks later, I heard a noise coming from under the car, which I had parked on our new driveway. I got the jack out, to raise it to have a look underneath it. I put the jack into the car's jacking point and it pumped up and down, but the car did not go up. At first, I was perplexed but then I could see the base of the jack was going deep into the tarmac. The Gypsies had not put a base down as I had asked them to, they had just laid the tarmac in the area over the grass! They had lived up to their reputation. Over the coming months, I had dandelions coming through the tarmac. I guess it was one of life's many lessons for me.

With some of the money we made from the sale of the house, we bought a newer car, but this time it was an automatic rather than having hand controls fitted. I always needed to ensure there was adequate space for my artificial leg to fit comfortably in, and would not impair me from using the pedals with my left foot. We ended up buying a Mark 2 Ford Cortina in beige. I decided to have the accelerator pedal put on the left side of the brake, to make driving with my left foot easier and to certainly make my right foot sit comfortably in the space created. Having used my left foot for the clutch, I was now using it for the accelerator pedal and getting used to using the brake with my left foot, not my right hand. It was all a change, but after a few mishaps, it worked well. It was a decision to change the accelerator pedal, one I would come to regret.

We had been married for four years and both thought it was time to start a family, and we waited and waited but nothing happened. I can understand a little of what couples go through when trying for a family because Ann was getting quite upset at not conceiving.

Life carried on, as did the daily commute. It took its toll on the car and eventually, I replaced it with an automatic Mini, bright orange in fact. It had relatively low mileage and the number of miles per gallon was much better than my Ford Cortina. It was, however, low to the ground and you were close to the front of the car, so you did feel vulnerable in the event of a crash. I decided I could just about manage without changing the accelerator over to the left of the brake like the previous car. This was where the problem started in making instant driving decisions and the millisecond of hesitation. It was difficult driving, and I would never recommend the changeover. It literally took about ten years of driving to retrain my mind to make the right instantaneous decision.

One of my work colleagues liked to go flying, and to keep your pilot's licence you must ensure you complete a minimum number of flying hours a year. He said that if I was willing to pay for the fuel, then he and his friend would take Ann and I up on two separate flights over the Portsmouth area. It was something I had tried to do before in a glider, in nearby Lee-on-the-Solent. During this previous attempt, I had just about managed to get into the cockpit and was waiting to take off, when the weather closed in and the flight was abandoned. This flight, with my colleagues, was to take off from Portsmouth Airfield, which closed shortly after our flight in December 1973 and where a large housing estate, called Anchorage Park, now stands.

Both Ann and I were looking forward to this, although I think Ann was more nervous than me. We arrived at the airfield, which was quite small and only had a grass runway to land and take off. There were two, two-seater light aircraft waiting with my colleague and his friend. We had a brief chat, and Ann got into her plane and I into mine. Ann went first, followed by our plane, which was very bumpy taking off from a grass runway. It was a fantastic feeling and gave us such wonderful views over Portsmouth and the surrounding area. I could see Ann's plane in the distance heading north and I was completely shocked to see her plane looping the loop. I thought how brave she was, doing that. I was offered the same experience but decided against it. We flew around for about an hour and it was amazing.

I had landed just before Ann's aircraft and watched her land and taxi to the terminal. She got out, but I think she struggled to walk in a straight line if truth be told. We thanked them and said our farewells, then drove back home. In the car, I said it was a fantastic experience and I was really surprised about the loop-the-loop. Ann owned up and said she thought the pilot had said, 'Are you enjoying yourself?' because it was very noisy in the cockpit, when in fact he was asking her if she wanted to experience a loop-the-loop. She said she would never have agreed to that in a million years, and her stomach was still three thousand feet in the air. One of life's experiences, but more so for Ann.

After nearly four years at Dunham Bush, I decided to look around for another position. I had finished at the Portsmouth Polytech, gained some qualifications and was continuing night school doing a two-year course for the Institute of Works Management Diploma, Parts One and Two. I did this off my own bat and paid the fees myself.

In 1973, I joined a contracting company called Southern Designs, as a design draughtsman, working on thin film technology for the space industry. I was also working on printed circuit board design. I was being taught quite a lot and really enjoyed the thin film technology used in satellites, for which I helped design the substrates for manufacturing.

I remember talking to one of the senior draughtsmen about my disability and he asked me if I was married, to which I replied 'Yes'. He replied, 'She must be incredibly special' and with those five words it brought it home to me how right he was. It would not suit everyone to be married to an amputee. I think those people who do are special, caring people. Even now, I always look at those in wheelchairs and empathise, but the person who is caring for that individual always gets my admiration.

In 1974, the miner's strike started and owing to the industrial action taken by the coal miners, the Conservative government at the time introduced several measures to conserve electricity. Two of these measures affected me because there were many power cuts, so at times we had no electricity at work, only a noisy generator and we were reduced to a three-day working week of thirty hours. To complicate matters, there was petrol rationing and I no longer lived in Portsmouth. To me, a car was essential as I could not use public transport because I could not walk far enough to the bus stop.

These were difficult times as inflation was high, my mortgage repayments kept increasing (at one stage by fifteen per cent.), I had a reduced income by more than twenty per cent. and the future seemed unsure. The Prime Minister, Ted Heath, refused to give in to the miners' seven per cent. wage increase demands and declared a state of emergency. He eventually called a general election, thought the country was in sympathy with him, and lost. The new Labour government soon reached agreement with the miners and normality was restored, thank goodness.

The work I was doing was quite selective and only two

people were involved in the thin film design, myself being one, and the other being a staff person at Marconi Space and Development. With some of this uncertainty on the work front there were inevitable delays in investment in new work, and therefore only enough work for one designer. My work there suddenly stopped, and the company needed to find me another role.

Fortunately for the company, some work had been won from Avery Hardoll for a designer to work in their electronic research and development offices in Havant. I was interviewed and accepted by them to start the very next day. They were manufacturers of petrol pumps and many other engineering products, such as fluid measurement systems. It was interesting working within a small team of six people at the cutting edge of petrol pump dispensing design. I helped with the draughting of the printed circuit board designs, not just for the pumps but also the dispensing motherboards in the kiosks. I often went with one of the senior design engineers to several BP petrol stations where the new pumps were being installed.

Havant is a town just northeast of Portsmouth and for me it was halfway home to Horndean. It was less mileage, and I avoided the early morning traffic jams too. There was a huge car park there and the R&D offices were alongside this. For me it was ideal, with little walking and in a single storey building.

All this time I was picking up a lot of knowledge in different industries, which, at the time, I did not realise would serve me well for my future career. I now had some qualifications but needed to make the jump from a draughtsman to an engineer. I had started looking around again for a new position and one came up as a product engineer in

Portsmouth at Marconi Space and Development. The interview went well because of my previous thin film work and I was offered the role of product engineer in the Broad Oaks Manufacturing side of the business. The downside was a salary decrease of ten per cent., but it was worth taking to get the engineer status.

We decided it would be nice to get a dog, being a few minutes from the countryside and saw a breeder advertising in the local paper, who had some red setter puppies available soon. The breeder lived in Exton, a lovely small village about twenty-six miles north of Portsmouth, so we phoned and made an appointment. It is almost always fatal to fall in love with puppies at first sight, and we were no exception because they were adorable. They were pedigree with all the associated paperwork, and I believe it cost me a week's wages to buy him. We called him Milo, after the Irish actor Milo O'Shea. He was a beautiful dog, but as a puppy their legs seemed to grow before their bodies. It soon catches up, and after being groomed he was so handsome.

One day, Ann and I went to Winchester, where there was a park area surrounded by a water canal about ten yards wide around most of it. We were playing with Milo, who loved chasing after sticks or a ball to bring it back to you only to be thrown again and again. One of us threw a ball, which went into the canal, and into the water jumped Milo. Unfortunately, there was a lot of smelly, gooey mud there, with little water where his ball had landed because it had not rained for many weeks. He was well and truly stuck in this quagmire and was in some distress. There was no way I could get to him with my artificial leg, so it was left to Ann to rescue him. I remember her lovely white top and sky-blue trousers absolutely covered in mud as she went about the recovery operation. Not to miss an opportunity, I took several photographs with my camera and none showed Ann smiling, she was not amused, which made me laugh even more. I do not think she ever forgave me for that.

We took Milo to dog training classes and he did quite well, with Ann doing most of the walking around the training hall. When I walked him, I could not walk far so would let him off his lead and he would run and run. I persevered with training and I could get him to sit about fifty yards away with just hand signals, lie down and come to me. He would come back to me nine times out of ten but that tenth time he would just look at me, cock his head, as if to say, 'I don't know you' and run off, not to be seen for an hour or two. I paid quite a bit out in rewards when people brought him back to me from the address on his collar.

Ann and I thought we would enter him for a show in Portchester, a few miles west of Portsmouth, where there was a fete. We groomed him well and he looked so handsome. Ann had been practicing how to hold both his chin and tail up, for when the judges would mark him. The fateful day came, and it was a huge turnout, being a glorious summer day. Ann entered the ring with many other dogs and walked all around as the three judges ran the rule over the entries. Red setters have a lovely stride and the flags on his legs just flowed as he walked and cantered. I felt quietly confident.

All the dogs were in a line about twelve feet apart and the judges were running the rule over each dog. They were getting closer and closer to where Milo was. Ann looked over to me and I gave her a reassuring thumbs up. It was now Milo's turn and Ann took her stance as the judges walked up to him. They looked and made some notes and then walked to his rear. Milo being a rather inquisitive dog then looked round to see where they were, with Ann still holding said tail and chin. As the judges moved around him, Milo followed and of course Ann had to so the judges walked around again followed by Milo with Ann in tow. Everyone was laughing at this dog going around and around in ever decreasing circles, with Ann trying to stop him. The outcome was that Ann was not amused and vowed never to show the dog again. Of course, we never won a ribbon of any sort and thank goodness they never gave one for the worst behaved dog of the show!

Milo was a scatter-brained dog, and where I lived in Horndean, they were building a small housing estate at the back of us, with what used to be our long gardens. I would walk with him, of an evening, and throw the odd piece of wood for him to retrieve. He loved that game and it helped exercise him. As the building works there continued, I picked up the odd stone, threw it and waited for him to bring it back to me. He brought a few back but not many and I thought nothing of it. The next day he did not want his food and seemed lethargic, so we thought he was just under the weather. The next day he was worse so a visit to the vets was needed. The vet examined him and could see he was not at all well so took some X-rays. These clearly showed the problem, he had been swallowing the stones and they had caused a blockage in his stomach. He needed to be operated on immediately to save his life. I remember the vet's bill cost me as much as I paid for the dog, but we did not mind. I just thought, 'No more throwing stones for this dog'. He did fully recover, but it taught me a lesson.

After about six months we took Milo back to Exton where we had bought him, to show the lovely lady there. We just went there by chance and unfortunately, she was not there but you could certainly hear her dogs when we rang the doorbell. We went back to our car and woe betide, the breeder was about fifty yards away walking with a red setter and what looked like an old golden retriever. She was pleased to see us and Milo, making a big fuss of him. I said the dog looks old as it was walking so slowly and ponderously, to which she replied it was only nine months old. Apparently, it had been very badly treated and she was helping with its convalescents.

This was our introduction to Monty and after some discussion, we decided to have him after his recovery. It was a good decision because the dog was just adorable and so obedient. How anyone could hurt this dog was just unbelievable. He used to walk alongside me with his lead in his mouth and when we got to a road to cross, he just sat down and waited for the instruction to move. He was good company for Milo too because they ran and ran together.

The one amusing thing was feeding the dogs together because Monty, being a golden retriever, would be like a hoover at mealtimes and his dinner would be gone almost in seconds. The opposite can be said about red setters who are very gentile eaters, and it would take a few minutes for Milo to eat his meal. Meanwhile, Monty would watch every mouthful Milo took, who in turn would give a cautionary growl to remind him whose dinner it was.

It was now 1975, and I was back working in Portsmouth again, commuting daily through the traffic. The job was different again, being involved in the manufacturing side of the MARK 24 Torpedo. It was this torpedo which sunk the General Belgrano, a navy light cruiser, in the 1982 Falklands War with Argentina in which three hundred and twenty-three people lost their lives.

The job itself was to be responsible for the control and monitoring of manufacturing cycles, both in-house and at subcontractors' works. I enjoyed the different variety of work to what I was used to, especially visiting other manufacturers to progress chase various components. There was, for me, however, a lot of shop floor walking, chasing up various issues, so I was constantly sore. The first six months were enjoyable but being a manufacturing production line meant things were repetitive.

Most people must work so it is important to enjoy your work as reasonably as possible. If you are unhappy it can affect your whole demeanour, and this was happening to me. After the first six months and the repetitiveness of the job, I felt there was little to learn apart from troubleshooting problems, so the next twelve months were the worst of my career.

Ann's brother, Keith, was a bit wild growing up and unbeknown to me, would often turn up at our bungalow having played hooky from school. Ann would let him in and cook him a meal, they were so close. The number of days he was having off attracted the attention of the school beadle, and a few other misdemeanours meant he was in danger of being sent away. None of us wanted that and his parents really could not cope, so Ann and I agreed he could come and live with us in Horndean.

One of the first things I did was to give Keith a front door key. It was to give him responsibility and accountability, which he was really surprised at. It worked and he never abused the trust I had in him. He was a lovely lad really, but just needed some guidance and structure in his life. Ann mothered him for about eight or nine months until he went back home. It had worked and he later went to work for a large do-it-yourself company, that had an outlet in Portsmouth, starting in the warehouse. Over the years, he worked hard there and eventually gained quite a senior position in the company, organising and managing major refits around the country. Ann and I were always proud of his achievements and to have helped him a little along life's journey.

The summer of 1976 was one to remember for many reasons, least of all to say it was the driest, sunniest and warmest weather of the twentieth century. There was a drought, a hosepipe ban was in place and the grass everywhere was parched yellow. I remember around seven or eight weeks of blue sky, with temperatures in the high twenties, low thirties, and of course we looked forward to our holidays with almost guaranteed good weather. The August bank holiday of that year sticks in my mind because rarely can you forward plan barbecues or garden parties with any accuracy in the UK, but this year was different, or so we thought. It rained all day.

The first significant rains were welcomed to replenish reservoirs and it meant the government's advice of sharing bathwater, using bath water to water the garden and placing bricks in toilet cisterns was receding. There were serious problems, though, with forest and heath fires because there was so little water to put them out, the firemen could not control them. Eventually normal English weather returned, and the crisis was over.

The highlight of 1977 was after six years of married life, Ann fell pregnant. The relief and sheer joy of that news still resonates with me today. I remember the day we found out; we drove down to my parents in Portsmouth to tell them, but halfway there we passed Margaret driving our parents in her car to see us that day. Fortunately, we saw them and followed them, met up and told them. It is so nice sharing the happiness we felt with them. By this stage, Arthur and Lyn had their two girls too, Christy and Kerry, so the whole family was growing.

Pregnancy during hot weather is no laughing matter, especially the last few months of gestation, and I remember Ann tossing and turning in bed at that time. From the first few months in the pregnancy, Ann was bleeding slightly and there was concern she could lose the baby. After discussion with the family doctor, she was given a monthly injection to try to avoid this possibility. This helped, but in hindsight it was nature's way of saying all was not well.

With Ann pregnant, we both knew life would change drastically and I needed to think about the future. The bungalow we had was not suitable, so it was time to think about moving again. Unfortunately, the housing market was somewhat flat, and in four years, the bungalow had only increased in value by six per cent., not one hundred and seventy per cent. as it did in the previous four years.

The race was on to change many things, but it nearly came crashing down around us when Ann started threatening to miscarry. It was a worrying time.

Chapter 16:
Good Decisions

At Marconi Space and Developments, I worked closely with several departments getting to know individuals well. One colleague was called Bob, who I interfaced with almost every day, and we ended up socializing outside of work with our other halves, Trish and Ann. It was a friendship that would last many years between our families as they grew up.

From the work front, life was becoming tedious and after only eighteen months there, I knew it was time to move on. One of the friends I had made there was a project manager called John, who had left a few months previous, and he got in contact with me to say he had recommended me for a job where he now worked. I also had the offer of work as a contract piping draughtsman earning good money being self-employed, but I still wanted to maintain the 'engineer' status I had worked hard for. It was a dilemma and I needed to think about it clearly to make the right decision.

We make many decisions in life. There are the day-to-day ones, the intermediary ones and the sometimes life-changing ones, like buying a house or changing your job. This was a crossroads for me and my soon-to-be-family, so I had to make the right one.

I decided to do some research on the company John worked for, which was called, Constructors John Brown or

CJB Ltd., based in Portsmouth. They had a lot of contracts for oil refinery and chemical plants in the UK and abroad, which included the engineering design, construction and commissioning of these plants. They were an established company best known by many for shipbuilding on the Clyde since 1899, and for me, it was local and employed nearly five hundred people.

I decided to take up the offer of an interview for a planning engineer role, although I knew little about planning. On the day of the interview, it was split into two parts. The first part was with the personnel manager and the second part, with the head of the department you would be working for. The personnel manager introduced himself, but I had to shake his left hand because the poor chap had an artificial right arm. In fact, his whole right arm was missing. We had a general chat and then he asked about my disability, which I was, and always have been, at ease talking about. I thought it went well and afterwards, was taken to the fifth floor of the eight-storey building to be interviewed by the head of planning.

The whole interview, I thought, went well and because the manager interviewing me was an ex-construction manager, the questions were focused on my construction experience. I mentioned I had been on sites when I worked at the Southern Gas Board, where they were laying large pipes through the countryside and in the design of governor stations. I also mentioned visiting vendors to progress chase components when I worked at Marconi Space and Developments, which went down well. I also think my background in HV&AC (Heating, Ventilating and Air Conditioning) and PCB (Printed Circuit Board) work helped too.

It is strange, sometimes, trying to look forward in your

career, as it can seem cloudy or even unknown but when you look back you can see the experience you have picked up along the way to bring you to the present point. The job of planning engineer meant liaising with many departments and my background covered some of those.

I did not know it at the time, but sometime later, one of the managers said the personnel manager had reservations about my disability and questioned employing me, but the planning manager overrode him. I thought it a little perverse when I was told this, as the personnel manager was himself disabled, and he never raised any of those concerns directly with me. The company did, however, make me an offer of employment.

When I received the letter, I was optimistic because it was a large envelope containing a lot more than one sheet of paper, which might otherwise say, 'On this occasion, you have been unsuccessful.' I opened it and read it out loud to Ann, where it said they were offering me the role of planning engineer. We both whooped with joy, but then I read on and realised the salary offer meant an increase of over forty per cent. on my existing salary. We were over the moon and straight away were planning for the future. It was a good decision to go for the interview.

Chapter 17:
My New Job

It was August 1977, and I was just starting my new job at CJB Ltd. I had been disabled for just over ten years and was adapting to my walking limitations, but there was a lot else happening. I had changed my job three times, I had got married, and I had a house and two dogs but all of these, in various ways, were affected by or impacted my disability.

Although I had come to terms with my disability, I was quite pragmatic about there being no return to how I was. There are many other factors you think about, which I would otherwise not even have contemplated. I would and still do, for instance, always look at the shortest possible route for any walking involved, as walking comes with pain. That means parking the car as close as I can to where I want to go or any type of shopping. It is difficult to apply to work, but I did limit my fluid intake to avoid having to walk too many times to the toilets.

It is this thinking in me which has fundamentally changed. When someone says, 'Let's go to such and such a place, it's only a couple of minutes down the road' or 'It's just around the corner', my heart races. Just a couple of minutes is nothing to walk if you are able-bodied, but for me personally, it can, on a bad day, be impossible to walk. I also need to consider if where we are going is upstairs and whether there is a lift or an escalator.

When I walk too far and that can vary day-to-day, it takes a lot of effort. I have always thought it to be three or four times more effort for me. I first get a slight headache, and this turns into something akin to a migraine. The cause is blood pressure and I have tried walking through this, but it is impossible. It is, after all, the body giving you a warning that the exertions you are giving the body are cause for concern. I can also get a stitch in my side from walking and have to stop. This sometimes goes away after a few minutes but can take longer. It is all manageable and centres around walking, hence the need to carefully plan any movement.

To manage this pain, I need to occasionally take a pain killer called Co-proxamol. They are powerful and can make you feel a bit heady after taking them. I remember a doctor suggesting to me in the early years that I should take about eight of these a day, every day, to manage pain. I did not want to be in a drug-induced stupor every day, so decided against that. These tablets only worked about two-thirds of the time and were not always effective.

It is a question of finding the right tablets to suit you. It can vary day-to-day, depending on the type and cause of the pain. I often use two paracetamol tablets with an ibuprofen tablet, which works quite well. Sometimes nothing works and those are dark times. The longest period the pain has gone on for me, both night and day, is five days and it is so debilitating, draining you completely. The only consolation is that after the bout, you sleep like the dead and wake up very relaxed, but it's scant consolation for all the suffering.

My artificial leg was always noisy in those early years of walking. It had many rivets and after a few weeks, one or more would work loose through the extraordinary stress and strain imposed on it when walking, and it would start clicking. Your artificial leg becomes an integral part of you, so you hear every sound it makes. It is somewhat like listening to your body and knowing when something is not quite right. The clicking sound I used to get every single step I took, to me was like the water torture you hear about with a drop falling on you every few seconds. It drives you mad and, in a much milder way, is the same as having a shoe that squeaks every step you take. Not only that, but it draws people's attention to you and your disability, which is something I do not like. There were many measures taken to try and stop it and I have personally used WD40, a fine lubricant oil spray and even talcum powder to try and erase the incessant noise. It is torturous, as I am sure other amputees will testify this too.

I had only been at CJB Ltd for just over a week when the news broke of Elvis Presley's death. It is a strange thing to remember where you were when major events happen. I remember when I was thirteen and had gone to see an X-rated picture at a local cinema, where you had to be sixteen to be let in, and on the screen, it came up that John F. Kennedy had been assassinated. Another memory was being with Ann in the car on Portsdown Hill, overlooking Portsmouth, when Neil Armstrong landed on the moon in 1969 on the 16th of July. Looking back, it was a major event personally joining CJB Ltd because it really started my career path and led to an eventful life.

My father had an old-fashioned approach to employment based on security, which you can understand, having lived through the 1930s' Great Depression, which was a severe worldwide economic depression lasting until the start of the

Second World War. I did understand where his concerns lay, but I was never one to worry about employment as I felt I would always find work and the world was changing. The youth of every generation are always headstrong, and I was no different.

I have learnt when you start any new job, it takes at least six months to get a grasp of their systems, processes, procedures and personnel, and this was the case at CJB Ltd. I enjoyed meeting people and there were quite a few disciplines or departments as they were called. These were Process and Mechanical, which included Machinery, Vessels, Heat Exchangers, Firefighting and Air Conditioning. Others included Instruments, Electrical, Piping and Civil. There was also the project management and project services side too, which I was a part of, so there were a lot of people to meet, form a relationship with and regularly liaise with.

Where I was located on the fifth floor of an eight-floor building, there were about twenty-five people in the department's offices, including my friend John from Marconi, who had recommended me for the position. About fifteen in the Planning Department and about ten in the Cost Control Department. They were nice people, a few characters, but the good thing was they had a pool of knowledge that they were willing to share. Other staff were seconded on different floors where project task forces were allocated.

There were two lifts and when I had to visit other departments on other floors, I applied a rule of thumb: if it were two floors or less from where I was then I would use the stairs. As I have said before, I do not like using stairs with people around me, so at each end of the building were stairwells which I used more than the main ones by the lifts in the centre of the building because fewer people used these. There were times I could not avoid it, but it was my quirky preference. Many people will not understand this, but I expect a few amputees will.

I enjoyed working there from Day One and realised very quickly how much I had to learn. The joy of this chosen profession is you are always learning and even though you can become a subject matter expert, I was still learning nearly forty years later. This was why I enjoyed it and if you enjoy work it makes it so much more palatable.

After a couple of weeks' basic training and the mandatory reading of Company Standards and Procedures, I was transferred to the first floor to work on Project 4327, an ICI Protein Plant project. It was a task force-based team so virtually all of the various disciplines were based on the whole of the first floor and my desk was opposite where the senior project manager's office was.

I worked with a young lady, who certainly knew how to prepare a monthly progress report, and she started training me. I was initially involved in the preparation of histograms and 'S' Curves, moving gradually to producing bar charts, programme analysis and reporting areas of concern. It was from this point my working life would always revolve around monthly reports and the collation, analyses, recommendation, preparation and submission. I even took timely holidays to avoid clashing with the preparation and submission of these reports.

As I got to know people on the task force a few started to ask questions about my disability, which I have always been open and willing to talk about. I was used to this and had the story off-pat. The project manager's secretary, who was about my age and attractive, was intrigued by my life story when she asked me about it. I explained how high the amputation was and tapped the socket near my hip bone. She did not believe it was this high and touched where I had tapped, whereupon she let out a shriek and ran back to her office. Some of the others laughed about it and I did too, but for me, it summed up how some would see my disability and it had quite a profound effect on me.

Ann and I had started house-hunting and with the increased salary we could afford a larger mortgage. Out of the blue, a three-bedroomed semi-detached house had just come on the market, it was in Portsmouth and was only one year old. We immediately asked for a viewing and found it was right at the end of a cul-de-sac and had a reasonably large garden for a house in town. It would be ideal, and we offered the full asking price of thirteen thousand, two hundred and fifty pounds, which was accepted. All we had to do was sell our bungalow in Horndean. We were lucky to get a buyer straight away with no chain, so everything was slotting into place and a First November 1977 move date was agreed.

Looking back, the timing of the move could have been better because Ann was now eight months pregnant. I could not carry and walk with anything heavy, so we engaged a local removal company and apart from one breakage everything went smoothly. My family helped us clean the house throughout and before long we were in our new house and Ann was preparing her nest for the new arrival.

On the twenty-seventh November, Ann's water broke and we drove to the maternity unit in St. Mary's Hospital in Portsmouth, which was only about half a mile away. Ann was in labour for many hours and it amazed me how she coped with the pain. There came a point where the midwife said 'Right, you can decide whether you want your baby on the twenty-seventh or twenty-eighth. If it is the twenty-seventh then a small scalpel incision is needed, or we can wait until things happen a little later more naturally'. Our family doctor had said the twenty-seventh so Ann decided this was to be the date. The sheer effort of pushing the baby into this world was astonishing to me, when I saw, from exhaustion, Ann's face colour would go from pink to red, to blue! The bliss of your firstborn is beyond words and to be there just filled me with pride and love for them both. I could not help but shed a few tears of happiness.

There are highlights in everybody's life and being at the birth of your child is right up there in neon flashing lights. It was fantastic and never to be forgotten.

Donna came into the world weighing just over seven pounds and was quite jaundiced so needed to get the bilirubin level lower by having phototherapy treatment. In those days, the baby usually stayed in the hospital for three days at least, and Donna and Ann were allowed home after four days. When you leave the hospital holding the special gift of a child, you feel not only proud but very protective too. I drove home very carefully, and the little voice crying could hardly be heard but that only lasted about four weeks until those lungs had developed, and the decibels increased.

I suppose I was a bit old-fashioned when it came to Ann working after the baby was born, but I decided I could manage and she would no longer need to work, just stay at home and, as they say, 'Keep house'.

Chapter 18: Counselling

It was now ten years since my amputation, and I was still going for check-ups every six months to make sure nothing was untoward. It was at these check-ups I met up again with Miss Cade and she was genuinely thrilled when I told her we had just started a family. It was her and Dr McEwan who I had to thank for saving my life.

When our new baby, Donna, was a few months old, we went to a local photographer who specialised in family portraits and had some lovely photographs commissioned. We gave both our parents framed photos and I also sent one to Miss Cade. I learnt later that she had several photographs of patients and their families near her desk whom she had helped during her career and mine was there too. She was a credit to her profession.

By now I had gained quite a bit of experience in living and coping with my disability and limited mobility. One day, when I was attending the ALAC for my regular repairs, Frank asked me if I would mind talking to someone who was only nineteen, had cancer like me and his whole left leg had been amputated. I said of course I would, and a date was arranged for me to meet him. I was not apprehensive to meet up with him because I had always been open and happy to talk about my disability if asked, but this meeting literally shocked me to the core. We were introduced and then just the two of us left to talk in a small room. He said straight away he would never, ever wear an artificial limb. I explained you must embrace your disability and set new goals in life, rather than the previous ones you may have had. I showed him my limb, how it fitted and how I could walk. He was not impressed but gave a tirade of hate as to how life had dealt him such a cruel blow. I had never met, even to this day, someone so negative about life and I was somewhat stunned by it. I have always been positive, with my glass half full, but his was empty and bone dry. The sad part for me was to learn cancer for him had returned and eleven months later he died. Maybe it was for the best because I could not imagine him coping with his life at all.

There were others I spoke to, probably a dozen or so over the years, who seemed grateful to be able to talk frankly and openly about the future challenges ahead of them. I suppose they could relate to another amputee who would give them first-hand knowledge, warts and all, of the path ahead rather than from a well-meaning professional without the actual experience.

I undertook the counselling mostly at the ALAC but did go to one patient's house near Southampton, which is about twenty-three miles west of Portsmouth, to talk to him and his wife. He had not long had his leg amputated, which was high above the knee and he had no transport. They were grateful to talk openly and frankly about many aspects of the life amputee's face and about some coping mechanisms too. These meetings were often with their partners because their life too would change considerably, to help and support each other through life's journey. I was more than happy to give my time freely to help these individuals, who all had high amputations and had many questions to ask. The main reason being was that I never had the opportunity to talk to anyone with a similar amputation and just found my own way of managing life.

Over the years I have spent many, many hours at the ALAC. It was first built a year before my amputation in 1967 so I have seen several changes. The name change is interesting as it really follows the increased awareness and knowledge of people with disabilities progressing. Some time ago it was renamed from ALAC to the Disablement Services Centre and much more recently changed again to the Enablement Centre.

When I think about the duration of time in my younger years, the average time for each appointment was around four hours. I go quite often for repairs and on average that is around every two to three months. Equating this to months, I can say that I have spent around five months of my life sitting in a waiting room. I have often wondered about entering this in the Guinness Book of Records!

Having spent a lot of time in hospital waiting rooms as well as repairs for my leg, it is not surprising to learn you build some knowledge of the human species and how they react to circumstances and surroundings. There are people who bring papers or books to read and most who bring and do nothing, having looked at the obligatory notice boards with ageing printouts of information. Then, of course, there are those magazines which have stood the test of time and I know because I once found a magazine that was fifteen years old amongst newer contributions.

For some reason, people often behave irrationally in waiting rooms. If they are told there is a thirty-minute wait, then this is more acceptable than an uncertain twenty-minute wait. The problem isn't the duration of delay it's how you experience the duration. I have seen all types of behaviour, from frustration and anger to calmness and serenity. It is a fact human beings respond about twice as strongly to the possibility of loss as they do gain. So, uncertainty can trigger stress. When you are waiting for a repair you have no idea whether they are working on your leg or it is in a queue of repairs. Minutes can drag on for hours on occasion. Then you wonder whether you have been forgotten, especially when other prosthetists say, 'Are you still here?' As waiting gets longer, satisfaction diminishes.

I always tell those whose first visit is to have a fitting for their first prosthetic leg that they should not accept the leg unless they are happy with it. There can be time pressures where they accept something they later regret, and another appointment is needed. Often transport ambulances are held up waiting for the patient and the patient does not want to miss the ambulance for fear of a long wait for another. The word patient comes from the Latin word 'patiens' meaning 'I am suffering', so the best advice is to be a patient patient.

I have some empathy with the prosthetist in carrying out the repair because it can be difficult to put a timeframe on them as there are so many variables, especially dealing with some of the patients. Some have learning disabilities so can have difficulty explaining the problems they have. Some too have high expectations of the service, but this mellows over the years as reality sets in. Others, you can see straight away, will never ever walk and stay in a wheelchair for the rest of their days. Some of the older patients just do not have the right mindset and have resigned themselves never to walk again.

Chapter 19:
Moving Forward

It seems the older you get; the faster time goes by and things seemed to be happening around us with some pace. Donna was growing fast, and then very quickly Ann found she was pregnant again. It was a wonderful surprise because we thought, having waited two years to conceive Donna, it would take the same time, but it took only five months.

The house had been redecorated and the back garden segregated to have a place for the dogs and separately a place for Donna's play area, which was just a swing and slide. The garden was not big, but more quadrant shaped as it was at the bottom of a cul-de-sac. We had decorated Donna's new bedroom as she was becoming a 'big girl' and would be able to have her own bed instead of a cot. By doing this, we paved the way for the new arrival expected in April of 1978.

In those days, people referred to all the old wives' tales of how the mother carried the baby to tell whether it would be a boy or a girl. I am not sure if any of it was true, but Ann did get quite heavy in her pregnancy and we felt it would be nice to have a boy after having a girl. Previously, we did not have the option, like today, to know the gender before birth, and I honestly believe it is still a part of the magic of that special childbirth moment.

It was a lovely first Christmas with Donna, seeing the

wide eyes looking at all the lights and opening the presents but preferring the paper to the contents, as babies do. We went to both our parent's houses to see everyone over the festive period and then before we knew it, we were back to the usual routine of work, but still cherishing those special moments.

It still amazes me how much parents must carry with them when they go visiting. From pushchairs to changes of clothes, then nappies, toys and the potty. The list of what you needed just seemed to grow. It was hard work, but wonderful times seeing your children grow.

Work at CJB Ltd., which was renamed John Brown Engineering, was going well and I was put on a project for the design, procurement and construction of a High-Density Polyethylene (HDPE) plant in China, closely followed by a Low-Density Polyethylene (LDPE) plant in South Africa. The experience was invaluable, and I was learning about planning these huge plants by drawing Project Evaluation Review Technique (PERT) networks, which is a project management technique used to manage uncertain activities of a network. Incidentally, this technique was developed by the US Navy in the 1950s to manage the Polaris submarine missile programme.

With the introduction of computers at work, our processes and procedures were changing. At first, we only had one calculator in the office that was cranked by hand with a paper printout and we had to fill out cards for the computer to run programme critical path analysis. I even went to night school with some work colleagues to study a computer programming language called Basic. My time was also taken up with an evening course I took on Conversational French.

At work, I got promoted to a senior planning engineer and

was put on a new chemical project in China to produce HDPE, where I was responsible for the overall home office network planning covering the monthly programme and progress reporting. I was working as much overtime as I could, to give the little extras in life, which are always needed. I averaged between ten and fifteen hours of overtime each week, sometimes working in excess of twenty hours at peak times and always working Saturday mornings. I enjoyed doing this but always liked dealing with figures, which I suppose stems from my father's insistence on learning my twelve times table parrot-fashion when I was around eight or nine years old. Little did I realise this numeracy ability set me up for life with a solid foundation.

I wanted to do an accountancy Open University degree course and I applied for the paperwork. I kept these papers in my briefcase for four years with the intention of joining the course, but because I was so busy at home and work, I never did get around to applying for it.

There was, however, a new role in the oil and gas industry coming to the UK from America, called 'Project Control'. This was combining both planning and cost control functions on projects to get a much better view of decision-making and its implications. I think John Brown was ahead of its time in many ways, and they decided to take someone from cost control and train them in planning. Likewise, they took someone from planning and taught them cost control. I was selected from planning and my colleague, Adrian, was selected from cost control.

I really enjoyed this time, learning the techniques and analyses of cost control, which I guess substituted for my accountancy degree. It was totally hands-on and not theoretical, which was a real bonus as you cannot beat on-the-job training. Adrian and I both adapted to the new roles quickly, and it proved a real benefit on projects to have this overview role of looking at the cost and planning side of a project. We were both soon promoted to project control engineers.

It was now April 1978, with Ann expecting the baby any day and I was expecting the call to be with her at any time. On the afternoon of Wednesday, 19 April, her waters broke, and I had the call to get her to the hospital. I phoned my mum to see if she could babysit Donna, and rushed to pick her up, then rushed home and took Ann to St. Mary's Hospital. Instead of going to the main unit, we were directed to the general practitioners (GP) unit. We did not care where we went but just wanted a bed and quick!

The labour lasted around eight hours and fortunately, Ann had a high pain threshold. I learnt from the last time to take off my wedding ring because Ann squeezed my hand so tightly at each contraction, I thought she would break my fingers, and the ring indentation left did hurt, but it was nothing to what she was going through. I had my work suit trousers on, having come straight from work and was coaxing her along with a couple of midwives when things happened so very quickly. One minute I was holding her hand and breathing in unison with her, and suddenly the baby came into this world in the early hours of the 20th April. I was absolutely covered in blood and gore, all over my trousers, which I had never seen the likes of before, but I had a beautiful baby boy, my son Darren, and nothing else mattered at all. It was, again, an utterly amazing experience and we were both in tears of joy. It was one of life's greatest experiences for me and melded us together.

I remember driving home that Thursday morning in the pouring rain, so elated and full of adrenaline. When I got home, I woke my mum to tell her; we were all so happy, as I had my first son and mum had her first grandson. Importantly to me was the continuation of the Paffett line, as I have always been interested in genealogy.

Back at work, I was congratulated, and we, of course, whet the baby's head with a few drinks at the local pub. Working in a carpeted office environment was nice but more often than not my artificial leg was noisy. When I say noisy, I mean noisy to me, not necessarily noisy to anyone else for the most part. Your artificial leg really becomes an integral part of you, so every squeak or click it makes gets accentuated, because to me every step taken in these circumstances is a reminder of being disabled. It is a strange way of looking at it but this is the legacy I have.

When I had a noise problem at work, I often carried a piece of paper to make some noise as I walked, which was a distraction from my noisy leg. Some people do not worry about this, but I certainly did and still do. It was around this time that developments in design and materials made quite a difference to my noise problem, thank goodness.

The twentieth century has seen the greatest advances in prosthetic limbs. Many materials such as carbon fibre, titanium and modern plastics have produced prosthetic devices that are strong and more lightweight than earlier limbs made of iron and wood. New plastics, better pigments and more sophisticated procedures nowadays create realistic-looking skin. It was, therefore, time to say goodbye to the aluminium legs and those darn rivets that lasted hardly any time at all and say hello to carbon fibre. Carbon fibre is a strong, lightweight material that was initially used to reinforce the socket but later used as central stems, in my case, to replace the tibia and femur. It was surprising when I first saw the tube because it was only about one inch (25mm) in diameter but, amazingly, the wall of it was less than one-eighth of an inch (2mm).

By using this new method of construction my new artificial leg was not only made lighter but less noisy. The leg was then covered with a sponge fairing so when covered with trousers felt more like a natural leg. It was a great advancement for me but never made any difference to how far I could walk, which was quite limited. I am sure there will be many advancements to come and of course, all amputees hope this will be sooner rather than later, in this field. I suspect one vast improvement in this area, which will come soon now, will be the use of graphene. This is currently the thinnest material known to man and yet two hundred times stronger than steel. Amazingly, it is only one atom thick. They say the potential for graphene is only limited by our imagination, so once manufacturing starts in earnest it will transform everyday products and applications. This will eventually spin-off to artificial limbs just as carbon fibre did, but I believe with far greater improvements.

Chapter 20:
The Growing Family

They say as you get older time passes by much quicker, but I was now in my early thirties and had a remarkably busy life with work and the family. The motto I adopted was 'Children first, then Ann and then me'. It is simple, but priorities, when both time and money are limited, ensure you stay focused.

The problem with work is that it engages you when you are at your peak energy levels during the day and then your family life does so, after work when you are drained of energy. The demands of this can be exhausting, but then, being at home looking after two young children also takes its toll. We were no different from millions of other couples raising a family and it has been going on in similar ways for thousands of years. We did look forward to weekends, having fun with the children and recharging our batteries, although I must say shopping for food or clothes with two young children has never been my idea of fun.

My parents and sister were particularly good to us, looking after the children on odd occasion but there was a routine we got into with the children going to 'Sunday School' at The Salvation Army. There were merits all around for this because I know as a child, I enjoyed The Army because it was so much more fun than some of the other churches, and it also gives you a good grounding in right and wrong. Donna and

Darren both enjoyed going there and Margaret would come to our house every Sunday and collect them around nine-thirty a.m. and take them to The Primary. Margaret, as she still does to this day, managed The Primary which is for children under five. The activities there are fun, but with a Christian bias. My mum was playing the piano or organ in the main hall for the more senior members and when The Primary finished, they would make their way into the hall to await the conclusion of the meeting.

Mum, Margaret and the children would then go home, where dad had been preparing the Sunday roast. Whether it's because mum was in The Services, I am not sure, but all her life, dinner was at twelve-thirty p.m. sharp. Sunday was no exception, so they always had a lovely roast dinner, which mum was famous for, plus a nice pudding. The children would then have fun playing with them all before Margaret brought them home to us around three p.m. This free time gave Ann and me time together to do the usual household chores and for me to do the gardening. The children loved the arrangement too, seeing their auntie and grandparents who they were awfully close to. We were so grateful to them for this.

It is difficult with young children because invariably they like running around and then being chased and I could do neither, so I had to be content to watch Ann doing this. I tried to make it up to them by playing with them without the physical exertion of walking on my part. I remember mum but mainly dad playing with Margaret, Arthur and me as children, running around and walking everywhere. When mum went to the Army meetings on a Sunday evening, dad would take us out to have some fun. We had several places we regularly went to which included the top of Portsdown Hill, just to the north of Portsmouth. We would be running up and down the hill, round and round the trees playing Hide and Seek. Other places included Canoe Lake, near the seafront of Portsmouth, to maybe go crabbing in the lake or catch a small ferry to Gosport just to the west of Portsmouth. Once over there, we headed for the green to play cricket. Dad would mostly bowl rather than field due to the bad knee he said he had, but it was a way to wear us out fielding methinks. Simple pleasures from simple fun but I was mindful I could not do this with my children.

Monday always followed Sunday and we were launched again into the weekly routine of life. At work, I had been on a few more overseas projects, learning my trade and I was put on a project for Rohm and Haas. The project was to build a Toluene Plant in the North East of England. This chemical is used as a solvent in paint thinners, nail polish removers, glues and correction fluid. I was given a promotion to senior project control engineer to be responsible for the overall cost, planning and interfacing with construction. Although I was given a salary increase for this new role, I did have to occasionally go to the site, which was not well received at home. With me being away, it was more work for Ann with the children. She did not like me being away but did like the additional money I was getting for my new role. More money equals more shoes and Ann certainly liked her shoes, so there was a compromise to be had.

It was nice to be able to drive across the city to work in about a quarter of an hour. No traffic jams were experienced this way and if there was a problem at home, or children's sports day and so on, I could be there quickly. I was also living about half a mile from the ALAC, so if I had an appointment, it was just down the road. Everything was going well but then

I saw an advertisement in The Telegraph for the same role I was doing with a competitor in Reading, Foster Wheeler. I thought I would just see what they had to offer and applied.

I was invited for an interview in Reading, which went well, and an offer was made to me a week later. I was in a real quandary because they offered me twenty-five per cent. salary increase. Ann and I spent a long time discussing this as it would entail moving there, which the company would have paid for, but it would be a major upheaval in our lives. Both our families were local, I could easily get my leg repaired if there was a problem, Donna was just about to start school and for me I was close to Portsmouth Football club too!

I had made the decision to let my present company know I had an offer on the table knowing they were busy with a lot of work and even trying to recruit themselves. I suppose looking back it was a good leverage ploy and within two days after an internal discussion they offered me a twenty-three per cent. pay rise to stay. There was no contest really because everything was on my doorstep so to speak, I did enjoy working at John Brown and I was still learning something new every single day. I made the decision to stay, which, looking back, was a crossroad in my life but it was the right decision.

Life was busy at home with young children doing all the sorts of things children do but looking back I remember we took Donna to ballet lessons. She looked such a cutie in her pink tutu and matching accessories. It was quite expensive at the time kitting her out, especially the special satin ballet shoes but she looked a treat. We took her to her first lesson, and she was nervous and started to cry, but they told us to leave as she would be alright. When we came to collect her, they said she had cried most of the time but then as a small five-year-old it must have been quite daunting. We took her every week for five weeks and every time she cried, and they told us the same story; she had cried all the way through the lesson. We had to stop as she was not enjoying it and our hope of a Royal Ballet dancer in the family faded into obscurity.

Ann's brother Dave was married to Ellen, and we used to visit them regularly in Swindon, which is about ninety miles north of Portsmouth. Dave was in the RAF and was working in Milan in 1980. Amongst other languages, he spoke fluent Italian and rented a floor of a farmhouse that summer in a small town called Varazze, between Genoa and Savona in Northern Italy. He kindly invited us to stay there with Ellen and their two children, Elaine and Paul, an opportunity we jumped at. The car I had, a Chrysler Sunbeam, at the time enabled the two back seats to fold down completely giving a nice area for Donna and Darren to play and, with a couple of pillows, sleep there too. In hindsight, it was so dangerous really because seat belts were optional. We took the car across by ferry from Portsmouth to Cherbourg and headed to Italy.

It was a mistake driving through France not using the toll roads. I plotted a route through France not using these, but I was a novice at it. I got lost so many times and I really wished I had a compass. It seemed every time you got to a crossroad it just pointed to Lyon or Paris. Do I take a right turn or a left? I ended up doing about one hundred and twenty extra miles due to this. The total journey was eight hundred and ninety miles. We stopped on route only three times for an hour each time and I drove eight hundred and ten miles without sleep. After going through the tunnel of The Mont Blanc Pass, I did feel very tired toward the end and so Ann took over the last stretch until eventually, we made it.

It was a typical Italian farmhouse and the owner, Lorenzo, was a nice old man, who spoke no English. We would sit outside on those hot evenings and as I spoke no Italian, we often drew things on the ground with a stick to try and make ourselves understood or we just shrugged our shoulders and laughed at each other. Dave had bought twenty-four bottles of a superb chianti from a friend of his who had a vineyard and so we indulged in red wine. Unfortunately, Dave said he had to work and return to the RAF Base in Milan, so he was gone most of the time.

It was very dark at night with virtually no ambient light around, so the stars were spectacular. We had gone out one evening and arrived back in the dark to park the car at the end of the track leading to the farmhouse. We had the two children and started walking to the farmhouse when I suddenly saw, about seventy-five yards away, four eyes looking straight at me. I could see the outline of two dogs, and they started bounding toward us. They were Doberman dogs. My heart was in my mouth, and I pushed the children behind me and faced the dogs, but my body was side on with my artificial leg facing them. I thought if they want to bite me then try my leg for starters. Just as they were about ten yards from us, I heard a whistle and they stopped in their tracks. I breathed a sigh of relief and a close neighbour to Lorenzo appeared smiling. I found it difficult to smile but she was nice, and those dogs were so well trained, that we ended up petting them.

This area was not too far away from where an Italian statesman called Aldo Moro was kidnapped in 1978 by the Red Brigade, a militant left-wing organisation responsible for kidnappings, murder and sabotage. I mention this because I learned only a few months after our Italian holiday, the neighbour was walking those dogs in the forest near the farmhouse when she stumbled across the police in the forest searching for members of the Red Brigade. Some of the police were armed and the dogs suddenly saw them and thinking they were a threat to their owner ran towards the police, who just shot them dead. Such a shame; they were so well behaved for their owner, and she was devastated.

We were fortunate to have a boy and girl, so never planned on any more children, but to our surprise, in 1981, Ann became pregnant again. It was unexpected but we were both thrilled, especially Ann who was a natural mother and so life took another turn. Her pregnancy went well but it was not easy, managing with the other two children, in the later stages because she got rather large and the waddle walk started.

In October, Jamie was born. I was there with Ann to have the wonderful experience of a new birth again and we were happy to have this unexpected bundle of pleasure arrive. Ann knew it would be her last so he would always be her baby. We bought presents for Darren and Donna to give to Jamie to help the bonding process. Donna especially liked her new dolly, which she thought was wonderful because otherwise she just wanted to cuddle Jamie in her arms all the time.

With another child arriving we realised the three-bedroom house would be alright because whatever the sex of the new baby, they could share with one of their siblings. It was around this time I started to draw up some plans for an extension to the house. I enjoyed doing this and went down to the Portsmouth council office to get details of what permissions I needed for planning/building regulation approvals. I decided to maximise the extension by going out twelve feet along the whole side of the house and started drawing the plans and submitting them for the process of approval, which took some time.

When you have a young family, a car and a mortgage, there is never enough money left over at the end of the month, so we decided to wait a couple of years before getting more money from the building society for the extension.

There was no rush and although the building permissions were slow in getting approved, we knew the extra space the extension would give us would be welcome with the family growing. We also had two large dogs, so space was beginning to be at a premium. The house was now about eight years old, and things needed replacing. The kitchen was on the cards for improvements. We decided to take the plunge and have a new kitchen at the same time as the extension was being built to get it over and done with more quickly. In hindsight, this was not one of our best decisions.

I loved the two dogs and they always played well together because they both had a lovely nature about them. We had previously read up on the breeds to ensure they were good with children. The red setter breed was marked as 'very good' and the golden retriever was 'excellent'. One day in the garden, whilst I was working on my vegetable plot, they were both playing together, as I thought. Donna was walking close by on the pathway when suddenly they were no longer play fighting, they were growling at each other. They had knocked Donna over and she was crying, and the dogs were fighting; it was mayhem. Ann rushed out and we were both distraught at this turn of events. Donna was taken indoors, and I separated the dogs, but it was alarming especially for the safety of our child.

The following week I went out to the garden as one of the neighbours our house backed onto was calling me. She did not need to tell me the problem as I could see one of the dogs had literally gone through a wooden fence. It was most unlike them but quite worrying. We could not continue wondering what would happen next so had to make a difficult decision, which, to this day, I still find painful.

I knew that Dave and Ellen from Swindon loved Monty, the golden retriever, as they made such a fuss of him when they visited us. I decided to ask them if they would like to have him. Milo, the red setter was too feather-brained for anyone else to have. They immediately said 'yes' without any hesitation. I consoled myself knowing he had a lovely home, was well looked after and was loved just as he deserved.

The tragic part of all this was talking with another neighbour, whose fence backed onto our house, about six months after we let Monty go, she mentioned that her Labrador was in season at that time and the dogs were just trying to get to her. We just did not know, and it was such a shame to split Monty and Milo up.

We had the usual children's ailments from colds to chicken pox and so on, but poor Donna seemed to have more than her fair share of problems. She was always of a small stature but as she was growing, it was noticeable one shoulder was higher than the other. The usual visit to the doctor ensued, followed by a referral to a consultant paediatrician, who diagnosed Sprengel's shoulder deformity. Basically, when the fetus is nine to twelve weeks old, both shoulder blades lower, but for Donna one did not, resulting in the problem. Donna needed surgery to have the shoulder blade cut in half, lowered and re-pinned. This was her third surgical procedure, and she was only six years old.

Donna's operation proved to be successful and despite a

nasty scar it hardly showed. It was good to get this done because the time was drawing near to her next school move, and that can be traumatic for some children.

In 1984, Margaret married Jeff, who was a warrant officer in the Royal Navy, and they had a lovely wedding in a church in the Portsmouth Dockyard. Donna was one of the bridesmaids, along with my nieces, Christy and Kerry, with Lyn as the matron of honour. Darren was the pageboy in his little waistcoat and bow tie; so cute. Weddings are great to see all your relatives because you normally only see them on these occasions or, more sombrely, at funerals, however, this was a joyous occasion.

Chapter 21: Life-changing Events

Holidays are easier to plan with an average family of two children, so having another meant rethinking our leisure time. Going abroad with young children can be quite fraught, especially if they play up and then of course there are the other passengers to think of. Even now, most of us cringe at the thought of a crying baby close to us on a flight, where there is no escape. We decided to buy a Trigano Translet trailer tent. This enabled us to go about in the UK as a family without any hassle, or so we thought. The body of the trailer tent was hard plastic and when it opened, we had an eighteen feet by fifteen feet covered space. This had two separate areas for bedrooms and a communal area too. It was good for our family size, and we did have a few holidays away in it, but we always seemed unlucky with the weather.

As the family grew, we knew it was time to build the extension. Without too much thought we embarked on this and thought we would update the kitchen at the same time. It was a bit unfortunate that, at work, the design phase of the pharmaceutical project I was working on was ending and the emphasis now moved to the construction phase in Irving, Scotland. I was, therefore, transitioning from the home office to the site just as the work on the house was commencing. It was hard work for Ann, who did not particularly like me being away, having three children under six, a large dog and the major upheaval of the whole downstairs of our house. I know I got the better deal, but I did manage to get back every weekend. I flew back from Glasgow to Southampton Airport, but did not get home until late Friday night, and then left home just after five a.m. on a Monday. Weekends were important to cram as much as you could into the two days, seeing family, and friends and playing with the children.

It was tough on all of us with me being away, but that is what the job entailed and why they paid me a good salary. We both accepted it, but when things go wrong with the building works it's difficult dealing with it from five hundred miles away. The first major issue started straight away as I had drawn conventional foundations on the plan, but it turned out, that when they started digging, the main house was built on a concrete raft. The builder was good and said he could get new detailed drawings done and approved by the council within three days, as he had his team of workers there, just hanging around. The downside was the building works were going to cost an additional ten per cent. of the overall cost, so my contingency fund for the extension was gone by the first day! I had no choice but to agree to it.

The second trauma I had was an early morning phone call at the site from Ann saying the dog was barking during the night as someone had climbed over the garden fence and tried to lever the patio doors open to burgle the house. Fortunately, they made their escape, probably after hearing the dog, but I felt terrible I could not be there with Ann. Thank goodness the rest of the building work and kitchen upgrade went well without any problems, so I was much relieved.

Southampton Airport was quite small at the time, so

parking your car was relatively easy and quite close to the departure zone. This meant less walking for me, but this was not the case at Glasgow Airport, which is a large international airport. I would often look out of the aircraft as we were taxiing to the gate for disembarking, hoping we would be close to the main building and not at the end. The difference was significant to me, from a walking perspective, especially as the travellators were often not working.

I was working in Scotland for just over a year, flying up and down each weekend so the walking did take its toll on me and my leg. It was creaking away and over the course of several months, I must have used a whole can of WD40, the fine oil spray, on my leg to help with the squeaks and creaks. It has its own pungent smell, so I also sprayed it with my aftershave to try and cover it up. The result was a strange wafting smell around me every step I took, and I am sure I must have had a few funny looks as people passed by me.

The other downside was the amount of walking I was doing had cut me open on my amputation scar line and I had no time to allow it to heal. When I was at work, I needed to walk on the site to assess progress and learn some of the construction techniques. When I was at home I needed to go out with Ann and the children and see to the garden and the dog. It did have an adverse effect on me and there was a lot of pain, but that went hand in glove with losing my leg.

I recall one journey where we were delayed for a long time because of snow conditions and did not arrive at Glasgow Airport until midnight. The snow was about three or four inches deep and, at that time of the night, it would have been treacherous to drive to Irvine, some twenty-five miles through the open countryside. My two colleagues and I decided to stay at the Glasgow Airport Hotel which is a short walk from the main terminal. Walking in snow is difficult for me, but not as bad as icy conditions. This was freshly fallen snow and I could just about walk in it, which is just as well, as I had no choice but to get to the hotel. After about two minutes of walking, I looked back and all I could see was a left shoe print and a continuous area of crushed snow, about the width of my shoe, all the way back. I could not lift my right leg above the snow so had to drag it through. It was exhausting but is one reason I now shy away from those wintry conditions.

Time moved quickly and I was soon back working in the home office and home every night, but then age caught up with my beautiful red setter. Our next-door neighbour, Trevor, used to run in the evening, and kindly offered to run Milo. Previously, Milo had often enjoyed this, but one day when he got back, he just collapsed outside the front door and was panting heavily. We patted him with cold compresses and after about twenty minutes, he was able to get up. It was really worrying for us, so we took him to the vet to understand what the problem was.

We came back from the vet devastated as they found he had a heart condition. He was eleven years old, which is a good age for red setters, but they said things would only get worse for him. The final nail in the coffin was the risk of him potentially choking on his tongue if he had an attack and if it was in the middle of the night we might not know or hear his suffering. We had to make the difficult decision many dog owners must when the time comes, to put him down. It is such a painful decision to make because all the dog has done all his life is give you unconditional love. I still think of Milo and Monty to this day.

We often went camping with our good friends, Bob and Trish, and this particular year we were with another couple of friends, John and Linda. It was a campsite about sixty miles west of Portsmouth and I had finally mastered how to reverse in the trailer tent. The children enjoyed playing with Bob and Trish's two children, Chloe and Sophie, and we were having a great time.

Ann had a hospital appointment in Portsmouth midway through the camping holiday to get the results of a chest X-ray, so we drove back to Portsmouth with the children happily playing with their friends on the campsite. We had a three p.m. appointment to get the results but like most hospitals were kept waiting and waiting. There were about twenty people waiting and even though we were before some of them, we were last to be seen at about four thirty pm. Ann suspected, but I did not, and she was told the biopsy she had previously had on her left breast showed malignant cancer cells and she needed a mastectomy. She was only thirty-seven years old! We were devastated and knew then why we were last to be seen, as we had to walk through the empty waiting room trying to come to terms with the worst news possible, both emotionally shocked.

Ann needed time to come to terms with this news and decided to go straight home. After making sure she was alright, I had the long, lonely drive back to the campsite, where our children and friends were enjoying themselves. It was one of the worst drives I have ever had, thinking of all the outcomes, how to deal with telling friends, and family and of course, what to tell the children.

When I arrived back at the campsite, the children ran to greet me and of course, were surprised their mum was not there. I explained she was not feeling too well so she stayed at home, but not to worry as we would be going home the next day. It was difficult hiding my emotions and it was not the time to tell the children anything, but I still had to break the news to our friends. Not seeing Ann there, our friends had an inkling of what I was going to tell them, and both were staff nurses so understood the implications.

Trish and Ann were good friends and I remember Ann always valuing her no-nonsense advice, after all, she came from Yorkshire, so she told her as it was. Many friends and relatives try to somehow put a positive spin on things to try to cushion the impact of what lies ahead, but not so with Trish. If Ann wanted to know something about her illness or medication then she knew she would get a straight answer, which she really valued.

It is hard telling people about a life-threatening illness, especially when you have a large circle of family and friends. Most were supportive, but there were a couple of reasonably close friends we had holidayed with in the past, who just could not handle it and they distanced themselves from us and strangely never made contact again. It is difficult to understand because when an illness like that strikes, the two most important things are your health and family, closely followed by friends.

When devastating news like this was told to Ann, she always seemed to retreat into herself for around three days before returning to normality. I believe it was her way of coming to terms with it and personally coping. I remembered when I was told I had cancer and the immediate shock of it and then needing a few days to readjust to what lay ahead. Until it directly impacts you none of us know how we would react to such dreadful news. What I would say is most people underestimate their own hidden strengths to cope with such things.

When we got home from the campsite the next day, Ann was in the bedroom and all the children ran upstairs to give their mum a cuddle and hug. It was lovely to see but I could see Ann struggling with it emotionally, as any mother would be, faced with an unknown future. The children then ran downstairs to play with their toys, as children do, and so we tried to be the normal family doing normal things until ten days later when Ann was to have her operation. It was difficult and raw.

Our next-door neighbours, Dave and Lesley, were the same age as us and supportive. This helped because she was a staff nurse and could talk freely with Ann. Of course, friends and family visited and offered their help and support, which was much appreciated, especially from mum and Margaret. Ann's close friends Teri, Trish and Linda were always there for her too and helped no end to lift her spirits at darker moments. When the front door closes and the façade we all put on is lifted, only then is the real pain, anguish and uncertainty felt.

My employers were very understanding and allowed me time to take Ann to the hospital. I told the children in as simple a way as I could, without alarming them, that their mum was going into hospital for an operation to make her better. Between mum and Margaret, they came to our house and looked after the children, collected them from school and fed them. It was invaluable help from them.

Ann had her mastectomy in 1987 at thirty-seven years of age. It was devastating to her, as it must be to any woman, as she said it took a huge part of her femininity away despite my reassurance. Ann was in the hospital for less than a week when she came home, and we had to keep telling the children not to bump into their mum. It took a few weeks before Ann would show me her scar, which she was very reluctant to, so in the end, I said, 'You accept me as I am, scars and all, do you not think I would not accept you?' I have always said when you love someone you see far beyond the physical self; it is so much deeper. It was so difficult for her to show me and so emotionally draining for her, but I knew it was a hurdle to jump and move forward from. Afterwards, we just hugged and cried together. It was a dreadful time of our lives together.

Ann started her radiotherapy to make sure the cancer cells were destroyed, and the consultants were optimistic they had caught it early enough. There were also Tamoxifen tablets to take daily and the associated side effects, which included mood swings, fatigue and nausea, amongst others. Basically, these tablets prevent any cancer cells from getting the hormones they need to grow, so the side effects were a price worth paying. Soon after this finished, Ann spoke with the consultant about reconstructive surgery, but she was reluctant for her to have this as the silicon insert might mask any new warning signs. It was decided to wait a year.

It was a long year to wait for Ann, but life goes on with the children and all their various activities, but it quickly came around. Ann was going every six weeks for a check-up and had the reconstructive surgery conversation again with the consultant, who reluctantly agreed to it, despite still expressing some concern. A few weeks later, we had an appointment to see a consultant at Salisbury Hospital, about forty-two miles west of Portsmouth, for breast reconstruction. Only a few years ago we were at this hospital with Donna who needed surgery to close a hole in her palate, so we knew it well.

Ann was pleased to see the consultant and they discussed the surgery in-depth, but his main concern was how taut the skin was because of the previous surgery and how he would try to do his best in the reconstruction. It was not like it is nowadays where breast reconstruction is commonplace surgery, this was over thirty years ago, so techniques and procedures were in their relative infancy. The procedure was booked for three weeks later and it lifted Ann knowing for her it would be an improvement to her body. It was good to see her being positive and relatively happy.

I was working in the home office on my next project for H. J. Heinz, which was useful not being away and able to be there for Ann and the children. It was also useful for getting speedy repairs on my leg, particularly as I was still going regularly every two to three months. It was about this time that carbon fibre was being used on artificial legs and mine was being adapted. Whereas in the past, I had sat in a plastic socket covered by leather this was thinner, stronger and lighter. Not only that, but instead of the leg being made from aluminium with many, many rivets, it was now a single carbon fibre tube from the hip mechanism to the knee joint and the knee joint through to the ankle. It was amazing how light this was, and the tubing was only two millimetres thick.

The use of carbon fibre revolutionised how artificial legs were made and paved the way for modularisation too. This enabled a whole hip locking, knee or ankle joint to be replaced rather than repaired and so improved the time spent waiting around for repairs. This made my visits, which were normally four hours on average, reduced to just two to three and freed up time for the prosthetist to see other patients. The biggest bonus to me was getting rid of the 'click, click' noise as I walked.

The two artificial legs I had, weighed between twelve and fourteen pounds each and by this time it was close to twenty years I had been walking on them. The downside of my mobility was slight scoliosis of my spine leading to some back pain, but the pain is relative to what hurts most and where that focus is; walking for me, hurt more.

The offices in Portsmouth where I worked had closed and we moved just outside of the city to Port Solent right by the marina. It was a lovely place and more befitting for international clients to come to than the previous dated 1960s building. The management team, in conjunction with human resources, thought it would be a good idea to give all their managers a yearly health check using a visiting nurse on the premises. There were numerous tests done and I received a printout giving me my scores and any recommendations. I think it was to catch any early medical problems as the industry is notoriously stressful.

My time came, to be put through the tests and as I entered the small room where the nurse was, my details were confirmed. I first had my blood pressure taken, so far so good, but then it was time for an ECG (electrocardiogram) test. This would test my heart's rhythm and electrical activity and entailed having sensors attached to the skin to detect the electrical signals produced by the heart each time it beats. The nurse said she would attach four sensors to me at my body's extremities, so she attached them to both hands and then both feet. Now there was a problem she had not encountered before because if she only attached it to my left toes there was no reading and if she attached it to my right leg, made largely of metal, the reading was off the wall. We had a good laugh about it and decided the ECG test was not for me.

When I got home, I told Ann and we laughed a lot about it, but for some reason, she did not believe me when I told her the nurse said I had the body of someone half my age and my wife was incredibly lucky. I may have misheard though!

Chapter 22:
More Bad News

Ann's reconstructive surgery went well, and despite the pain and discomfort she was in, she remained in good spirits. We visited her at Salisbury Hospital and the children were well behaved and did not jump on the bed to give their mum a hug and kiss. I lifted them individually to give her a kiss and treated it as a game. Ann was only in there for a few days before she was allowed home and she loved her home; it was her sanctuary.

A few days later, Ann showed me the results of her surgery and I was shocked but had to remain positive for her sake. I told her how good it looked, and she was reasonably happy with the result, but I was not. It did not look good and was a different shape to her left breast, but it did not matter what I thought, if Ann was okay with it, then I was. It was certainly better for her than having a silicon prosthesis in her bra, which was quite heavy and made her shoulder ache.

We carried on as normal for the children's sake, so as not to burden their young minds with the problems their mum was having. Little Jamie was too young to understand, Darren was quite astute and asked questions, whist Donna was not aware of the trauma going on. It's always a balance of what to tell children and it was new territory for us and we were without the support that exists nowadays.

We saw Ann's brother, Keith, and his partner, Lorraine, quite a lot. We got on well together and Ann really liked Lorraine a lot. Ann needed a lift from all the bad news, so we went on a lovely holiday to Tunisia, which we often talked and laughed about because they were great memories with a great couple. Ann was well for the week, bar a couple of days where the side effects from the tablets that she was on took hold. Mum kindly came to stay for the week at our house to look after the children, and with their nearby schools, it was ideal. Soon we were home again, thanking mum and cuddling the children, who were so happy to see us. It brightened our lives for a few days.

Keith was doing well at his job and getting promotions, but this entailed working in other parts of the country where the stores were, so we did not see each other a lot, but when we did, it was always good. He would often phone Ann, and her being so fond of Keith, she always looked forward to their conversations to catch up on the latest news. We were proud of Keith and how he had turned his life around.

Darren had a school friend called Daniel and they got on well as both loved football. His mum, Linda, and Ann got on well and she proved to be a true friend from the very beginning. Tragically, her husband died around this time, and it must have been difficult for them both. Darren had, like Daniel, joined a local football team called Meon Milton and they played in the same team. This meant every Sunday morning taking boys in the cars to the matches. Linda was always there, and Ann often came too, so it was quite a meeting point for a few of us. Jamie liked football too but followed a few years later, so I watched them both play collectively for seventeen years.

It was almost two years, all but a couple of months, from her mastectomy when Ann said her chest was itching and did not quite feel right. We did not want to wait another six weeks for the now three-monthly review, so contacted the consultant's secretary to make an appointment, which, because of her medical issues, came quickly in just a couple of weeks. We never saw the senior consultant, only one of the consultants under him. His doctor/patient rapport was awful, and he talked down to us with a supercilious air about him, saying there was nothing to worry about and he knew best. Ann did not take prisoners lightly and she said there was a problem, that she knew her body better than he did! The platitudes rolled out from him, and he just left. The nurse in attendance just raised her eyebrows to confirm her own thoughts of this man.

We went home quite annoyed. I decided I did not want other couples or individuals going through this health uncertainty and to have this negative experience, so I reported him to the secretary of the senior consultant to get it on the record. He soon phoned me back and was a nice man who, I felt, spoke genuinely about his concerns regarding what we had experienced. He also spoke to Ann and assured her she would not be seen by that particular consultant again and that he would personally talk to him about this matter.

We knew the next check-up was only six weeks away and during this time Ann still felt things were not right and she was getting more and more concerned. I always went with Ann to her appointments, not just to understand what was happening but to ask any questions Ann did not ask and to give her the support only a partner can.

Finally, the appointment came and off we went again to

see the senior consultant this time, not his junior. He listened to Ann as she described the symptoms she was experiencing, the burning sensations and itchiness which would not go away. He examined her and felt the lymph nodes under her arm and said they were swollen, and further tests needed to be made. If breast cancer spreads, it typically goes first to the nearby lymph nodes under the arm or around the collarbone. They decided that day a needle aspiration from the node was needed and so we waited for the results a few days later.

It was an agonizing wait but eventually, we were called to the hospital and spoke with the oncology consultant this time, whom we trusted. She told Ann the news that cancer had spread, and a radical mastectomy was required. It explained her reluctance for Ann to have her reconstructive surgery because the silicone prosthesis can mask any swelling, which may not otherwise be found. The radical mastectomy meant that cancer had spread to the breast muscles and lymph nodes, which all needed to be removed.

We came home and Ann went straight to the bedroom, she was devastated again. She stayed there for around three days, all the while coming to terms with the threat of her mortality. I had to tell friends and family the news and it was hard repeating the same awful news to everyone, whilst balancing it with family life and protecting the children from the fallout of this.

The surgery happened quickly, as time was of the essence, and we were going through the same worrying times again. Throughout all this tragic news, Ann was very brave once she came to terms with it, and her priority was always the children. Friends and family rallied around once again, and they were all a great help through those dark days.

After the surgery, Ann was prescribed several tablets including steroids, but the oncology consultant said chemotherapy was also necessary to help kill any remaining cancerous cells and it should start within a month of surgery. The period for Ann's chemotherapy was six treatments every three weeks. This treatment entailed having the drugs inserted directly into a vein through a needle and took nearly an hour each time. Chemotherapy medicines affect the whole body, stopping any cancer cells from dividing and growing but they do kill the good cells too, so the effects are very debilitating. The next day after treatment was bad and Ann took to her bed and within a few treatments, she started finding a lot of her hair on her pillow.

Ann always took pride in her hair and to me seemed to spend ages getting it just so, like many women I suppose. We knew it would probably happen, but it came out over a few weeks until there were just straggly bits left. Ann started to wear a turban scarf at first but then decided a wig would be better. We bought one locally from a shop dealing with similar chemo patients and they were helpful. Ann's pallor had changed because chemo is basically poisoning the body by killing off the cancerous cells, which also kills the living cells too. The wig looked quite good and gave her confidence in going to the outside world. It was hard on her and the bouts of sickness after each session were taking their toll.

My job was quite intense, but I enjoyed the challenge, variety and learning side because in Project Control you must know what each function does. I needed to understand what information they needed and why, then what information they provided and to whom. Added to that was the programme effect on any delay and the overall cost to the project amongst many aspects of controlling a project. I was promoted to project controls manager and given a company car, which sounded great, but I had previously been paid for overtime, and now I was not. I think it took about four years to catch up on what I had been earning, but it was another step on the promotion ladder.

Once Ann had finished her chemo, I needed to lift her spirits a bit. It was early May and I had booked a farmhouse in the Dordogne, France. It was a huge place and had its own courtyard, a side barn with games, like table tennis plus a swimming pool overlooking a beautiful field with wildflowers. Although the temperature was hot, the water in the pool was quite cool and I remember offering the children some money for the first to get in. Darren took the opportunity to dive in and it just took his breath away and I have never seen anyone get out of a pool so quickly. We all laughed and it was a lovely family time.

The barn itself was a bit spooky with lots of pictures of Christ being crucified scattered throughout the house. It was typically French with dark wood everywhere and being in the countryside there was no ambient light so once the house lights went out it was pitch black. The children did not like it being so dark and their imaginations ran wild. I was last to bed and the stair light switch was at the bottom of the stairs so to turn it off, I had to walk up the stairs in total darkness as we did not have a torch. I must admit it was a bit spooky too!

The other unusual thing for all of us was to get to the barn there was a long, winding road several hundred yards long with grass verges on either side. These verges were being cut by this chap who I can only describe as a lookalike for the harbinger of death, and he was using a scythe to cut the grass too. He really looked the part with his very wide-brimmed black hat and as we passed him, he would just stop and stare at us, which was eerie. Daily, he was slowly making his way toward the barn, cutting the grass with his scythe and the children were spooked by him. I took the initiative and when we next passed him, I waved. He just looked and stared at me. Next time I waved again, and he smiled and waved at us. Job done because the next time all the children waved at him and he waved at them.

Right in the middle of the courtyard was a lovely oak tree and one day I sat Darren on my knee in the car. Like all young boys, they want to drive a car, so I let him steer whilst I used the brake and accelerator pedal, and we went round and round the oak tree in the courtyard. He loved it and Ann was smiling away. The smile from her made everything worthwhile after what she had been through. It was a memorable holiday for all of us for many reasons.

Chapter 23:
Bad News Continued

Family life continued for us, and we had some great parties at the house. Not just our wider families getting together for birthday and Christmas celebrations, but also New Year's Eve parties. Having the extension built on the side of the house meant we had a large L-shaped lounge so could accommodate quite a few people. When you have children, it is near impossible to get babysitters on New Year's Eve so we often invited relatives and neighbours to our house and said they could bring the children too. The children played upstairs, and the adults stayed downstairs. I tried not to think too much about trampled food and spilt drink upstairs because we had such a great time downstairs. They are great memories of everyone being happy.

When it was Ann's 40th birthday, we had a lovely party at home and our good friends and family were all there. The beer and wine were flowing, and Ann liked her red wine. She always told a good story where she held the audience in the palm of her hand, embellishing with each sip and the audience was captivated. I watched her in the garden that day chattering away until her glass was almost empty, and she walked toward the patio doors to get to the kitchen and replenish it with the lovely merlot she enjoyed. What she had not seen, though, was the patio doors were closed. She hit it with some force, bounced back and landed on her bottom. I rolled up, everyone looked around at the noise and she nonchalantly got up opened the patio door and entered the kitchen. We have all done something like that where you just want no fuss made and Ann was no different, but everyone was in hysterics. The amazing thing to me throughout this drama was she never once spilt the remaining red wine in her glass!

Darren, like Jamie, enjoyed his football, but Darren was also quite good at tennis and was in the Priory School Tennis Team. They had a good set-up there, which was well run by the deputy head. The school team were entering a tournament in France, so we paid for Darren's trip over there for a week to help with the French he was doing at school too. Darren also liked golf and they went to a golf course whilst over there to play. It was a large course, so they hired golf buggies to get around. The saying 'boys will be boys' comes to mind because I would probably have been doing the same thing myself at their age, but it turns out they were racing around the course up and down the mounds, going too fast when they overturned. The phone call we received, early one evening, was quite frightening. One of the teachers was saying Darren had been on a golf buggy with his friend Ben, which had overturned. Darren had banged his head, briefly lost consciousness, and had blood coming out of his ear. He was in the local hospital and being kept in for observation. They said they would phone me the next day for an update.

It was a sleepless night following the news and Ann was going through all sorts of scenarios as most mothers would. The worrying part was the blood coming out of the ear and I assumed the hospital was worried about a clot forming. The phone call the next day said he had a good night but would be kept in the hospital. I started looking at flights across to this place in France, but the nearest airport was some way away so a hire car would be necessary. The next flight was the following day, but I wanted to see whether he would be discharged. It was quite a dilemma because Ann was not feeling well at the time, but still wanted to travel with me and we were not getting any prognosis for his condition. Every call we got said he was likely to come home the next day, so I never did book a flight. I wish I had booked the flight straight away because Darren was in the hospital for five nights, eventually travelling back with a teacher by car ferry. It was traumatic for Darren over there with no parental support as he often reminds me! The outcome was Darren had damaged his eardrum; hence the blood and it has left him with tinnitus for the rest of his life.

Around this time, Ann was having regular appointments at the hospital with the oncology consultant, whom we trusted, and she always spent time with both of us. I had known her when I had my cancer, and she did my annual check-ups, so we had a history. We had hoped with the radical mastectomy, the steroids and chemotherapy that this would be the last of the issues we faced, but it was not to be.

Weight for most women is an ongoing issue and Ann was no exception. The steroids did not help with the weight and she, at times, had a bloated stomach but said this time it was not going away, in fact, it was getting worse. We made an unscheduled appointment with the oncology consultant who immediately referred her to a consultant gynaecological surgeon. By the time we got to see this consultant in a matter of a few weeks, Ann looked as though she was four or five months pregnant. He confirmed our worst fears that it was ovarian cancer, and an immediate operation was required to remove the tumour.

A week later Ann had her operation, removing the tumour and at the same time, she had a hysterectomy. When the consultant visited us, he said the tumour was the size of a football and that regular three-monthly visits, plus more chemotherapy, would be necessary. It was a terrible blow and Ann felt the clock was ticking on her life. I brought the children in to see their mum in hospital, which, by now, they were unfortunately getting used to, but it was lovely to see them hugging and talking to her about everyday things.

It was around this time there was some devastating news for our next-door neighbours. Leslie, who was a great friend to Ann and always a picture of health, had suddenly collapsed and been taken to hospital. We had a call to say we should visit now as a brain tumour had been diagnosed and she had days to live. We rushed to the hospital and their distraught relatives were there. Leslie was unconscious, with some tubes inserted and we said our goodbyes. She passed away a few days later. It was dreadfully sad as Dave had three young boys to bring up.

We went to the burial at Warblington Cemetery, just eight miles east of Portsmouth. The church of St. Thomas is from late twelfth century and overlooks Emsworth harbour. It was an incredibly sad day, especially so when someone has not lived a full life. The setting, though, was lovely at a quiet cemetery looking out to sea.

There was too much time for negative thinking, and I needed something to change that. I decided to get a second mortgage to free up some of the accumulated capital on the house, and with part of the money I booked a holiday to

Disneyland, Florida for the whole family. When Ann told our friend Linda, she said she would love to take Daniel too, so there were now seven of us going. It was exciting and just what we all needed; Linda included.

Before we knew it, we were on a holiday. I planned the three weeks we were away to maximize the places to see. We stayed in Orlando, International Drive to be precise, where a lot of tourists stay. We ate out all the time and went to a place where you had a buffet breakfast for about four dollars and kids ate for free. At the time, the dollar/pound exchange rate was nearly two to one, so it was cheap dining. The children all enjoyed themselves, particularly the drive-thru for Dunkin Donuts, where they served coffee and thirty-two varieties of doughnuts.

Upon arrival at Orlando, I had hired a large transit to transport the seven of us around and it was ideal until I went to drive it and my right foot was in the way of the accelerator pedal. There was no room to move it to the side, so I was stuck. The rental company did not have any other large vehicles so Ann said, 'Don't worry, I will drive.' I must admit I prefer driving to being a passenger, but to give Ann her dues, she drove over 1300 miles during the holiday without incident.

It was quite a busy holiday in many ways, travelling around to places like Daytona Beach on one side of Florida to Clearwater on the other side. We also went to Busch Gardens, Cape Canaveral and nearby to our hotel, we found Typhoon Lagoon. We had a memorable moment there that my children often laugh about. It was a warm, humid day when we visited Disney's Typhoon Lagoon, which is a water theme park located in Lake Buena Vista. There were lots of water slides, children's areas, diving to a wreck (very shallow) and a huge pool that created a large wave about four feet high every fifteen minutes. It was a tropical oasis and to cap it all off, it had a lazy river which you could just swim and drift in, or as everyone in our group did, acquire a large rubber ring each to sit and float in. It went around the whole park and took about twenty-five minutes to float around.

I could not do this with my artificial leg on and somebody needed to look after all the separated piles of clothes scattered nearby, so I sat down and watched everybody excitedly depart with their rubber rings into the shallow lazy river. I just sat back and relaxed, watching the lifeguards walking around, which enjoyably reminded me of the TV series Baywatch. I did notice, however, that the skies seemed to be darkening!

Nobody was worried, when, about fifteen minutes later, a few drops of rain appeared, mainly because almost everyone had their bathing costumes on. I had a few palm trees nearby but as it was so hot and humid, did not give it a thought as I would soon dry out. Suddenly, the rain turned from a few spots to a full-blown tropical rainstorm and there was I, getting soaking wet as I rescued the various piles of clothes scattered around. I found a small changing area and put the clothes there and still it poured. I was absolutely drenched and could not get any wetter, so I just sat in my chair in the rain. It was novel being so warm in the rain and being a tropical rainstorm, it was soon over, and the sun was shining when the entourage arrived back. Everyone was rolled up with laughter at the drowned rat before them, but they really enjoyed the ride and seeing me wet through, but worse was yet to come.

I got up to greet them but found the few steps I walked quite difficult, which was strange. I soon realised why, as the trail behind me showed. My artificial leg had a carbon fibre tubing above and below the knee and this was covered by a sponge liner shaped like a leg. The sponge had soaked up so much rainwater that I was leaving a trail of water behind me as I walked. I believe they thought I had had an accident and had wet myself. I squeezed it through my trousers and water poured out, much to the hilarity of everyone. I thought sitting in the sun might dry it out, but it did not. Even back at the hotel they are geared for hot not cold weather being in the Tropics so leaning my leg on the air conditioning unit did not help at all. Every day I wore trousers which quickly got wet from the sponge in my leg, even the car seat got wet when I sat down in it, and everyone seemed to find it so funny. It took five days to dry out!

We had a week's pass to visit Disney World and I was shocked to find you had to pay an adult price for children nine years old and over, and tickets there were expensive. I had read a book about how best to use your time around the theme park which was almost circular. It turned out that if you go through the entrance, like a clock at six o'clock and go straight to the twelve o'clock position and walk clockwise visiting the attractions, this was the most efficient way.

I just could not walk the distances involved so hired a wheelchair for the week, which proved an excellent asset for all of us. The queues can be quite long at many theme parks and Disney was the same even with its amazing efficiency. They had markers along the queue line for every fifteen minutes of waiting and some queues there were over an hour, which really eats into your available time. Being in a wheelchair, the ride attendants let me in to the front of the queue but not just me, they let our whole party through, all seven of us. They were very disabled-aware and made a point of talking directly to me not the person pushing me. We went on many rides; some several times and the children were in seventh heaven. It was a magical place, and they did cater for adults not just children to enjoy themselves. I remember there were themes on the ecology of the planet and that was thirty years ago, so it was all interesting between Ghostbusters and Ninja Turtles, to name a few.

One of the many things to make an impression on the holiday, aside from all the fairy tale themes, occurred when we were all driving later than we expected and got lost. We were about twenty or so miles from Orlando and somehow took a wrong turn off somewhere along the way and headed toward a few lights in the distance. The few lights turned out to be quite a large area of poor housing, where everyone in the township was black. I did say to Ann I could ask the young lady, swinging her bag and standing on the corner if she could offer some directions, but for some reason she dared me to do it. We made it through there and eventually back to our hotel.

The next day, I was talking around the hotel pool about our experience of getting lost and they said where we went was where most of the workers live, who work at the Disney resorts. Sometimes the magic can fade away when the façade of the American dream is revealed.

The holiday had to end sooner or later but it achieved what I had wanted and created a small diversion along the precarious path we were travelling. Linda was a good friend, and I am sure it helped her and Daniel too. A little escapism is good for all of us but what really made a difference was having three weeks off work rather than the usual two-week holiday, so I too felt refreshed.

The normal routine of back to work and back to school

came quickly enough, and I found I was having to visit the company's other offices in Warrington and Stockton quite regularly to review their projects, on a monthly basis. It was a necessary part of my job but hard on Ann, particularly with her health issues. All I can say is, thank goodness for family and friends.

It was decided by the company I worked for to create a pharmaceutical business and this initiative meant having a separate business stream. I was invited to be part of the dozen or so people to set up the group, including the financial control and reporting systems. We met up for three days at The Langrish House Hotel, about fifteen miles north of Portsmouth, which is a lovely 17th century manor house that accommodated business functions. At the end of a lot of hard work in getting our business plan outlined and a clear way forward, everyone was enthused and excited about moving forward. On the final day, the managing director came along for us to present the work we had done. He listened, nodded and we all felt positive and waited for his final rubber stamping of our plan. He spoke briefly, acknowledged our hard work and then said he had three things to say to us, 'Marketing, Marketing, and Marketing'. With that, he packed up and left, leaving us all looking at one another quite deflated. We all knew marketing was necessary but it was not a good performance by one of our best managing directors I have worked for.

Chapter 24: The Day You Always Remember

No matter what problems you face, life just continues as normal around you, and so it was in our house. We wanted normality to escape the nightmare medical condition Ann was facing and to protect the children from the traumatic ongoing issues ahead of us.

By now, we had the builders extend the house once again to give us five bedrooms, one of which we converted into a shower room. As any growing family knows, you need space, and we were fortunate enough to have a separate shower room and a separate bathroom. Over the years, we often faced the decision to stay or move to a new house but opted to extend and sometimes upgrade the house. Looking back, it was the right decision because we were close to family, friends, schools, hospitals and Portsmouth Football Club. The house was at the bottom of a small cul-de-sac so offered a safe environment for the children to play in and we knew many of the neighbours.

One summer's day, Ann organised a party outside where we lived and got most neighbours to pay a few pounds towards the hire of a bouncy castle. There was enough to buy some food, and many helped in making cakes and sandwiches to feed the many children there. The adults bought their chairs and sun loungers out and the drinking and merriment began on a beautiful sunny day. Phil and Teri from around the corner came, and Linda too. The children loved it and we all had a great time, to make a special memory of a happy day.

At work, I was put onto a project in the home office for a PTA (Pure Terephthalic Acid) Plant in Taiwan as the project services manager, which included overseeing the project control, finance, commercial, accounts, estimating and foreign currency transactions. The client was ICI (Imperial Chemicals Industries), and they were good guys, very professional and demanding, as any client is. The project was known as T9 and it went well, and we were awarded a follow-on Project called T10. In many ways, I threw myself into the work to escape, for a few hours a day, from all the problems mounting with Ann's health at home. It was always a balance getting work, Ann and the children right in equal measures as circumstances dictated. The company was particularly good during these difficult times and allowed me to attend every medical appointment with Ann to support her. I remember one of the directors saying to me 'John, it is payback time for all those occasions you have put yourself out for the Company'. It was well received and again excellent man-management by the company, which is only as good as the employees managing it.

I remember going to watch Pompey play a football game, one Tuesday night with my dad and getting a tannoy system call in the ground to return home immediately. I got home as quickly as possible to find Ann in excruciating pain, so we immediately called the doctor who administered a morphine injection to quickly ease the pain. I foolishly said to her she would never suffer pain like that again and spoke to the doctor who started her on phials of five millilitres Oramorph solution, which contained ten milligrams of morphine sulphate. Every time she had a pain, she could just break open a phial to take the medicine. This replaced the TENS machine, which is basically electrical nerve stimulation to help block or suppress pain messages to the brain. They also stimulate your body to produce higher levels of your own natural pain killer called endorphins. For some it works but it never worked for Ann, and when I had tried it a few years earlier to block my phantom pains it never worked for me either. Ann's health was deteriorating and the tablets she was on seemed to be increasing, it was a difficult time.

We were lucky to have many great neighbours but there were two who helped me tremendously and I am forever indebted to them. They were Gita and Mano, who lived about four houses away and were both consultants in local hospitals. Ann was getting breakthrough pain as the cancer spread through her body. It was getting progressively more painful but not in a way you could just take more medication. There were spikes of pain when the medication was not sufficient, and she was in agony. If this happened during surgery time, I would phone for the doctor to visit but this could take a few hours. During the night you would get through to a locum physician to come to your house, which on average would be two to three hours, meanwhile Ann would be in agony, and I felt helpless, always remembering the promise I gave her when I said she would suffer no pain, as the medication would rid her of that. Although it was out of my control, it still haunts and pains me a lot as I could not fulfil the promise.

Our local GP was Dr Patel, a real family doctor you rarely see today, who knew all my family including mum and dad. He kindly gave me his phone number and said if Ann had a pain breakthrough, he would come out and give her a morphine injection, even in the middle of the night. I did phone him four or five times and he would come, no matter what the time of night it was. Mano and Gita also offered to give Ann an injection to ease the pain during the night and I also called on them a few times, because it was so quick for Ann to get relief with them being just a few doors away. I am forever grateful to them for this true act of kindness, which meant so much to both of us.

We were shopping with the children once and Ann held a clutch bag. As we strolled through the shopping centre one Saturday, suddenly, the clutch bag came flying in front of me. We all laughed at this because Ann said how weird it was because it was an involuntary spasm which caused it to happen, and she had no control over it. Looking back, it was the first sign of things progressing.

Ann often went to play bingo in the afternoon. On one of those days, I had a call at work to say she had been driving home and had an accident and was being taken by ambulance to the local hospital. The accident happened only a few hundred yards from where we lived, and Ann had blacked out in the car, which had continued along the road before veering off and demolishing a garden wall. Fortunately, no one else was injured but we needed to understand what had happened.

Ann was kept in overnight for observation and they thought she had suffered a TIA (transient ischaemic attack), which is basically a mini stroke with the symptoms fading away quite quickly. She was allowed home the next day, but her driving days were severely limited now. The car insurance sorted out the wall and car damage.

Strange things like this were happening and the consultant

sent Ann to Southampton Neurological Hospital. She previously had a syringe inserted carefully into her spine to get her spinal fluid tested and this visit was to get the results. It was February 1995 and the consultant there said it was not good news as there were cancer cells found in her spinal fluid. He called it leptomeningeal disease and there was no cure for it, just radiotherapy and chemotherapy to slow it, but the prognosis he gave Ann that day was six to nine months to live. It was devastating news, the worst you can get and haunts me to this day.

I remember driving out of the hospital with such a feeling of utter despair, with tears rolling down my cheek. Ann was tearful but we could not talk because we were both desolate and lost in those darkest of dark thoughts. I held her hand most of the way home, but we barely spoke during the forty-minute ride home. When we got home, the children were still at school so they could not see the visible sadness we were engulfed in. Ann went to her bedroom and like other times stayed there for two or three days to come to terms with the reality of the news.

It was not all new ground for me, receiving progressive bad news and then having to tell family and friends, but now it was what to tell the children without too much trauma affecting their immediate fragile lives. It is a fine balance and I told them individually to suit what I thought was the best way to tell them their mum was extremely ill and would soon no longer be a part of our lives. Donna was eighteen, Darren sixteen and Jamie eleven, such impressionable ages and so sad.

Ann started more chemotherapy, but the side effects were not good and certainly affected her quality of life. The cancer cells were attacking the brain hence the way the clutch bag went flying. Walking was becoming difficult, and she needed crutches.

There was a surreal moment one afternoon when I was working in the company's offices at Port Solent. Ann liked to play bingo and went two or three times a week, plus it was a good distraction for her. I personally cannot stand the game, but we are all different. I was in a meeting with the project manager and client, talking through some changes worth several hundred thousand pounds, when I had a call from reception to go and pick Ann up at a bingo hall a few miles away, as she was unwell. I immediately left and went there expecting Ann to be outside for me to pick her up, but there was no sign of her. I feared the worst and thought she may have fallen, so I quickly parked the car and went inside. When I spoke to somebody on the door and explained I was looking for my wife who uses crutches and is not well, she said to go through the door opposite. I opened the door to be met by hundreds of people, mainly women, playing bingo and Ann just a few tables away, playing too. I asked how she was, and she said she felt poorly and if I could take over her last two games as there was a potential big cash pay-out. I could not believe my ears, but what could I say or do? I picked up the pen and started marking the card as numbers were called out. It was surreal because half an hour ago I was negotiating variation orders to the contract worth hundreds of thousands of pounds and now I was playing a game of bingo, which I thoroughly dislike. We didn't win on the last two games anyway, and I immediately took Ann home.

It was getting more and more difficult to manage work and home life, especially when Ann had bad nights. I was getting exhausted even though Margaret and mum were helping enormously, but I managed to find someone locally for a few hours a week to help with the cleaning and ironing, which helped tremendously. The family doctor also arranged for some home-care for Ann. Every bit of help was welcome during those difficult months.

Ann was on a real cocktail of tablets to stop or ease certain conditions and then other tablets to offset the side effects of those. I did get quite knowledgeable about the tablets because, at times, she was hallucinating, seeing butterflies or horses galloping by, so dosage versus pain control was important.

Keith and Lorraine visited Ann, even though they lived far away, and of course her good friends Terri, Trish and Linda were all seeing her regularly too. Ann had her own car and was able to get out with her friends for tea and coffee mornings with a lot of retail therapy, particularly shoe shopping. There was no repeat of her TIAs and we got medical advice about her ability to continue driving.

As the disease progressed it must have been attacking her brain cells through her spinal fluid, which started to affect her walking capability. She already had to use crutches to support her as she walked, but we both knew she was struggling. Add to that the effect of all her medication, particularly with the increased Oramorph and she was really in a twilight world at times. We could all see the slow deterioration, but Ann was one brave woman who kept going and going. Donna had her first job at a care home and Darren had just been made head boy at his school, so there were lovely things to celebrate. She told me she wanted to live, to see her children grow to adulthood, to cuddle her grandchildren and to grow old with me, but fate had cut her a cruel deal.

The nursing help increased, and they were coming three times a day to help her and give her medication. By now, Ann could no longer manage the stairs and was sleeping downstairs in what had been our study. It was a large room with patio doors leading into the garden, and the bed was positioned so she could look out into the garden. If Ann was unwell during the night she would call out and I could be straight down to her. I remember Darren, who was sixteen then, saying he would sleep downstairs on the settee to help his mum during the night, if needed, to give me a break. Ann was calling during that night, so I came down as Darren had been fast asleep. He always slept soundly, and the next day Ann and I both laughed about it.

I found Ann at this time was asleep for almost twenty-two hours a day, with all her medication so I talked to Doctor Patel and he agreed a palliative nurse would visit to discuss the medication because she was on a huge amount of morphine by now. Following this visit, Ann was very quickly transferred to the Rowans Hospice a few miles north of Portsmouth for a week. They are marvellous places, so caring and they quickly sorted out her medication, which enabled Ann to be awake about six or seven hours a day. We both knew how precious time was and it was really pulling Ann back from the jaws of death to spend a little more quality time with us.

It was during this time that Ann planned her own funeral service; the hymns, the passages and as the curtain of the coffin closed, she wanted the song, 'Wish me luck as you wave me goodbye' played gently on the organ. She had a wry sense of humour.

The other aspect of her hospice stay was that I was also fed when I visited her, and the food was good. One thing I will always remember was when we left to go home all her dirty washing had been cleaned and ironed, which I thought was marvellous as it saved me time too.

We had been married a long time by now and our silver anniversary was fast approaching in a few months' time on the twenty-first of November. I did a bit of research and decided to take her to a beautiful hotel on the shores of Lake Garda in Italy. I had costed it, but just in those few weeks of planning it the deterioration was apparent and I knew we would never go there. It was desperately sad seeing the once vibrant, beautiful woman I loved just fading and drifting away from me and our children.

We had another visit to the hospital in early October where they looked at recent tests and recommended another course of chemotherapy to slow down the now rapid growth of cancer through her body. Ann listened and asked how long she would last with the new round of chemotherapy treatment, and they said it would be three to six months. She felt the quality of life was awful going through another round of this and then asked how long she would have if she did not have any treatment, to which they replied 'Four to six weeks'. It was inevitable, dreadful, dreadful news but Ann took it stoically, she was one brave woman. She declined further chemotherapy.

As her condition worsened and the breakthrough pain continued, there were exceedingly difficult conversations between Ann and me. She had really reached the end of the road in terms of pain and poor quality of life. I really tried to empathise with her but only she knew how bad it was. One evening, she said she had had enough and wanted to leave this life and asked me if I would help her. I was stunned and never expected to be asked this. I really do not believe in suicide, but how dreadful a state of mind hers must have been in to ask me that, and what pain she was going through. I must admit I was in tears as I said I just could not do that because I loved her too much, to which she said if I did then I should help her. It was an awful dilemma and one I had to face a few days later when she asked me again. I felt guilty not helping her, but in all conscience, I knew I could not live with myself in doing that. I felt I could not talk to anyone about it, so I kept it to myself.

I believe Ann did have more TIAs because when she was looking at you, one eye was not quite aligned as the other and she couldn't see but a short distance. By now the morphine was four hundred times more than when she first started taking it to help manage the pain. Our family and friends were truly wonderful and with the clock ticking they decided to have a silver anniversary party toward the end of October. All the family were there, as well as friends and neighbours. Ann was now confined to bed, but like the trooper she was, her storytelling continued around her bedside talking as best she could to her friends with a glass of champagne in one hand and a smile. I did take a video of the day here and there, but Ann, for some reason I never fathomed, did not like any photographs or video taken of her. It made me smile because even with her impaired vision she still caught me taking the video from a distance and called out for me to stop it. It was the last video I have of Ann.

Ann loved the party but was exhausted by it and when everyone had left, she wanted the children to give her a big hug before she went to sleep. Sleep must have been welcome from the frightening journey ahead, but the amount of diamorphine she was on did give a euphoric feeling, so it was some small consolation. The night nurse soon arrived and tended to Ann, made her comfortable and stayed the night by her bedside. They were lovely caring people who looked after

Ann incredibly well and enabled me to sleep knowing she was in good hands.

A few days later, Ann had stopped eating, was hardly drinking, and unconscious all the time. There were no final words of goodbye because we had spoken before and said everything, we needed to say to each other, which were very special words between two people facing the final separation. The nurse, based on her experience of dealing with dying people, felt the time was close. The children always kissed their mum first thing in the morning and last thing at night, and it was so difficult watching them, knowing the end was soon.

I phoned Keith the next day and he took time off work and came to stay with us. Those final days, and shared pain both Keith and I felt, bond you together for life and eventually the inevitable day of Ann's death came.

It was the ninth of November 1995 and Ann was very peaceful in her bed. We had not spoken for several days as her condition weakened and her medication increased. Darren and Jamie had kissed their mum goodbye as they both went to school and then Donna left for work and kissed her mum goodbye too. Keith and I took turns to sit with Ann and at about two-thirty p.m. Keith said he wanted some fresh air and went for a short walk. Maybe Ann somehow knew we were alone, but I sat with her and at two forty-five she started perspiring whereupon many beads of sweat suddenly appeared on her forehead. I had never seen anything like that before and knew something was happening. I held her hand, told her I loved her, and her breathing got shallower and shallower until at three p.m. she peacefully passed away. It was a smooth, painless transition from this life, after so many difficult years, but so terribly sad for all those she left behind.

I tried as best I could to compose myself and phoned the place where Donna worked to get her to come home. I phoned my mum and told her the news and asked if she would come over to me later. I knew Margaret would bring her, they were such a help. I also phoned Ann's Mum to tell her the sad news and she called a taxi to say her goodbyes to her only daughter. Unbeknown to me, Jamie had not gone to school on this day but was first to come home at his usual time. I was looking out of the lounge window down the road and saw him coming so I opened the door to him and told him the sad news. It was so hard telling your child that their mum had died and trying to comfort them. I said to go and give his mum a kiss goodbye, and with that Darren came through the door and I had to repeat the painful process and tell him. I looked out of the window and saw Keith walking down the road, and I opened the door for him, and he just knew what had happened and just fell to his knees in the road, completely distraught. He was so upset he was not there, but maybe Ann had not wanted it that way. I then saw Donna walking down the road and opened the door for her and she also sensed what had happened. It was awful breaking the news to the children, and I will never ever forget the raw pain for me or for them on that day.

The other painful memory was phoning friends and family to tell them the news of Ann's passing and sharing the grief repeatedly. I comforted the children as best I could, but even though we knew the day was coming it is still the finality of death, knowing you will never see your loved one again and all that remains are the memories. I felt their grief.

I remember having to phone the doctor's surgery to get a doctor to certify the death. This doctor came quite quickly and certified her death. I know it's a formality to get the certification enabling other things to follow, such as funeral directors and registration, but later to have a bill come through, at the time for £65, to confirm my wife was dead was somewhat surreal when I had been there at her death, anyway these were the formalities to follow.

I had a few visitors that evening, and mum and Margaret were marvellous in comforting the children. I needed some time by myself and said I needed to go out for a short while. It was eight p.m. and I drove the car to Old Portsmouth overlooking the harbour and sat on one of the benches. It was raining and my mind went over everything that happened for the next hour. I looked around and saw life was just continuing around me. It was a strange feeling because I almost wanted the whole world to acknowledge the loss of Ann Paffett. Life just continues and the circle of life for Ann was complete. I needed to get home, so drove slowly back.

The next day was a Friday and the children stayed at home. I phoned the schools and Donna's workplace, so people understood the situation. Keith was there too, and his girlfriend, Lorraine, came to see us. I talked with the children and tried to explain how difficult it was to lose their mum but to try to understand she was no longer in pain. I then realised I had to try and be both a dad and a mum to them and there was no training for this, nothing to help you, all you can do is your best for them.

My employers were incredibly good, and I took time off to plan arrangements. I needed to register the death and get several original death certificates to let various companies know, so there was a lot of correspondence. There were, of course, the funeral directors to appoint and arrangements to be made. They helped in booking the cremation and follow-on service at Warblington Cemetery and I contacted them about a plot and having a stone made. Ann had decided on Warblington because her friend and next-door neighbour, Leslie, was buried there following her untimely death and she loved the peace and tranquillity of the location.

Ann had arranged her own order of service for her funeral, which was lovely because it was her closure on her life and a fitting finale. I wrote a eulogy, which was filled with the fun parts of her life, amongst the sadness of her passing. I met with the vicar before the cremation to speak about Ann, her life, her achievements, her family and the fun we had. It meant a lot to have the discussion because we weren't regular church-goers, but did believe in God, so in a small way the vicar very briefly got to know the person Ann was.

The next few days were a blur really, because there was a lot to do in organising things, as well as talking with our many friends and family. It is, of course, always sad when someone dies, but when they are young, we are often more affected. We all hope to live a full life of at least three scores and ten, but life can be, on one hand, so exciting, vibrant even, but then so cruel and unfair. I knew how I felt.

The cremation was arranged for the twentieth of November and I was pleased it was not on the twenty-first, which would have been our silver anniversary. This would only have compounded the grief I felt. I had to put the obituary into the local paper, The Portsmouth News, and when it was published, nearly half a page was filled with friends and family's contributions of condolences. A few days after, there was to be a service at Warblington Church with the internment of the ashes for close family and friends.

I kept thinking what was best for the children in their grief, with my parents and Margaret helping enormously to support me during this life changing transition of trying to be both a dad and a mum. It is strange, in many ways, the mix of emotions you go through because, on one hand, I was dreading the funeral as I found it hard to manage my emotions at those times, but on the other hand it meant a full closure of Ann's life and I did not want that either.

I had a bad experience of going to see an aunt of mine in the Chapel of Rest when I was seventeen. I remember looking at her there and hardly recognizing her, as death had taken its toll. I vowed never to see another person like that and just remember them in happier times. I never went to see Ann, but I was told she looked very peaceful by those who did.

The dreaded day of the funeral came, and I remember seeing the hearse slowly driving down the cul-de-sac and then parking outside our house. It was such a sad sight, as outside was Ann in her coffin with flowers leant against it spelling the word 'mum' and inside the house were her children all visibly upset at this cruel twist of fate robbing them of their much-loved mum. We got into the hearse and the funeral director slowly walked the length of the road in front. It was very solemn, and I remember as we left the house, there were some neighbours kindly paying their last respects lining the road. We drove the seven miles to the crematorium, but one kind act stayed with me and that was a lollipop man getting ready to ferry the children across the road, stopped, took his hat off and bowed his head. It was a lovely, thoughtful gesture and one I will never forget because in that simple act it showed a statement of true compassion.

When we arrived at the crematorium, it was lovely to see all the faces of friends and family there to pay their last respects to a special person. In front of us they slowly took the coffin out of the hearse, and we all got out of the car. To me, it was an exceedingly difficult moment, knowing Ann was just a few feet away from me and the children, so I started taking deep breaths to get my composure back. We made our way into the chapel, which had around one hundred seats all filled, and I noticed later about thirty or forty people standing, so it was well attended.

With the eulogy spoken by the vicar and the songs Ann wanted sung, the curtains closed on the coffin to the lightly played tune on the organ of 'Wish me luck as you wave me goodbye'. I learnt later the children did not like the finality of the coffin lowering as the curtains closed, and I know many services nowadays leave the curtains open and the coffin stays there.

We walked through to where a sea of flowers was laid out and read a few of the displays before everyone filed passed us shaking hands, hugging and crying together. It was a sad day, but we got through it together and a few days later we had the private ceremony at Warblington Church. Here, we made our way through the pathway surrounded by burials long past in the grounds to the church. It is steeped in history, a lovely old place and we sat in the front seats along with about fifteen close family and friends. I was comforting the children when suddenly a trestle table was put by my side, and I looked at the children and then back to see the urn of Ann's ashes placed on it. I never expected that, I stared at it for quite a few seconds, thinking all the time it was the essence of Ann and all that remained of her. It was so upsetting but the short service soon started, followed by a slow walk to place the urn into the ground where later a small plaque was put. It was what Ann wanted, something simple she said to me, just to show I was once on this earth. Her final wish was granted. We all miss you so much, Ann.

Chapter 25:
Life Carries On

Life carries on, but it would never be the same for any of us. This is what life is about, change and how we manage it. People were incredibly good to us, but each one of us were trying to deal with a new way of living without Ann. I do dislike the saying 'time is a great healer' because it certainly never applied to me. All you do is adjust to the pain of loss for the rest of your life.

I liken losing someone to the action you take throwing a pebble into a pond. The biggest impact is when the stone hits the water, as it was for us, and then the strong ripples spreading out from the epicentre, gradually weakening the further they go. Ann's death affected many people in many ways but now the children were my responsibility and I had to do the best I could for them in this unchartered life I now had to lead.

Immediately after the funeral, Keith took Jamie back home with him for several days. Jamie always looked up to his Uncle Keith and I knew Keith would spoil him. I hoped it would perhaps soften the immediate blow a little. It helped Darren and me a lot because there was a lot to do and organise.

Donna was now back at work, Jamie, after a few days, had returned from Keith's and went back to school and Darren was getting ready for his A levels, whilst earning some spare money working at a local supermarket. I returned to work, and

I remember telling the senior management team about events over the past few weeks, which was difficult, but we were quite a close-knit team. They were all very supportive and in many ways it was good to get back to work and have a different focus. Adrian, Julian and Lynn, three of my colleagues, had all come to the funeral as they had often met Ann at the company events such as the Christmas Dinner and Dance. The year Ann died, I felt it impossible to go to the company Dinner and Dance as it was all too raw for me with the previous memories I had there. Work was a good focus, but there were dark moments.

Our close friends and neighbours were particularly good, and I remember Sue, a friend and neighbour, bringing a lovely lasagne meal for us to eat. It was such a kind gesture when words could never convey how they were feeling at the time either. Friends were visiting, but deep down I knew it would never be quite the same without Ann, nevertheless, I will always value their help and friendship. Linda was a great help and a good listener too, and I will always be indebted to her for her help and kindness to us in the first year of losing Ann.

I had been getting some pain for a while in my knee and thought it was just wear and tear, which you would naturally expect when the one must work harder than if you have two. The pain was increasing, and I was fortunate enough to have private medical cover through work, so I asked my doctor to refer me to a knee specialist. My appointment came through quickly and I had some X-rays done. The consultant diagnosed degenerative patellofemoral osteoarthritis, which occurs when the cartilage on the underside of the knee wears down and becomes inflamed. It was no real surprise because of the pounding just the one knee takes, but I did need to manage it.

My way of managing it was to only use the stairs at work to travel up or down one floor, otherwise I used the lift. On the odd occasion I would take anti-inflammatory tablets, but I do dislike taking tablets unless necessary. When this happens it's a realisation of age, with wear and tear a biproduct of it. You must embrace it and adjust a little, but it was easily manageable. The consultant had said the time will come when the pain gets too severe and a knee bone scrape would be required, but that could wait.

I was trying to get into a different routine at home after work, regarding cooking, washing, ironing and cleaning. Then, of course, there were sandwiches to make in the morning for the children's packed lunches. I was quite domesticated through necessity as Ann's illness had progressed and she became less able to do the necessary chores. Our friend, Teri, knew someone who would do some cleaning and ironing for four hours a week on a Friday, which does not sound a lot, but it certainly helped. Mum and Margaret helped an awful lot with the cleaning, which helped me too, so our new life was getting organised.

I talked to the children about their mum and things she would have done or said, but it was not easy. Once doors are closed none of us knows what goes on in other people's lives and so it was with the children. They were all dealing with their grief in their own way because we had no real guideline or professional help to assist us, unlike today.

The first Christmas without Ann was right upon us and hard for everyone in the family, but with my parents, Margaret and Jeff, Arthur and Lyn we got through it. It was not easy but time marches on, and the adjustments to change were now underway.

I remember one day at home, and Donna said to me she was leaving home to live with her new boyfriend called Andy. I really had no idea Donna was seeing anyone because she had been meeting him from work for a few months. She never brought him home and never spoke about him. I did not want Donna to rush into anything, but she was determined to move out and it was a re-focus for her from the dark days before. I said I wanted to meet him and went to visit their bedsit, which was an eye-opener in meeting Andy. He had not had it easy in his early years, recently losing his own mum, so I could understand the bond they had. What I did see was how happy they were together, and I knew he would care for her in his own way. It wasn't ideal just a few months after losing her mum, but she was nineteen now and getting independent so, reluctantly, I agreed. It was sad in many ways to see her leave home, but I did understand how foolish young love can be, having been there before.

Keith and Lorraine had unfortunately split up and gone their separate ways, which was sad, but Lorraine so wanted a family and Keith did not. They cared so much for each other but unfortunately Lorraine's maternal needs drove the decision. Lorraine later met Steve, who owned a nursing home in Norwich and within a short time they were getting married, and we were invited to the wedding. We had always been and will always be close to Lorraine, so I took Darren and Jamie to the wedding. It was lovely to see both Lorraine and Steve enjoy their special day. I did find it difficult being at this type of function, when I would normally be with Ann, so there was some sadness too, but I was glad we had made the effort to visit Norfolk and celebrate with Lorraine. When we were in the church, it poignantly reminded me of our own wedding, when taking our vows and saying, 'in sickness and in health, until death us do part.' I did get upset at this point. It was also a new focus for a few days for me and the boys, which was most welcome.

I went regularly to the football matches with my boys on Sundays, and so it continued with Jamie, as Darren was now focusing on his exams. I met some good people there and it was nice to meet socially and chat. I had not realised, but Ann had allowed Jamie to stay home a few times from school in the last year of her life. It would have been hard to stop it if I had known because those moments of being with her youngest child were so precious to her, knowing the clock was ticking, but the legacy of missing schooling is sometimes hard to recover from and so it proved for Jamie.

I missed Ann dreadfully and the interaction you have as husband and wife. I missed female company, so I went out with a few ladies for companionship. I went out with Linda our close friend and she helped me a lot to get through those early days just talking about many things from our holidays to the children, who she knew so well. I owe her a huge debt of gratitude, she was a lovely, fun person to be with. About a year later the other ladies, too, were a nice distraction from the loneliness and heartache I felt.

Life certainly changed quickly for me in the early summer when Donna told me she was pregnant. I believe she wanted to start a family quickly to help in some way to compensate for the loss of her mum, and it was quite a shock for me, but in her own way she and Andy were happy, so I could not deny them that. It meant my first grandchild was on the way, which was a happy, yet sobering thought.

Darren had passed his A level exams and had got a place

at Bristol University in the South West of England to study International Business Studies with a German bias. It was a good course for him, and I thought it would be a good stepping-stone for his future. I also thought it would be a good idea to take all the children away, one last time together, so we took a holiday to Turkey, joined by Arthur and Lyn. They both helped look after the children with me, and Donna would not leave my side. Her pregnancy was quite visible by the time we went on holiday, and I first noticed a few people looking at us both strangely until it dawned on me; Donna looked younger than her years and there she was, pregnant with a middle-aged man. Goodness knows what they were thinking, but it never bothered me. The same thing happened, only more so, when we arrived in Turkey. There was no hiding the blatant staring, but it was their problem to deal with, not mine.

We had a nice break with Arthur and Lyn and the weather was hot. The hotel was lovely and the beach close by. We visited a few places there to soak up the local heritage, but one visit sticks in my mind, which was to Pamukkale. This visit was quite a distance to travel but this small town in Western Turkey is known for its mineral-rich waters flowing down the hillside, which, over millennia, has turned the cascading petrified limestone a beautiful white. People can swim in the shallow pools that form there, but I would rather bathe at the top than lower down where their water flows. We were watching and enjoying the spectacular views there in the hot sun when a real commotion occurred in a pool a few feet away from me. A young German man with Down Syndrome was suddenly found floating face down in the water. Goodness knows where his carer or parents were, but there was pandemonium for a while whilst they carried him out of the pool and gave mouth-to-mouth resuscitation. Fortunately, it worked, and he was breathing again, hopefully a lesson was learnt there.

When the coach first arrived there, it drove around a small hotel at the very top of the hill to drop us off, however the following year this place was given World Heritage status and the coaches had to park a few hundred yards away to conserve this beautiful place. We travelled back through small rural villages seeing the devastation local earthquakes had caused, which made me realise how fortunate we are not to live in an earthquake zone. It was a long, tiring journey but we eventually arrived back at the hotel in time for our evening meal.

Most evenings, we all ate in the outside part of the hotel's restaurant. It was lovely to dine al fresco, but the only downside was mosquitos, and they took a fancy to all of us, especially Donna. One night, about seven p.m., we were tucking into our starters, when, on the road running parallel with the hotel, you could hear a noisy lorry. At first, we saw some smoke and thought it was from the lorry, but the smoke and fumes just grew and grew and just swept over everyone eating outside. It was awful and people were coughing and leaving their food. It turned out the local council, to reduce the troubling mosquitos, had, in their wisdom, decided to spray the whole town in the evening when the mosquitos come out. I believe they used DDT spray, which they say is relatively non-toxic for humans if taken indirectly but this was certainly directly and, on our food, and no warning was given.

Holidays like this remind me of the concern I have when you need assistance from the plane to the luggage carousel. It does seem better nowadays, with the odd exception, but I have encountered real difficulty. I remember, one time, arriving back at Gatwick Airport on a business trip, having requested wheelchair assistance, which meant waiting on the plane until assistance arrived. All the passengers got off and still no assistance had arrived. The flight crew were leaving the plane and said they would be there soon. They also said if I could walk up to the seating area through the plane exit it would enable the cleaners to clean the plane. I walked up to this area, and it was around eleven p.m. and the place was deserted. I waited and waited, nobody came, and nobody was around. I had no alternative but to walk to passport control. What compounded matters was the travellators you can step onto, to save walking, were all turned off. Not only was I exhausted, but my leg had cut into me, and it was bleeding. One of those trips to forget.

I have had many experiences travelling through various airports around the world, and of course in the early days of passing through metal detectors with my artificial leg, they often, but not always, set the alarm off. Nowadays, it nearly always works with the odd exception. One of the most rigorous checks I had was going through the Charles De Gaulle airport in Paris. I often went this route to go to one of the company's offices, called Sofresid, for regular meetings in Paris. I went through the metal detector, which was set off, so before I had the quick frisk, I explained I had an artificial leg that was high. I believe they rarely see people with an artificial leg this high walking through these detectors, so there is a novelty factor. They frisked me, felt the hard plastic seating and leather around my waist and gave me the strange look I had become accustomed to. I was quickly marched away from the area and suddenly had four armed policemen closing in on me. They took me to a small room and asked me to lift my shirt up and closely examined the leg. They even asked me to undo the straps around my waist to make sure I was not carrying anything untoward. It was intimidating, but from a security perspective you can never be too sure. Afterward, they said I could continue my journey, so I smiled and walked away.

I was still going to the Disablement Centre at least every two to three months for adjustments to my artificial leg. It was almost like a second home, the amount of time I spent there, but you do get to have a good relationship with your prosthetists. I have only had a few my whole life, from Ted, to Alec, to Eddy, to Steve, to John. They were all experienced guys and we learned together all the foibles a leg like mine can have, and like all amputees, the uniqueness of their own artificial leg. There is also the relationship I had with the technicians who undertake the actual repair or rebuild. Again, Malcolm literally knows my leg inside out and has a huge amount of experience, having worked on my leg for over thirty years. Danny is now currently following the learning curve on my leg and building up the inherent knowledge required. Things have improved over the years because my usual stay in the waiting room was averaging four hours but nowadays it is just over two.

My mum and dad were celebrating their golden wedding anniversary and we went on holiday to Menorca with them in September of 1996. Margaret and Jeff, and Arthur and Lyn joined us too, so it was a nice family break from the routine. It was good fun and lots of banter at the expense of mum and dad, but they took it well as they both had a good sense of humour too. The only strange thing to me was being on holiday in a single room, which was a new experience. I believe this was the start of going away with them every year and for all of us it was a time to enjoy and cherish those family moments together.

My spirits were lifted in November of 1996, a year after Ann's passing, when Donna gave birth to my first grandson, Luke. It was lovely to see new life, even though I recall Ann saying in one of her darker moments, all she ever wanted was to see and play with her grandchildren, but it was not to be. Andy and Donna looked immensely proud that night and it was so nice to welcome an addition to the family circle. Knowing Donna's threshold for pain, I thought we may have problems through the birth process, but she was a natural and really surprised me. I believe having lost part of her family she was now starting her own.

Chapter 26:
The Wow Factor

During the first year of losing anyone, it is a string of dates and reminders of where you were or what you did, which can be difficult. I had been out a few times for a meal or drink with about four of five women, whose companionship I really enjoyed. Even though you have friends and family around it can still be lonely, and suddenly being on your own, not as a couple with friends, can be quite different.

It was a lot quieter at home with Donna now living with Andy, and Jamie out a lot, playing with his friends. I remember the day I was saying goodbye to Darren as he first drove away to university and feeling quite sad as I waved goodbye to him, but I thought it would be good for him to have a new focus in life. Jamie's close friend Matthew, who he had known since he was five and had started playing football in a team at six or seven, was also a great help to him. Matt's parents, Barry and Jacky were particularly good to Jamie, even Jacky's mum who lived locally was a help too and he sometimes ate there. I had known Jacky for quite a few years, and she also went to the St. James's Hospital Social Club where Ann and our family used to go, often on a Friday night because it was only a few hundred yards from where we lived. She mentioned to me, that there was a Christmas function at the social club happening a few weeks before Christmas and asked if I would like to go with them. It was a friendly place and I admit to playing the one-armed bandits there while Ann was playing bingo. I decided it would be nice to go.

The day of the function soon came, and I met up with Barry and Jacky at the social club. We had a drink and chatted with the friends we knew there. I remember Jacky, who worked in the hospital, saying that her friends, Brenda and Lyn, with whom she worked in the hospital, were also coming that night. With that, the ladies walked through the entrance door and said hello to us. I knew Lyn but it was the first time I had seen Brenda and my first impressions were 'Wow!' I could hardly keep my eyes off her as she was so attractive or 'drop dead gorgeous' as you might say! They sat on the other side of the room chatting away, occasionally dancing to the seasonal Christmas music, with Brenda and me snatching a few glances at each other.

Having drunk a few pints, midway through the evening I needed to go to the gents. It might seem strange, but I held off going because I did not want Brenda to see me walking out, knowing my disability would show somewhat. Even though it was, by now, thirty years ago that I had lost my leg and meant I had had the artificial leg twice as long as my real leg, still these hang-ups persisted. I am sure it might have helped having some form of psychoanalysis, but I have just accepted my own insecurities in dealing with times like this. It has never really left me.

The evening was over too quickly, and I never really had the chance to speak with Brenda, but I did want to meet her again but was not sure whether she wanted to see me. When I met with Jacky, a few days later at the usual Sunday morning football match with Jamie, I did ask her if she would let me have Brenda's phone number so I could ring her. She said she would get it and let me know.

Christmas was a lovely family time with Darren returning from university and my newly-born, one-month-old grandson, but we all knew without Ann it would never be like it was, so we were all adjusting to the difference, some better than others. Once Christmas was over, it was back to the old routine of school, university and work. I still had not heard from Jacky with Brenda's phone number, so at the next football match I mentioned it again.

February was typically bleak, and watching Jamie's football in cold, windy, rainy conditions would be testing to any parent, but I did, at last, get a business card from Jacky with Brenda's phone number. It had taken two months to get it, but I just hoped it was worth the wait. In the evening, I phoned her and invited her out for a meal, and she agreed to go with me. It is strange how certain dates stay in your mind because I remember it was the 17th February 1997 when we had our first date. It felt strange calling it a date because by now I was in my mid-forties not my teens, but what else do you call it? It is also strange going out with other woman when you had been committed to one person for twenty-seven years. My emotions were in turmoil, but it was nice to feel excited about going out with Brenda.

It turned out Brenda only lived about half a mile away from my house and I made a reservation for a nice old, secluded country pub called The Barley Mow about five miles north of Portsmouth. I had looked forward to seeing Brenda again and that day had been a rainy one too. I picked Brenda up from her house and headed for the countryside. It was quite dark out there, especially when you live in a city with all the ambient light, and the dark roads were full of puddles, but we found our way there. I never thought about it, but Brenda was very nervous that night on our first date. Brenda had some previous traumatic relationship problems coupled with her very overactive imagination and later told me she thought to herself if I had tried to attack her in the middle of nowhere, she would just push me over and run! Well, I could not run anyway but I would never have that intention.

The evening went very well and Brenda, being a hairdresser, in addition to being nervous that night, never stopped talking. I have always thought her tongue was afraid of the dark, and to that she has always replied 'You look better in the dark.' Not a lot you can say about that! It went well for both of us, and the lovely meal, open fire and easy conversation could not have gone better. We found we had a lot in common with shared values and as I did not attack Brenda that evening, we arranged another date a few days later.

I remember going to my parent's house, which I did every week, and talking to mum about the new woman I had just met. She was excited for me and could see how happy I was talking about her, after those dark days behind us. The only thing I did not like was Brenda being a smoker. I have always disliked it and never smoked myself. I can still recall using the outside toilet at home when I was a child after my dad had been in there when he smoked. It was awful and he was warned by the family doctor to stop smoking after he started coughing up blood. He was then only in his mid-forties and he was of an era when most men smoked, and I am sure it helped a little, getting through the war too. He did eventually stop, but it was difficult for him, and I wondered whether Brenda would ever be able to stop her twenty-a-day habit.

We went out again the following Saturday, to a local fish restaurant called Flounders and had lobster thermidor as Brenda had never had lobster before. It was delicious and the easy conversation flowed as we talked about her boys, Russell and Lewis, my children and everything else from politics to religion. Before we knew it, the waiter politely reminded us that the restaurant closes at eleven-thirty p.m. and, looking around, everyone else had left the restaurant. Where the time went, I do not know, but it was the beginning of a special relationship again.

I had not told Brenda at the time, but I had been seeing about four other women and did let them all know about someone I had just met, who I wanted to see again. It would have been unfair for everyone to keep on seeing me and it was the right thing to do. I must have been smitten.

The year was starting out well for my work as I had been promoted to a senior project controls manager. I had thought things were going well for my eldest son, Darren, at university and he would immerse himself in the course. He had a nice flat in Bristol we had sourced together and I was paying for each month. This, he shared with three others, and he also had a reasonably new car which had been Ann's, so transport was not a problem. We talked every week on the phone, but I never realised the difficulties he had in coming to terms with the loss of his mum and the continuing impact it was having on him, until one day in late 1996 he told me he wanted to leave university. I was shocked and disappointed that he wanted to leave and tried to get him to realise the importance of completing the course. I couldn't persuade him, and the most important thing was not what I wanted but what he wanted, including his own wellbeing. So, Darren left university and came home.

It was good to have Darren back home as the house was so quiet with just Jamie and me. As a parent, you sometimes long for a quiet life, but when the children leave home, it is quite an adjustment with reasons both for and against. I managed to get Darren a job in the Estimating Department where I worked, which suited him for a few months, before going back to Portsmouth University to do an Accounting and Business Information degree course. Coming back home was good for him because he was close to his friends and family.

Brenda and I continued seeing each other on a regular basis. I introduced Brenda to my mum and dad and straight away they hit it off. She called them mum and dad from their first meeting. Mum liked being smartly dressed and had lovely silver hair, which in no time Brenda was cutting, setting and perming. She also met with Margaret, Arthur and my friends over the next few months and of course the children.

Brenda originally came from Stroud, which is about one hundred and fifteen miles north of Portsmouth, and was the seventh child of the seventh child, which supposedly means she is gifted with 'second sight' also known as the gift of prophecy. It also meant eventually meeting her four brothers and two sisters. I first met her mum and sister, Mary, who lived in Stroud. It's a beautiful part of England below the western escarpment of the Cotswold Hills, at the meeting point of the Five Valleys. The natural sandstone there has been quarried for millennia, so as you approach the area you see houses in the distinctive light sandy colour and because it is a sheep farming area, all the walled boundaries are made from the local dry stone. It is so typically English and when I visit there, I always think of the song Jerusalem and the words ‘on England’s pleasant pastures seen’.

Like Brenda, I called her mother, ‘mum’ from the start but her dad had died many years ago, so I never had the chance to meet him. Brenda was the last child to be conceived, when her mum was forty-five, which meant her mum was now in her eighties. She was a lovely lady, and I could clearly see where Brenda got her looks from. The conversation was easy with her and Mary, and it was lovely to meet them. Brenda told me she had spoken to her mum on the phone before and said she had met someone nice called John, to which she said, ‘All John’s are nice!’ An incredibly wise woman! Then Brenda said that I only had one leg, to which her mum replied, ‘So what!’ She was quite a character and like my mum in many ways, especially being the matriarch of the family.

Brenda had sold her hairdressing shop before she got divorced and was now doing mobile hairdressing and working part-time in the kitchens of St. Mary’s hospital, to make ends meet for her and her two boys. Brenda had boundless energy and I could see how hard she was working. She started in the hospital at six-thirty a.m., finished at ten-thirty a.m., and was then straight into her mobile hairdressing until four p.m., when it was straight home to feed the children and housework before going back to the hospital between six p.m. and eight p.m. For her, Saturdays were always busy hairdressing and she worked in the hospital on a Sunday from six-thirty a.m. until one-thirty p.m. doing all the overtime she could. I then appeared on the scene, so it was quite a demanding time for her.

I mention the busy life Brenda led because of some of the places we visited. I enjoy the odd musical such as Les Miserables, so decided to take Brenda along to the Chichester

Theatre for a bit of culture. It is a lovely place to have a meal and a nice glass of wine before the show, which we did. I had previously been to London with Ann to see this musical, and we enjoyed it, so was looking forward to seeing it again here. The lights dimmed and the show started. It was a good performance, and I was enjoying it but when I looked at Brenda after about fifteen minutes, she was asleep. I think the food, wine, low lights and general weariness had caught up with her, poor thing! She tried to stay awake, but the nodding duck syndrome was there. At the end of the show with lights up and snatches of the musical seen, Brenda apologised for falling asleep. I said not to worry but her snoring and dribbling was noticed by those around her. She did not believe me.

I always use the saying 'The sun is always shining behind those dark clouds' and for me it was a lovely feeling to have someone special in my life. I can never forget the past because it is there almost every day, in so many ways, but you do continue throughout your life adjusting to the pain of loss. It must have been difficult for the children seeing me with someone else, but I hope it was compensated by seeing me happier than I had been in ages. We were all dealing with our grief in our own ways. Donna was really feathering her nest, as they say, by starting a family, Darren was at the age when he was going out with girls and Jamie was well supported by his friends.

Work, for me, was busy and I was asked to be part of a three-man audit team to visit the offices we had in Greenville, South Carolina in America. A sudden loss of half a million dollars in a month for the office had got the attention of our CEO. By the time we were organised to go, the forecasted loss had increased to one and half million, so alarm bells were ringing. I travelled from England with the engineering director, and we flew over on a business class flight, which was rather nice. Our other colleague to join us was a financial director from our Florida office, who had a shorter flight than us. I enjoy doing audits because, having started from the grass roots of the industry, I know the building blocks to apply whilst understanding what good processes, practices and procedures should be applied.

Greenville is a lovely city and the people there were genuinely nice to us. We started immediately when we got there and the three of us agreed how and what we would be looking at. For me, there were project reviews to attend, which entailed a detailed overview of the financial and commercial status of all the projects being undertaken by the office. I have been in situations like this before and it is a little daunting when being reviewed, especially if you have prepared the detail and collated the reports. Sure enough 'Murphy's Law' prevailed because, within a minute of being introduced and starting the reviews, I noticed an anomaly in the figures. I asked them to explain, and the people were looking at each other for the explanation. They acknowledged the query and why I had questioned it, but they had to take it away and come back to me as no one could answer it. I felt for them, but I had to do my job and get answers, but more importantly we had to ensure the financial forecasts were accurate.

We were there doing the audit for eleven days in total, which meant we had a weekend free. My colleague from England and I hired a car, which was an automatic and a bit sporty, so I did the driving. We were recommended to drive to Asheville in North Carolina to see Biltmore House, which is the largest privately owned house in the United States.

Apparently, the well named, George Washington Vanderbilt bought seven hundred parcels of land, fifty farms and five cemeteries for this estate and completed the build in 1895. The Vanderbilt family were immensely wealthy, having made their money from the railroads, so the house was very opulent as money was no problem. During the Great Depression, in 1930, the house was turned into a museum and nowadays attracts more than 1.4 million visitors each year.

It was a sixty-mile journey there, but what fascinated me was for most of the journey, the road and surrounding land we travelled along was owned by this one family. We eventually arrived there and being late November, they had several, quite old-looking Christmas trees decorated. The whole house seemed to be in a time warp around the 1890s and we could hear several 'ooh's' and 'ah's' around us from the many American visitors. Then I heard one person behind me say, 'It is so incredibly old here.' I almost spluttered and laughed out loud because my parents' terraced house back in Portsmouth was built ten years before this one. I suppose we Brits take history in our stride, especially with the imprint the Romans made on England, but the Americans do not have that kind of history, only going back to the Jamestown Settlement in 1607.

We enjoyed the trip and travelled about three hundred miles that weekend, visiting some historic sites of the Civil War and local attractions. It is unusual to have spare time on a business trip, which normally entails car to airport, plane, and taxi, place of work, taxi, airport and home, with no spare time.

While we were there, it was Thanksgiving and staff had been invited to bring along a dish to eat or pay three dollars for a buffet meal. We offered to pay but they kindly insisted we were their guests. We went to a room where there were tables in a ‘U’ shape and were passed plates and told to help ourselves. I am quite a fussy eater, and I could only recognise a large, cooked turkey. There must have been around fifty dishes there along the tables and one was ice cream with dollops of peanut butter in. There were so many local delicious dishes I had never seen before, and they made us feel so welcome.

The audit went well from our point of view, but not for the local Greenville office. We uncovered poor forecasting and commercial exposure on projects including some unauthorised spending. Each office in the company’s business model was its own profit centre and the final forecast had risen from half a million dollars to a five and a half million dollar loss, which was bad news. When we got back home, my colleague and I were summoned to the CEO at our Paddington offices for an audit debrief. There were only the three of us at the meeting, which lasted just less than an hour. It was thorough and we both presented our observations with some recommendations. The outcome made by the CEO was to close the offices, which, from a business perspective, was the correct decision, but must have been awful for those people who worked there and were so welcoming to us.

It was good to get back home to see my loved ones and to avoid the amount of walking necessary on business trips, especially at airports. As usual, I was pretty sore, and needed to book an appointment to get my leg adjusted. I do not think my two artificial legs, which were bespoke for me, were as robust as I needed them to be because they were in constant need of repair. I think people with high amputations do little or no walking, but at times I had to walk quite a bit, hence testing the limits of their construction.

You do meet some real characters at the Disablement Services Centre, as it was then called, and around this time I remember sitting, as usual, in the waiting room whilst I waited for a repair to be completed. In came this chap, who I later learned was fifty years old, using under-arm crutches and not wearing a leg. I was intrigued, because not many people use these like I did, most use elbow crutches. I wrongly assumed he had just had his leg amputated and I noticed it was quite a high amputation. We passed the time of day, as you do in places like this, and he told me he lost his leg in a motorbike accident as a teenager. He was now a welder, which entailed standing for the most part of the day. I said this must be difficult, but he said he positioned one of the crutches under his stump while working to support him. I was amazed how he had adapted to counteract his disability.

In between, the prosthetists coming to see us both, you cannot help but hear what everyone's issues are, and I learnt this was his first fitting for a new artificial leg. He had managed for over thirty years with crutches, but these had taken their toll on his shoulder ligaments and he was struggling with pain to walk with them. I felt sorry for him because to suddenly start learning to walk at his age with a high amputation was no easy task, but he had no choice other than be in a wheelchair. From time to time, you see many familiar faces there, but I have never seen him since and often wonder how he managed the herculean task he had to face.

My youngest son Jamie had just completed his GCSEs and did not do well. I did get Jamie quite a few months of private tuition to help prepare him for the exams, but it was to no avail. I guess the combination of missed schooling during the latter stages of his mum's illness and coping with the aftermath of losing her had taken their toll on him. I also managed to get him a week's work experience in the office where I worked, but I don't believe he enjoyed the inside environment. I spoke with him, and the decision was made to send him to the local college for more education and re-sit the GCSEs he needed to. His attendance at the college was poor with the net result; he did not take his exams again, which was disappointing. Darren had managed to get himself a job at the local supermarket too, so he did have some money to spend. I also agreed with Jamie for him to have another go at furthering his education so signed him up again at the local college, but after a few months, he decided it was not for him.

It is quite a dilemma for a parent when your child's education is not being pursued because there could be negative repercussions if you force the issue. The old adage of 'you can't put an old head on young shoulders' certainly applied to Jamie as I tried to get him to understand the benefits education can give you. He had made his mind up and had to make his own way in the world without a robust education. The one saving grace was that Jamie did have a good work ethic, so he would not just lounge around.

Brenda had been saving hard as she was determined to take Lewis and Russell abroad for a holiday to Spain. We had been getting on well and when I asked if I could join her on the holiday, she readily agreed. It was a nice week away and an unexpected holiday on the spur of the moment. It also helped to get to know the boys a little too. I knew, too, that I would be away shortly for about a week as the project team I was working with had a meeting coming up in Egypt.

My life at Kvaerner, the company I worked for, which had several names over the years as mergers and acquisitions occurred, was mainly made up of projects you worked on. The current one at this time was in Egypt, where we were doing the conceptual, preliminary engineering design and execution plan for a secondary pharmaceutical plant owned by Pfizer. I was part of a ten-man team who went to Cairo for a week to present our work. It was my first time in Egypt and quite an experience.

Upon arrival, I found the security there very lax, but when we exited the airport in our taxis it was an amazing sight as we entered the motorway heading toward our hotel. It appeared to be mandatory to sound your horn every ten seconds, so the cacophony of sounds from so many vehicles, coupled with the air pollution, was a stark introduction to Egypt. When I was there, in 1999, Cairo had a population of eighteen million with two million doing the daily commute in and out of the city. We found the three-lane highway we were in merging with a five-lane highway, but the cars were so tightly crammed together it turned out to be a five-car-wide highway merging with a seven-car-wide highway. I had never seen anything so disorganised and so noisy. It was an incredible sight to behold. Our car was at the point of merging from the five lanes into the seven lanes when I saw a local man on a bike weaving in and out of the cars and ringing his bell! It was an amazing sight to see, almost unreal, and I admired his tenacity in the face of all those cars. I thought I had seen it all but as we eventually got through this, no doubt thanks to the taxi driver sounding his horn about a thousand times, we suddenly had to brake hard due to the car in front. We were in the fast lane, and he had decided to change lanes, so we could then see the cause of the braking. I thought the cyclist had great belief in his self-preservation but the sight of a donkey and cart in the fast lane of a highway just blew me away.

We arrived at the Sheraton Hotel, which sits on the west bank of the River Nile, and it was here where we were going to have our meetings. My room was on the fourteenth floor and it was large and comfortable with a veranda. I went to bed that night but was awoken some time before five a.m. with the calls to prayer. At this time, each mosque delivered their call to prayer or 'azan', as they call it, via loudspeakers, so it seemed they were in competition as to who could do it the loudest and longest. The minarets and prayer halls were all suddenly alive to this discordant bellowing and although it was supposed to just be a couple of minutes it sometimes went on for forty-five minutes.

I am a light sleeper and decided to get up, take a shower, sit on the veranda and prepare for our morning meeting. Being on the fourteenth floor, I had a wonderful view of Cairo and the bridge across it, but unbeknown to me there was also a four-storey police station opposite the hotel. I know this because you could see the police arriving around seven a.m. and then proceed to the roof where they stripped off and changed into their uniforms. It was a bit of a culture shock, to say the least.

The meetings during the week were not going too well because there was the usual misconception as to how much the new pharmaceutical building would cost. The business model was based on selling the old building as it was originally built on the outskirts of Old Cairo, but as the New Cairo grew it became part of the city and its value increased. The director of the plant we were dealing with had told his employees they would have an ultra-modern facility on the outskirts of Cairo, funded entirely by the sale of the existing facility. He was revered by his employers, and they all looked up to him. The only problem was an additional fifty million pounds was required to fund their expectations, and as usual they were shooting the messenger.

We normally finished the day around four-thirty p.m. , and midweek one of the process engineers I got to know had said to me he always had an ambition of riding a camel around the pyramids. We had got to know the taxi driver we used quite well, and as usual they had all the contacts. It was an incestuous relationship with his contacts because they were either his brother, uncle, or third cousin once removed it seemed. One evening, we said to him that we wanted to go to see the Great Pyramid of Giza, which today borders Greater Cairo and he said he would take us there as his brother had two camels, he could lend us, for a price I might add. It was around five p.m. and our journey in the taxi began.

On the way to the pyramid, the taxi driver asked if we had seen any papyrus art to which we said 'No'. He said he had a cousin who owned a gallery and would do us a great deal if we bought something there. I did not particularly want to go there, but my colleague was so enthused about the whole visit he said, 'Yes please.' We arrived and looked around the shop for ten minutes, but there was nothing I liked, and the tourist prices were high, so we left. I said to the driver I wanted to buy Brenda a gold ring, so of course he said, 'My uncle has a shop, I will take you there.'

When we arrived, the jewellery shop was quite large and had a huge selection. I looked and eventually found an eighteen carat gold ring with some precious stones in, which I thought would be an ideal present. The ordeal of haggling, which I do not mind, started and lasted about twenty minutes, with me walking away a few times. Eventually, I bought the ring and matching earrings for about twenty-five percent. of the original asking price and both parties seemed happy. Now it was time to visit the pyramid.

We arrived literally on the edge of Cairo because suddenly the housing stopped, and the desert began. We stopped in the taxi about fifty yards from the desert and, lo and behold, two camels were there, lying down waiting for us. I got out of the taxi and my colleague had bounded straight to the camels, with a huge smile on his face, I assume because he was about to fulfil his childhood dream. There was no price negotiation, he was on the camel straight away, which was rising, and I had not even reached them yet. There were two young boys leading the camels and his 'relative' on a horse leading the way. I got onto the camel, which for me was a bit daunting with my leg and found that the stirrup is only used to get on and off. I sat on the saddle and had to let my right leg dangle from the saddle, which was quite uncomfortable. Then there is the unique way a camel gets up, which at first throws you forward and then backwards, until you are level around two meters above ground, on a beast of burden weighing around five hundred kilos.

The journey around the pyramid was a unique experience and one I will always treasure. The guy on the horse spoke good English and had a lot of knowledge about the near one hundred and fifty metre high building, built for the Fourth Dynasty Pharaoh Khufu in two thousand, five hundred and sixty years B.C.. The sun was setting, it was warm but not too hot and the place was magical, oozing with history. It took forty-five minutes to slowly move around the pyramid, but what an experience it was. One of the reasons to remember it was not just the scenic beauty, was when we got off the camel and they said that would be eighty pounds. We duly paid it and met the taxi driver, who had been waiting for us to take us back to the hotel. He said his cousin owned a perfumery shop and if we wanted to buy some. We both said 'yes', so just around the corner was this shop with a huge display of perfume. We were both hot and the owner asked if we wanted a drink, which we were wary of and so said, 'Yes but no ice'. He brought us out a bottle of beer each and two glasses, which were still wet, where he had washed them. The beer was well received, and he went into his sales spiel, showing us various perfumery concoctions. He then demonstrated it was genuine perfume oil by putting a few drops into a glass of water and seeing the droplets float to the top. I bought some lotus oil because if it was good enough for Cleopatra, it was good enough for Brenda. The price was about twenty percent. of the prices charged in Paris, he told me, so what a bargain I had. It was a lovely perfume and lasted Brenda a few years because she only used it on special occasions.

Eventually the taxi driver had run out of relatives but must have made enough commission to be a good day for him and we arrived back at the hotel. In the early hours of the morning, my stomach started hurting and got worse as the night wore on. Then, what the local ex-pats called 'Rameses Revenge' hit me. I had been careful not to eat any salad that may have been washed in the local water, which you just do not drink, but my stomach was really gurgling. It then dawned on me what probably caused the problem was drinking from the freshly washed glasses we had our beer in at the Perfumery Shop. I had to starve myself to get rid of it.

During the design side there were several variations to the

contract the client had requested, and I was negotiating with the director to pay for seven changes, amounting to just over four hundred thousand pounds. There were a couple of changes we thought would be difficult to get approved, so were prepared to lose them. Eventually, after some discussion we agreed the sum of two hundred and eighty thousand pounds for five variation orders to the contract. I prepared them and presented them for formal signing by the director. He said to me, 'John, I will pay you. I do not need to sign these. Don't you trust me?' It was a dilemma for me and instead of saying 'Of course I trust you, but company policy states a signature is necessary', I shook hands with him, looked into his eyes and said 'Okay, I trust you'. It was a huge lesson for me because he never did pay the money. Giving him the benefit of doubt, I believe it was a cultural issue rather than blatant dishonesty. In future years, whenever I was giving a lecture on project change control, I always quoted what happened and the mistake I had made so it would not be repeated by those listening.

The meetings, because of the cost issues, were not successful and on the last day, a Friday, we were just going through the motions. I did a presentation and finished around three p.m. and there was a flight to catch at nine p.m.. Others were wrapping up, so I bid them farewell and left with a colleague a little early and we went straight to the Egyptian Museum in Cairo, which was close by. We got there at three-thirty p.m. and it closed at five p.m. The taxi drivers said locals can visit for free, but tourists pay, which is fair enough. He said he had never been there, which can be typical if it's on your doorstep.

The museum has one hundred and twenty thousand items

there and we had an hour and a half so we each went our own way and agreed to meet when it closed, by the front doors. I looked at as much as possible at the time, but what amazed me was not just the excellent workmanship of the jewellery, but the intricacies of the chairs, particularly Tutankhamun's furniture. To think they made this around 1,300 B.C. underlines to me how underrated we think our ancestor's skills were. It was a whirlwind visit but worthwhile and so we made our way to the airport.

We arrived at the airport, and everything was again very lax there. We passed through check-in quickly and joined the short queue for going through security and into the main seating area. We were just about to be security checked when the call to prayer happened. Everything stopped, the three guards left and joined about two hundred people kneeling, saying their prayers. We could not believe it. It took about twenty minutes before they returned and just carried on as normal. Another culture shock!

We arrived back at Heathrow and because of my own pride, I would not ask for assistance from the plane to the luggage carousel so walked with my colleagues. For me, it's a long walk and the repercussions by way of cuts to my scar line and the following days of associated pain were difficult, but it was my decision.

It was lovely to get back home, to see the children and, of course, Brenda. It was always easy buying for Brenda because she had hardly any jewellery, so I could not go wrong with the gold ring and earrings. In her past relationships, she had never been spoilt, had hardly any jewellery and she rarely had a birthday or Christmas card from them. When she saw what I had bought her she was excited and particularly liked the lotus oil perfume. She was, after all, my Cleopatra.

It was strange, in many ways, having someone else so special in my life again and I had to deal with the guilty feelings of being with someone else because I was no longer a married man, I was a widower. The adjustment took quite a while, but it was so nice to be happy again after such a bleak period in our lives.

Chapter 27:
A New Century

As we approached the year 2000, life felt good again. I had a grandson, Luke, Donna was happy with Andy, Darren was at Portsmouth University and had also met Anita. Jamie had decided he did not want to work in an office, preferring the outdoor life and, having tried numerous jobs, decided on fitting double glazing. Then, of course, there was Brenda, who had lifted me so much from the gloom of bereavement and brought a lot of fun into my life. Her two boys were doing well at their education and Lewis was doing a foundation course at Portsmouth University, before going on to do a degree in Communication Design.

My work had entailed periods where I was away from home and the coming year was no exception. I had been asked to go for an interview with a GlaxoSmithKline project director to work in their offices, near Heathrow Airport, on a major project they were undertaking. I arrived and the project was explained to me as being part of the one point two billion dollar Strategic Master Plan whereby fifty-four global sites around the world were being core and business rationalised. It stemmed from the merger of Glaxo Wellcome with SmithKline Beecham and they initially wanted me on their team as the analyst manager. The interview went well as I had quite a bit of pharma experience and I was offered the role on secondment from my parent company, who received a daily rate for my services plus all expenses paid.

I had to start the following week and stayed in a hotel about a mile and a half away from their offices. I left early on a Monday to be in the office by seven-fifteen a.m., which was a way of missing the congestion on the M25 and likewise I left around quarter to four on a Friday to beat the traffic yet always hit traffic jams on the M25 around Heathrow and the M4 interconnection. It was a close-knit team, filled with a lot of experience and I shared an office with Steve, the project controls manager on the project who was an American seconded over.

It was a great project to work on and I learned a lot about the business and working on this type of project. Max, the project director was good at his job, and we got along well. I remember every time he had a high-powered meeting, he would always eat a banana half an hour before, as he said it helped him to concentrate. There was even a sweepstake when the first email would appear once his boss's plane had landed from any destination, any time of the day. It was always around twenty-five minutes; such was this high-powered environment.

The project was going quite well and some of us in the management team had to give presentations to the board in the Research Triangle Park offices in North Virginia. We flew out business class and the hotel we had was lovely with huge rooms. One lasting memory of this visit was going through the front door of this impressive building into a lift. What caught my eye was the huge array of different veneer wood on the four walls of the lift. I asked the lift attendant about this, and he said quite matter of factly, the wood came from all parts of the world and was specially commissioned. Arriving on the top floor, we walked along the corridor to the board room and the whole corridor was covered in oil paintings of past chairmen and CEO's. It was luxurious.

The meeting went well, and we came back, but the difference in working for a contracting company like I did, compared to a blue-chip company such as GlaxoSmithKline was quite stark. The other point was many people had worked for this company all their lives and had no idea how fortunate they were and their tremendous working conditions many took for granted.

After a few more months it became apparent why I had been brought in because I was called into the director's office one morning. He said that Steve, the incumbent project control manager, wanted to return to America and asked if I would take over his role. I agreed without hesitation. Steve left six weeks later, after doing a particularly good job and I was trying to follow in his footsteps.

Every few months I had my line manager, Adrian, visit me to make sure everything was going well. Perhaps I should not have enthused over the role so much because the feedback I had was the company thought I was going to leave them and join GlaxoSmithKline. I had been with the company well over twenty years by this time, but there was a great disparity between both companies such that I could have been tempted, in hindsight. I never really had the time to contemplate because I had a call from my home office saying I needed to return there to work on an important project. They also said I had been promoted to general manager of project controls.

In many ways it was disappointing not to see the project completed, but it was a good career stepping-stone and the company's way of not losing me. It was good to be home again for a little while before the next assignment, to be close to the family, and of course Brenda.

I took mine and Brenda's children, apart from Donna, on holiday to Turkey for two weeks. We went with her friend Lyn and their family too, so there were ten of us all together. We had a great a time there, the weather was over one hundred degrees Fahrenheit and all I can say is thank goodness we went all inclusive. It seemed as if the youngsters had just discovered alcohol, judging by the glasses outside their room. We went on a few excursions but there was one trip with Captain Jack, which springs to mind as memorable for several reasons, one of which was me surviving!

This trip was on an old galleon styled boat, which sailed from the harbour, where we were, to a small inlet along the coast. Here in the lagoon, you could dive and swim from the boat, before having lunch and free drinks on board. We all arrived at the harbour by coach, having been picked up at the hotel on quite a sunny, warm but windy day. We saw this nice galleon at the end of the pier and were told to go there for boarding. When we got there, looking out to see it was quite choppy and the gangplank from the pier to the galleon was moving up and down about four or five feet. This meant one of the crew walking with you, very quickly, across the gangplank, timed to avoid this rising several feet. I thought, with my leg this is going to be challenging because I cannot suddenly walk very quickly, like the forty-odd people who were now boarding. My time came to board and the crew member looked at the next rolling wave and timed the move for me by holding my waist and virtually frog marching me onto the boat. My group, who were all on board by this time gave me a big cheer. I was not looking forward to the return walk, but that was to be later.

Everyone went swimming except me, but I enjoyed watching everyone have fun. By the end of the day, the chairs were getting uncomfortable for me, so I was glad to up anchor and head back to the pier. It had been a bit choppy travelling there, but when we entered the lagoon it was quite still, and the return trip seemed even rougher. It was a nice trip back on a beautiful sunny day, even if the wind had risen with the sea spray cooling us down a little. It only took about ninety minutes to get back and we could see the pier in the distance. As we neared the pier, there seemed to be a lot of discussion by the captain and crew. We then dropped anchor about fifty yards from the end of the pier. The captain had made the decision it was too rough to use a gangplank and we would all be transferred by a small boat to the end of the pier. I am not of a nervous disposition, but the thought of getting into the boat from the galleon and then the boat to the pier did fill me with trepidation.

The waves were now rising about six or seven feet, and everyone was slowly taking turns in boarding the small fifteen-foot boat and being taken to the pier. Our party got on the boat and the crew, because of my disability, decided I would be last to leave so they could help me. Everyone was off and our group were all waving and laughing on the pier, although Bren looked nervous. I was being loaded on the leeward side, so the waves weren't so big. With the rise and fall of the boat, and assistance from the crew, I got into the boat. The first part was done but worse was to come.

The small boat was moving about quite a bit and as we approached the pier, there were a lot of people watching as conditions seemed to have worsened. Lots of smiles and remarks like 'nice knowing you' and 'I will start the collection' were heard coming from them. I even remember Darren with a big smile on his face, with my video camera recording, I assume for posterity, my final moments.

We got to the side of the pier and the rise and fall was significant. I would estimate the boat was rising close to eight feet then dropping down, so when the boat was at its highest you had to grab hold of this metal ladder attached to the side of the pier and climb up. I thought 'What am I doing here?' but could see the funny side and all those smiling faces on the safety of the pier. I just thought if I did fall in the water, my leg would act like an anchor, as it weighed nearly a stone and I would soon be down visiting Davy Jones's locker. Oh well, with cameras rolling, the crew ready to push me toward the ladder, I waited for the next wave swell which soon came. It was almost like a fairground ride and with my heart in my mouth at the peak of the wave I grabbed for the ladder and hung on as the boat dropped away. It is a good job my upper body strength was good, so I quickly ascended the stairs, two at a time, to a big cheer from everyone and a big hug from Brenda. It was quite an experience, perhaps not to be repeated.

One day on the holiday I was sat on the deserted beach with Brenda, who, by this time, I had known for around eighteen months. It was a perfect blue sky, lovely and warm and it felt so right being with her that I said, 'I would like to marry you.' She was absolutely stunned and did not quite know what to say. All she said was 'Well yes, sometime in the future.' I did not actually mean there and then because I thought it was too soon for us and the two families, but I just wanted her to know how much she meant to me. I think she was in a state of shock.

As usual when I returned from the holiday, I needed some repairs to my leg. It was about this time it was suggested to me that getting rid of the two leather straps and buckles around my waist would be a good thing to do. The socket I sit in has a belt around four inches wide around the left side of my waist and these straps and buckles enable me to pull the socket tight into my body. Changing from buckles to Velcro strips is changing something that is almost an integral part of you and somehow seemed quite daunting to me. I did think it would weigh slightly less and look flatter on my stomach, so with a leap of faith I said to go ahead. It is an amazing invention that stemmed back to the 1940s, based on cockleburs which attach themselves to you and especially dogs. It took a while for this hook and loop invention to be used but NASA did in the 1960s. It worked well for me and is tremendously strong and more durable than leather straps and buckles.

There have been times when I have been far away from home, just walking and suddenly one of the leather straps have broken. It means you do not have the support you expected and the additional stress on the remaining strap could cause that to fail too. I have had to use all sorts of temporary arrangements, when this happened, just to be able to get back home or to the car. There have been so many incidents where things have broken, or weird noises have emanated from the leg. You do wonder sometimes if you have exhausted everything that could possibly happen, but I dare not test fate.

I did find falling over a problem at times, as you must fall in the direction the leg twists you because it is around your waist and there is no compromise. This usually happens two or three times a year on average. You try to avoid banging your head, but sometimes it cannot be helped and of course you try to get up quickly because of the embarrassment from people watching at the time. The worst for me is falling backwards, which has happened a couple of times getting across the threshold of the back door from the garden. If you look at a double-glazed door, the threshold is not level but made up of ridges, and although I constantly look out for the day-to-day hazards, if you get complacent or just slip a little, then away you go. When I fall backwards, I invariably bang my head and all you hope is, it is not too hard.

When I first met Brenda, she was often going to bed late and getting up early, not just for work but to take Russell to his swimming lessons. Russ was a particularly good swimmer and was in training at a local pool where they already had an Olympic swimmer there. It was very intense, and he was a tall lad built for swimming. There were competitions which he performed well in, and he did this for nearly three years, but one day he decided he just did not want to do it anymore. All that time and training, but if he were not enjoying it anymore then there is no point continuing, but you can't help but wonder how far he would have gone if he had continued.

Darren enjoyed being back at home and he had a great holiday with his niece, Kerry, when they went over to Ireland for a week. He did not complete the degree at Portsmouth University, he left and worked for a travel agent in Chichester for three months. I managed to get him a job in the Estimating Department where I worked, as I knew Kevin who managed it. Darren was like me, quite numeric and after a year at Kvaerner was interviewed and offered a role as an accountant at IBM in Portsmouth. I was pleased for him because it was a good company, and they would support him to become a

Chartered Accountant.

Jamie had found his niche installing double-glazing and despite leaving home at eighteen to live with a girlfriend, had since returned home for a while when the relationship broke down. Once you start having independence it can be difficult to comply with somebody else's rules. I think my rules were somewhat at odds with his, so it was not too long before he moved out again.

As we approached the new millennium, Donna told me she and Andy were expecting again, so my second grandchild was on its way, and I was pleased for them both. Donna was moving to another house but did manage to get a council flat, which certainly helped them as Andy was working in a butchery factory and the money was not great. I think all my children were still struggling coming to terms with losing their mum, but we were all trying to cope in our own different ways and Donna's way was to start her own family.

One day I will never forget, was the welcoming of the new millennium. Brenda and I were invited to her friend, Lyn's, New Year's Eve party. It was a good night as many were there drinking and dancing as the clock slowly moved toward twelve a.m. with the dawn of a new century. Brenda and I went outside to see the firework display and welcome the New Year in. We were so lucky that Portsmouth had put on three sites for spectacular firework displays, with one just a short distance away from where we were partying. It was marvellous to see and as I held Bren close with the firework display above our heads, I proposed to her with an engagement ring. It was magical.

We had been away for a few days to Jersey, about four months prior to the party, and had been looking in a large jeweller's shop at rings. Brenda had pointed out one particular ring she liked with an unusual, coloured stone, and then we moved along looking at many other things. I said it was time to go but then she needed to go to the restroom in the shop. I thought, 'Now is my chance,' and I had about two or three minutes to do the deal. I quickly went to the counter where the ring was, which Bren liked so much. I said to the manager there, I wanted this ring, but I would make him just one offer, which he could either accept or reject, as I only had a small window of opportunity to buy. He hesitated, but fortunately agreed to my offer and I quickly paid for the ring. He understood what I was doing and gave me the ring in a bag, and separately another bag with a pair of earrings in. Brenda came towards us and knew I had bought something because she had a wry smile as we headed out to the carpark and into the car. Once inside, I said I had a surprise for her, and she was quite excited as I passed her the bag with the earrings in. As she opened it, I was really laughing inside because she thought it was the ring, but she still had to keep up the pretence of being happy, with a sickly smile as she saw the earrings.

When I gave Brenda the ring on New Year's Eve she was over the moon, especially knowing it was the one from Jersey. We went back inside to the party, and she was showing the ring to everyone there with lots of back-slapping, handshakes, hugs and kisses. It was such a happy, memorable moment in time, never to be forgotten.

Being home, I decided it would be nice to do something positive to help others, so I contacted the Samaritan's who were on a recruitment drive. I went along for an initial interview, and we discussed why I wanted to join and what it would entail. They said it involved a commitment on my side of doing a ten-week course of three hours, one evening a week, managing suicidal conversations, talking with vulnerable people and sometimes in difficult situations. I enjoyed the course and of course the scenarios of a trainer on a phone call and how you talk to them. What I really enjoyed most was being with like-minded people who cared about others.

The course soon finished and most, but not everyone, were accepted, with two or three not lasting the course. The commitment I made was for four hours every week, in my case from seven p.m. to eleven p.m. at night, once a week and an overnight stay once a month. If the phone rang, we took it in turns to answer or we were both on the phone. It was always different and interesting, with no two conversations the same, and I found it both humbling and rewarding in so many ways. The support within the centre I went to was good, as it can be emotionally draining on you too.

The biggest problem for me was the one night a month sleep over. There were a couple of beds to sleep in, but the phone could and did ring at any time during the night. At night I need to take my artificial leg off to rest my body but there was no way I could do this in any privacy, so I just kept my leg on and dozed on the bed. It was not ideal at all for me and caused me problems with pain the next day. I only lasted nine months as my job was moving me on to another site in Ireland, but I like to think I did help some people whilst there. I always hoped to go back to the Samaritan's at a later date, but constantly working away from home was just not conducive to being a member of the team. I do, however, cherish the memories of the wonderful people I met there and admire their commitment and care for their fellow human beings, as there are some very troubled people out there.

I was now working in our home offices in Port Solent near the marina, which is to the north of Portsmouth, so commuting was once again easy. The project I had been brought back to work on had been going for around six months and was a pharmaceutical plant being designed and built in Cruiserath, Dublin for a company called Bristol-Myers Squibb. I was helping to collate the estimate, which was several hundred million pounds, before going over to Southern Ireland for the construction phase. It was interesting work and there were some great people on the project whom I knew and had worked with before.

Before long, I was put on assignment in Ireland and flew over from Southampton to Dublin every Monday morning, on the 'red eye shuttle' as they called it, before returning late Friday evening, every week for well over a year. I was fortunate to have a company car over there so getting around was not a problem. I had found lodgings in Skerries, which was about a thirty minute drive to the north of Dublin. The place I stayed at was quite nice with a fantastic restaurant. Apparently, it was owned by a TV celebrity chef over there and even Bertie Ahern, the Irish Prime Minister at the time, had eaten there. The breakfasts were superb too and it's one of the things, when you are away from home, you look forward to a nice evening meal at the end of a long working day.

When you spend time away from home, you form good friendships as did I with David, the project manager. We both worked hard on what was becoming a difficult project and two occasions spring to mind. It was a February day, in fact, to be precise, it was the fourteenth, Valentine's Day. We decided to go for some Chinese food at the local Skerries restaurant, which was a small, terraced house converted to a restaurant.

As you walked in, there was a hatchway for getting your takeaway and through a side door into another room there were about six tables. Not the best restaurant I had been to, but we sat down and ordered. There were a few couples in there, looking into each other's eyes, and then there was David and me. We were missing our wives, but David then asked me to be his Valentine that night, so we had a good laugh about it and to this day he still refers to me as his Valentine!

Another time we had worked nearly twelve hours without a break and David said in the evening 'We need a break from all this, how would you fancy going to Cruiserath and watching a film?' So off we went and into a multiplex, bought an ice cream each and sat in the back row of a cinema watching a Harry Potter movie. It was surreal and a complete change from what we had been doing, but great fun.

During my time in Ireland, I remember the dreadful news of 9/11. It was frightening as events unfolded and planes were crashing into buildings and many lives were lost. We had no idea where it would end, and when you get moments like that, all you want to do is be close to your family to help and protect them. Being far away just heightens your concern for everyone.

When I worked in London for a year, I managed to collect points at the Best Western hotel I stayed at, and these points can later be exchanged for free nights at any hotel in their chain. I said to Brenda, 'We should make the most of this', and arranged a tour of Southern Ireland for a week in late summer. I was also able to use the company car for this, which was a bonus. It is a beautiful place and outside of the larger cities, it is in a time warp going back sixty or seventy years. It is called the Emerald Isles because of its rolling hills, vales of green and lush landscapes, but in places it is absolutely stunning and none more so than the Beara Peninsula. I have seen many places around the world, but this is one of the best. The day we arrived it was raining on and off and a bit blowy, but the magnificence of the large Atlantic rollers crashing into the cliff sides, the different hues of the countryside peppered with sheep plus beautiful rainbows, is something you just cannot forget.

The first night we arrived at one of the hotels we found it was full, which was surprising as there seemed to be a lot of young people around. We were quite tired so ate in the noisy restaurant and headed back to our room via the lift. Just as the doors were closing a young girl in her late teens, full of tattoos and earrings, jumped into the lift with us. I asked if she was with the large group of people there and she said, 'Yes, they are a great bunch of people, and we meet up every year because we are the Drug and Alcohol Rehab Group.' Bren and I just smiled and then we looked at each other. Enough said!

One day after visiting Waterford we were travelling through the scenic beauty, about two hundred feet above sea level overlooking a bay and thought it would be nice to stop for a coffee. I saw a small sign which said 'Tea, Coffee and Snacks Here'. There was no shop, just a bungalow up several flights of steps, so we parked up alongside this dilapidated building. There are many such buildings in Ireland, which date back to the mid-1800s when the potato crop failed, and between emigration and death from starvation, the population was reduced by some twenty-five per cent. We tentatively knocked on the door and as the door opened you could smell the peat fire. This lovely smiling face greeted us, with her beautiful lilt and invited us in. The lady had a white pinafore on that had seen better days and her hands were very black as she had been cleaning the fire. We asked for a coffee and tea and declined the offer of her homemade cakes after seeing her hands. Just then an old chap, who was around eighty years old popped into the room and sat down. He was smiling and chatting to us, reminding me of a leprechaun. He was such a character, again with that lovely smooth Irish lilt you get in the south, and he spoke in limericks; it was really entertaining. Brenda asked to use the toilet and he looked out of the window and said to her, 'Do you see that bush over there?' to which she said, 'Yes', he replied, 'Then just go behind there.' She looked at him, then me, and just was not sure until he burst out laughing and said, 'It's just through that door over there', winking at me.

We stayed, being entertained for nearly an hour, and during the conversation Bren asked if the dilapidated barn we parked alongside was theirs. The old chap said, with a glint in his eyes, 'It was, but because of the high tides they needed to move higher up the hill to this bungalow.' Brenda said, 'Really!' and I just burst out laughing and then she realised we were over two hundred feet above sea level. We all laughed; he was such a character, but it did help to make for a memorable holiday.

I was part of a team that had to fly out to China to give a presentation to a client for a project worth several hundred million pounds. There was quite a bit of walking for me, so it was daunting, but I had never been to China. We flew firstly to Schiphol and then, flying with KLM, onto Beijing with another connecting flight to Shanghai. From there, we travelled for another hour and a half by car to the large town where the presentation was held. It was an exhausting journey and amazing to see the different culture. In both major cities there was so much air pollution it was a constant smog, just seeing the sun slightly through a haze. What was noticeable to me was how yellow the grass was because the light from the sun could not feed the chlorophyll for photosynthesis.

All the team were tired, but the hotel was a bonus as it was five stars but in the middle of nowhere. It was odd because the staff all wore pristine uniforms, but if you looked at their shoes, they obviously had to provide these themselves and it showed. We had a nice meal with our interpreter and then wearily headed back to our room. I really needed to get my artificial leg off as I was cut and bleeding because of the excessive walking for me. I had a nice shower and laid on the bed when the phone rang. I picked it up and someone was talking to me in Chinese and the only thing I heard was her name, Mi Ling. I said for her to phone reception as she must have the wrong room number. Five minutes later, the phone rang again, and it was the same woman speaking a little bit of English this time and saying what I thought was her name again, Mi Ling. I repeated for her to phone reception and put the phone down. Another five minutes and yet again the phone rang and this time her English was understandable, and she clearly said to me, 'May I come in!' So, my interpretation of Mi Ling was explained but I did say, 'No, thank you." About twenty minutes later there were several knocks on the door, so she was certainly persistent. I looked through the keyhole and there was a young, attractive woman in her mid-twenties waiting for me to answer. It had been a long day and I did not answer.

The next morning at breakfast I mentioned the persistent call I had and each one had the same experience, even the female translator. During the few days we were there, the translator confirmed it was a poor area and the hotel was mostly for business people and occasional tourists. She said in winter it was very cold and the main food supplement during these times was dog soup. I am glad it was a fleeting visit.

The first day went well and we outlined our proposals to the client before we started presentations. During this meeting we all had a cup of tea and as soon as you took a sip, there appeared someone alongside you holding a large kettle full of tea to re-fill your cup. You really had to pace your tea intake at these meetings!

We decided to go out and eat where the locals eat and found quite a large eating establishment to dine in. It turned out you had a choice of 'a la carte' or a buffet option. We went to have a look at the buffet but, unlike in England, most of the buffet was still alive. There was a large room you went into, about twenty yards square, filled three aquariums high with a staggering assortment of seafood and other animals. You chose, they then killed and cooked it. I really felt like becoming a vegetarian but did notice three largish soup urns in the foreground so asked the translator what was in each one. She said the first was chicken and lettuce soup, the second was just many vegetables thrown in to form a soup of sorts and the third she declined to tell me. I pressed her for the third, but she steadfastly refused. The business manager, Andrew, heard the conversation and said she had to tell us and taking a deep breath she said it was 'bull's penis and turtle soup'. Everyone declined it, but we did smirk as we got back to the table and ordered a boring steak.

My presentation was on day three and this was important for me to finish then because the following day, after I arrived back in England, I was flying again the next day to go on holiday to the Canary Islands. The client wanted a much-shortened programme than we were offering, to make product earlier but I knew we could not because we had to spend several months developing the Front-End Design. I said we could not improve on this, and they then went into a huddle and said if they gave us one of our competitors' Front-End Design could we then improve? It was so blatant, and any contractual terms of copyright protection held no sway there. It was an eye opener how nonplussed they were in making the offer.

After my presentation, I left on my own in a taxi travelling to Shanghai Airport. Arriving there I was stared at quite a bit because there were hardly any non-Chinese people around and I was at least six to nine inches taller than most. I looked around to find the check-in desk and noticed many large barrel shaped containers around the airport. I did not have to wait too long before I understood their use! The Chinese have a habit of clearing their nose, throat and chest with a large snort bringing up from the depths whatever lies there and spitting it into these barrels. A different culture, which is entirely accepted by the masses it seemed. I just thought about the poor cleaners there.

I checked in on the flight and went through the security check. A young security guard looked me up and down, then at my passport and proceeded to pat me down. I tried to explain about my leg, but he had no idea of my language, just as I did not of his. He felt around my waist and suspicions were immediately raised. I could see the alarm in his face as he made me raise my shirt for him to see this contraption around my waist. He shouted something and I was suddenly surrounded by six of his colleagues, whereupon he insisted on showing them my leg strapped around my waist. Not only this, but every Chinese person around me decided I was an interesting specimen to look at because I wasn't Chinese either. It was rather embarrassing, with what seemed like hundreds looking at me and these security people prodding and poking my artificial leg. Eventually, the penny dropped, and they let me through, but it was one of the worst experiences of airport travel I ever had.

I finally boarded the plane to Beijing and caught a connecting flight the next day to Schiphol. As we took off from Beijing, it was astounding to see the Great Wall of China, which is huge, but we made our way further north over Siberia and I could no longer see it. What I saw for the next two thousand miles was just snow and ice with the occasional fir tree poking through. I have never seen anything so vast, so clean, so unspoilt and almost uninhabitable.

The connecting plane to Heathrow was running late and after landing I eventually got a taxi home. I got indoors, exhausted, around eight p.m. and it was lovely to see Brenda again, but I was tired knowing a taxi was arriving at three-thirty a.m. to take us to Gatwick and on holiday to Tenerife in The Canaries. It was a hectic time, my leg was cut and really hurting, but I thought a relaxing holiday would be just the job. We went away on holiday regularly with my mum, dad, Arthur, Lyn, Margaret and Jeff. We had arranged the early morning minivan to take all eight of us to Gatwick, and Brenda, unbeknown to me, had sneaked the wheelchair on too. I really did not like the wheelchair but by using it I was able to be with Brenda and the family in exploring parts of the island I would otherwise never see. We caught the plane to Tenerife and got the coach to take us to the hotel.

Arriving at the hotel and walking through the reception area my artificial leg had metal fatigue across the knee joint and sheered. I could not walk on it as it was a catastrophic failure and I needed the wheelchair, which I did not want to bring, to take me to the room. It was a disaster, but I was able to buy a pair of crutches that can break down and be carried in your suitcase, so for the whole week I was wheelchair-bound, using the crutches in the room. I needed them to get onto the coach and move about in the plane, so they were a necessity. I have always tried to be pragmatic about situations I've faced and realised how much worse it could have been if it had happened a few days before when I was completely on my own in Shanghai Airport. With that thought, I had a week of not wearing my leg and enabling my damaged skin to heal, which was a real bonus.

As I had no choice in the matter, I used the wheelchair all the time there. I also used a spare pair of Arthur's swimming trunks and Brenda sewed the right leg up so I could swim every day in the pool. One day, my mum and dad were also in the pool with us and all of us were taking turns in supporting them. Mum had some floats so was quite mobile, but dad wanted to swim. Dad was eighty-six years old and had never been a strong swimmer, but he was up for it. Arthur and I were supporting him, and he was trying to do the breaststroke. We asked if he wanted us to let him swim on his own and he agreed so we eased away. He stood up and then off he went swimming the breaststroke, only instead of moving forward as he moved his arms, he just sank down, still moving his arms but getting nowhere. We rescued him and were all laughing so much, but poor dad did smile after the initial panic he had and realised his arm strength had gone: his swimming days were over.

When we returned to the UK, I immediately went to the Disablement Centre to get my leg repaired and get back to work. They had never seen a break like it and said it underlined the immense stresses and strain the leg is under when I use it. They fortunately had a spare knee joint to replace my broken one and I was soon mobile again, remembering yet another episode in the trials and tribulations of my life using an artificial leg.

Chapter 28: Time For Change

With the start of the new century, we were looking forward to planning for our future lives together. Brenda, Lewis and Russell had already moved in with us about a year or so before, so we told them of our engagement and all our family the next day. Everyone was happy for us, but it is never easy merging two families together. Brenda has always said she could never replace my children's mum and would never try to, but just be there for them if they needed her. She has always been supportive to them, and I felt the same way toward Lewis and Russell. With any couple getting together with their own children, you cannot just embrace the one person, it must be the whole family.

It was initially extremely busy for Brenda at home with five grown men to feed. I remember her using two loaves of bread every day for making sandwiches in the morning. The amount of food young lads eat is amazing as they grow. Before you know it, the family have reached adulthood, which you hope you have prepared them for with the same values you share. Bren was putting her own style of décor into the house and making it a lovely place to live in. My idea of cleanliness was not always aligned to hers and my explanation was it's a 'man thing' but she did keep the home really clean and tidy for all of us.

The family were making their own way in the world, with Darren becoming engaged and then marrying Anita in 2000. It was a lovely wedding and they had bought their first house in Portsmouth, which Anita's father, Des, being a builder, had spent a lot of time working on, to modernize it. Jamie was learning his trade in double glazing and seemed more settled doing this. Donna was pregnant again as she always said she wanted a large family. Russell was now embarking on his A Levels at a Portsmouth College just a mile away from where we lived, and Lewis was doing really well on his degree course.

I did need to think about the future though, which I wanted to spend with Brenda. She helped me through those early days, and we were planning all sorts of things ahead, instead of looking back. Ann had died at the house we lived in, and it held some lovely memories of our past lives with her, not just for me but the children too. On the other side of the coin, those last few months were the most difficult in my life, containing some painful memories and likewise for the children. With this in mind, we thought it might be time to move to a new house and have one on neutral territory, where Brenda and I could make our own history together.

The children were slowly going their own way in life. Donna had left a few years before and had fallen pregnant again, but there were problems with the pregnancy, and it aborted at twenty-four weeks. It was a baby girl they wanted to call Joanne. They were both upset and wanted to have a cremation for the baby. Arrangements were made for the cremation and service at Portchester Crematorium, where Ann's service took place five years earlier. It was a very private service and on the day of the service Donna and Andy were too upset to attend, so I was the only one in attendance at the small North Chapel. It was quite upsetting being the only one there representing this small soul's family as they brought the miniature casket in. I do struggle with my emotions at the best of times but being so close to where Ann's service took place brought a lot of painful memories back too, but it was the right thing to do in difficult circumstances.

Donna quickly fell pregnant again not long after and again there were complications. At twenty-two weeks the foetus had not developed properly, and the brain had not formed so the pregnancy was aborted. They were going to call the baby Michelle, but under the circumstances, there was no funeral service this time. Perhaps they should have listened more to mother nature, who knows when things are not right.

It was around this time I learnt from reading Donna's notes that she had a mild form of Klippel-Fiel syndrome. I was absolutely astounded by this revelation as Ann and I had seen so many consultants throughout Donna's childhood and no one had ever mentioned this. To this day, I do not understand why it was never discussed or even mentioned in passing, but it did explain so much about Donna and some of the health and learning difficulties she has.

The timing was right to move so we put our house on the market. We had three valuations and naturally tried for the highest price. Meanwhile, we found a nice new-build four bedroom detached house about three hundred meters from where we lived. It was part of the new estate being built by Bryant Homes on the grounds of the local hospital where I used to exercise my dogs twenty years before. There were four others ahead of me who had shown an interest in this house, but I was the first to put a deposit down. For a house in the city, it was a reasonably large plot with a long drive up the side to a double garage. Anyone who lives in Portsmouth knows the difficulty you have in parking your car, but I could get seven cars on the driveway, so it was ideal. It was the most expensive style of house on the estate, but it was what we wanted; we did, however, need to sell the house we lived in too.

There was some interest over the first few weeks, but no firm offer on our house, so I reduced the price, but now I was under pressure from the sales team of the new house to close the deal. They kept it open as long as they could but eventually, one Friday, they returned my deposit, much to our disappointment. On the next day, we had a viewing by a lovely couple who were cash buyers, and they made an offer on our house, which we accepted. Now was the race to the sales office to see if anyone else had bought the house we wanted. Fortunately, no one else had, so we reinstated our deposit and eventually the transaction went through allowing us to move into our new house.

I am not sure I would ever move into a new house again as ours was beset with problems from the very start. The handover was poor, and we noticed so many defects, some significant, like an attic hatch which you could not get into as it was placed over the stairs. There were numerous leaks, some behind walls, nails sticking through the ceiling and brickwork not cemented in; the list seemed endless. We had a lot of dialogue with the site agent who kept sending so-called tradesmen around to correct things, but a lot of it was down to shoddy workmanship. One of the worst parts was after having had new carpets laid down, the ceilings needed to be filled in places where nails showed through and these were rubbed down before being repainted. There was dust everywhere and it was a nightmare we were living through. We had several months of this and in the end, I contacted the area director with a ten-page list of faults, and he arranged to meet me. It was a friendly meeting with no bad feelings, just acceptance, on his part, of the problems we had. He agreed to rectify everything to our satisfaction and as compensation agreed to build a fifty-foot, six feet high wall at the side of our garden for free.

It has taken many years to resolve the problems in the house as some do not come to light immediately. One happened ten years after we moved in, with what we thought was rising damp behind a radiator but turned out to be where some plastic pipework had not been pushed together properly. With the continuous expansion and contraction occurring daily, it finally resulted in enough escape of water to be noticeable. The only way to get to it was to make a big hole in the wall, and this was just one of many examples.

The new house was quite detached, so on the side where the lounge was, we decided to have a conservatory built with a door leading into it. Conservatories look very nice when first built, are light, providing a lovely place to sit and enjoy the garden, but there are downsides to them. The downsides are you can only use them for about six months of the year because they are either too hot or too cold. If you open doors and windows there is an ingress of flies, bees and wasps that do not seem to know how to escape through the way they came in. Then the major problem for Brenda was the lurking spiders, which seem to love conservatories and find all sorts of places to hide, but like a lot of people we tried to make the most of our conservatory.

Brenda and I were happy and enjoying being together. We

had known each other for nearly five years by now, we were engaged, and the children were gradually leaving to make their own adventures in life. We decided it was time to get married and started planning the event. I never realised what an industry it is, there are so many aspects to it and the devil is in the detail. Brenda is very logical and would have made a good planning engineer because she thinks every step through, this, coupled with my work background, meant we spent a long time preparing it. The date was set for June 2003 and we had about fifteen months to plan it.

Our immediate family was growing again as Donna and Andy had their second child, Matthew, a good-looking boy, so they decided to move again. When you have five children between you, then my parents and associated family, we were finding time difficult to manage, especially with me being away with my work quite often.

As usual, time flew by, and I was still having to get my artificial leg repaired on a regular basis of every two to three months. In the waiting room I was able to take work in with me or read reports there, so not all the time was wasted, but you do get some characters there, some of whom just want to talk. I always try to give words of encouragement to those who have recently had an amputation, especially the older people where it must be quite daunting to learn to walk again. When I am not wearing my leg, I can be quite agile in hopping around and I remember Darren saying he was always amazed how quickly I could chase him up the stairs without my leg on.

There are patients attending who have learning difficulties, which can be challenging to a prosthetist in understanding how comfortable a new leg is, or whether there is some resulting pain from the fitting of the leg. Sometimes you just know individuals will never walk with their legs because you do need to have the right attitude and endurance to manage your expectations and pain control.

One day, I was sitting in the waiting room when a soldier walked in, a commando in full marine uniform. He walked very well so I knew he must have had his leg amputated below his knee. We got talking and it turned out he lost his leg in the Falklands War and he was there to get a special titanium leg made because the conventional legs just kept breaking due to the rigours, he kept putting them under. If you are in the Forces, you are not under the same financial strictures the NHS impose and new innovative designs for legs can be more easily obtained. This was the case for this marine sergeant and eventually the prosthetist arrived with his new titanium reinforced leg. It was his second fitting, and he was really pleased with it. We talked a bit, and he was a strapping guy, quite muscular and said he really wanted this leg because tomorrow he was going on a twenty-mile yomp. I thought, 'Good for you' and only wished I could walk just part of that distance, but his conquering spirit was not letting his disability halt him in any way, which reflected the ethos of a marine.

When Bren and I could snatch a free Sunday, we would go and visit her sister, Mary, and her mum, who lived together in Stroud. 'Mum', as I called her from our first meeting, was quite a character and had been a hard-working woman, bringing up seven children. Her early years were hard, and she would regale us with tales from her early childhood. I could see so much of Brenda when I looked into her mother's face, and the strength of character she had inherited from her. One story she told us was as a young child she would wait with her brother for her father to walk home from the pub along the railway lines. He was the worse for wear from his visit there and they would purposely trip him up to try and get a few coins from his pockets to bring back to her mother to help feed the family. She would also pick-up coal along the railway lines, which had fallen off the freight trains carrying it, to bring home for their fire. They were hard days indeed, but it gave her the strength to raise a large family and work hard for most of her life.

The latter years were difficult for her with arthritis, and she really struggled to walk. We did take her out for Sunday lunch a few times when we visited them, and I remember she liked nothing better than playing on the one-armed bandits. Gradually, the combination of things caught up with her and her toe was looking gangrenous, but she was trying to clean it regularly. She was in a lot of pain and an ambulance was called, so we immediately drove up to Stroud Hospital to visit her. We walked into the room she was in, and we were greeted with such a lovely radiant smile. Most of her children were visiting and she was there holding court and laughing and smiling at us. The time came for us to go and her parting words, with a smile, were 'Goodbye, see you in the morning'. Mum passed away a few hours after we all left, but what a lovely way to say goodbye to her children.

We learnt later that she had been suffering with breast cancer for many years, but never wanted to make a fuss. She missed her husband, Ernest, who died aged sixty-seven, very much and just wanted to be with him again, as she said in her own words. Bren's mum, like my mum, was the matriarch of the family and it leaves such a big hole in your life when it's their time to leave. We miss her a lot.

On the home front in 2002, Donna and Andy were over

the moon because their third child was a girl, whom they named Joanne. We were both pleased for them and the number of grandchildren we had was certainly growing. Russell seemed to have settled in Bath and had a girlfriend, Natalie. He was in shared digs, working as a barista and happy with life, even though Brenda worried about him.

The bond I have with Keith will always be special, not because of the early days we spent together or how much he loved his sister, but because of those last difficult few weeks of Ann's life. It was during that time when Keith insisted in being there with us, where we shared the raw emotion of losing someone so special to us. The closeness, the sense of grief we both shared is something that lasts a lifetime and beyond.

It was good Keith had found someone after Lorraine, who was by now married to Steve and starting a family. Joy was a lovely, bubbly person who worked for the same company as Keith and they were happy together. Joy was very keen on skiing, although Keith did not share the same passion, so she went abroad with her friends. Unfortunately, Joy had an accident on the ski slopes and damaged her cruciate ligaments and this was at the beginning of the holiday. She then had to endure everyone having a great time, with her leg in a brace and it must have been so frustrating.

Keith and Joy were getting married in May, which was only a few months after the skiing accident. I know there was some concern about walking down the aisle, but she did manage it, holding unto her dad's arm and looked as radiant as any bride would be. It was a lovely wedding and good to see Keith settling down to married life and buying a house in Taunton, Somerset. Living so far away, we do not see Keith as often as we would like, but we always know when we meet up

there is a warm welcome and always lots to talk about.
Our wedding was fast approaching, and as you start organising things you realise what an industry it is. We had been to wedding fayres where everything imaginable was on display and we had a huge amount of literature. Firstly, we booked John Pounds Church to get married in and the twenty-eighth June 2003 was the date set. From this you can then start booking other things, with the next most important thing being the venue. We had gone through the guest list and had around ninety people for the sit-down meal and double that for the evening. Brenda had been heavily involved in Morris Dancing in her earlier years and thought it would be a good idea to have a ceilidh. I had previous ideas about Morris Dancing but having been to many dances with Brenda I understood the fun, history and good old English heritage of it, which dates to the fifteenth Century.

The search was on to find a place to seat the number of guests we had coming and have a square dance floor for the evening's festivities. We felt, at our age, a disco was less appropriate and by having a ceilidh more people would join in, especially after a few drinks. We looked at many places until we found the Royal Beach Hotel in Portsmouth, which was in a great location, opposite South Parade Pier and was the ideal place.

We then started booking many other things, like a vintage car to take the bride and groom to the church and onward to the Garrison Church in Old Portsmouth for the photos. It was a super place for photos because most of the church roof had been bombed in World War Two, so the natural light and bright stonework was an excellent backdrop for photos. We booked the photographers, someone to video the whole day, a harpist to play during the sit-down meal and so on. It was like shucking peas as you keep paying out for everything, but it was a special occasion. The best investment, however, was to employ a Master of Ceremony. He said, 'You won't see ninety percent. of what I do, but I will make everything run smoothly' and he really did. Of course, he knew the protocol and announced each guest as they entered the hotel room as we met them and then supervised the speeches and so on; he was excellent.

I had known Kim for many years as her boys had been in the same football team as Jamie and Darren. She is an excellent cake maker and we asked her to make us a three-tiered wedding cake. Kim never disappointed us and made a beautiful cake, so expertly decorated. She is incredibly talented.

One of the most important things for any bride is the wedding dress and Brenda was no exception. Every bride wants to be radiant and naturally look beautiful on their special day. We managed to find a dress designer who was first class and after several fittings Brenda was so pleased with the dress, but of course like any groom I had to wait until the wedding day to see the fruits of all their labour. We decided for myself, my best man, Arthur, and the four boys it would be nice to have matching black morning suit tailcoats with a gold waistcoat and cravat. It was a good choice and following the fitting everyone looked very smart.

The next big outlay was choosing where we would honeymoon. We wanted somewhere exotic and decided after much deliberation on a beautiful hotel in Bali with seven koi ponds and six restaurants. Neither of us had been that far east so it was an exciting venue to visit.

With Arthur as my best man, between us we arranged for a stag night with quite a few friends. I did not want to go from one pub to another because of the walking involved, so we started off at a nightclub called Jonglers, which was a comedy cabaret down in Gunwharf Quays in Old Portsmouth. We stayed there for a few hours and it was a great show, especially as the drinks flowed. It turned out the more we drank the funnier the acts were and eventually it came to an end, so we then got taxis to go to a Gentlemen's Club with some exotic dancing. It was a unique experience and best left there, but all that drinking left us hungry. It was now the early hours of the morning and with numbers dwindling to about eight, we went to a local curry restaurant, which to me was a great way of finishing a memorable night.

The wedding day finally arrived. I had stayed the night at Arthur and Lyn's house so Brenda, with her bridesmaid, could get ready by themselves and of course, as tradition has in, I would not see the bride until she walked up the aisle. I would not say I was nervous, more excited by the whole day, followed by a honeymoon abroad. We were blessed with a beautiful summer's day with clear blue skies as we made our way to the church. Our friend, Barry, had offered to drive me to the church in my Jaguar car, so Arthur and I arrived in style.

Before the ceremony in the grounds of the church, it was so lovely to see friends and relatives who you care for enjoying the special day, especially as they knew the difficult times, we had both had previously. We made our way into the church as time was marching on, saying hello to the many guests, then after a short wait the wedding march sounded, and Brenda came in. She looked spectacular to me, not that I was biased, in such a beautiful dress, followed by her bridesmaid who also looked stunning. The bridesmaid, Bryony, had travelled over from Spain where they lived with her mum, Ellen, who was Bren's niece. Many others had travelled far and wide to celebrate with us.

As we went through the order of service, I remember thinking how special the day was, not just because we were getting married but to see all our friends and relatives happy, smiling away and enjoying the time together. With the ceremony over and having signed the marriage certificate, we made our way up the aisle to the front of the church and awaiting transport, a vintage 1930s car, for the photographs. We had a few photos taken outside the church, having been showered with petals and rice as is the tradition, then off for more photographs.

We soon arrived at the Garrisons Church for the photographs. It was originally built in 1212 by the Bishop of Winchester as part of a hospital and hostel for pilgrims. It has quite a history and was even used as an ammunition store after the Reformation in the mid-seventeenth Century before it became part of the Governor of Portsmouth's house during Elizabeth I's reign. It was restored in the nineteenth Century and in 1933 the church came into the care of the Office of Works, but a firebomb raid in 1941 destroyed the nave. Nowadays, the nave ruins stand divided from the intact chancel by a modern screen wall. With no roof over most of the church, the light is brilliant for photoshoots and so ours started.

The photographers and videographer were busy getting the right light, the right positioning and of course the right people together. It was quite a warm day and we did not realise we would be there for nearly two and a half hours, otherwise we would have arranged refreshments. I do believe the public house opposite the church did rather well with our guests that day. With the photographs taken, we got into the vintage car to take us to the Royal Beach Hotel for our reception. There was a lovely surprise waiting in the car for us, as the chauffeur produced two champagne fluted glasses and popped the cork on an ice cool bottle of champagne. It was well received and so enjoyable after all those photographs in the heat of the day, and so we toasted the very beginning of our marriage.

By the time we got to the hotel all the guests were there, mostly in and around the bar. We went to the large function room where all the tables were laid out and positioned at the door as guests were introduced to us as they entered the room by the Master of Ceremony. We duly, shook hands, kissed or hugged everyone as they made their way to the allotted tables; it was such a lovely occasion. I did think about all our children and how they felt about having a stepfather or a stepmother, hoping they would all be happy for us because they could see how happy we were together. I also half expected my dad to give me a few pearls of wisdom because I remembered when I was first getting married to Ann, he said to me, 'Son, always remember in your marriage, if you do something well, you will do it for the rest of your life.' True words I often remembered as I washed up plates and cutlery many times over the years, wishing I had rued his words! I think he must have thought I did not need any advice this time.

We then had to walk together from the door, through the tables to the long, head table where the speeches were about to begin. Everyone clapped us as we walked until we sat down. This was one moment I did not like, to be honest, because of my own innermost feelings in showing my disability as I walked in, even though I had known many of the guests for years and years. Once sat down, I relaxed and looked around at the smiling faces, acknowledging as many as I could before we tucked into several courses of delicious food. The speeches started with Arthur, and everyone listened as I occasionally cringed at the tales, but all in good humour. I then gave my speech and presented presents to various friends and relatives for their help, before we all moved into the bar next door so the tables could be cleared ready for the evening ceilidh.

The ceilidh was the right decision as many joined in. It was light-hearted, and part of the fun and enjoyment is in making mistakes and just laughing at yourself. The evening went well and before long it was ending. All the detailed planning had paid off to make it a memorable time for everyone. We seemed to spend ages saying goodbye to the many guests and those invited for the evening celebrations, but it was in the early hours of the morning we decided to head for the Honeymoon Suite.

The Honeymoon Suite is on the fifth floor, so we made our way over to the lift and to my dismay found the lift had broken. We had to go up five flights of stairs with me going up two at a time. I was exhausted after the day and those steps nearly finished me off, but a man has to do what a man has to do. We entered a huge room overlooking the sea, gave each other a lovely kiss, threw back the bedclothes only to find we had been sabotaged by friends and family with petals all in the bed. We just could not stop laughing. It was the end of one of the most memorable days of my life.

We only had a few days before we were on the plane to Tobago. I had previously planned a trip to Bali but eight months before our wedding there had been a terrorist attack.

Brenda and I were having a long weekend away in France and Bren was in the shower when a newsflash said two hundred and two people had been killed in a bomb explosion. We could not risk going there so I changed the destination. We wanted somewhere safe but exotic to remember. We were mindful of the approaching summer hurricane season, so in the end we chose Tobago, a small, almost unspoilt island almost one hundred miles from the coast of Venezuela and away from the hurricanes.

We flew Virgin Atlantic, which was a nine-hour flight direct to Tobago. The hotel we chose was right on the shoreline and from our room the patio doors could be opened onto the beach with the water only about seventy-five yards away. It was a paradise island and virtually unspoilt, unlike Trinidad with its industries and associated pollution. The food was quite good too and I remember us eating breakfast, watching hummingbirds feeding off the flower nectar no more than six feet away.

I had put some elbow crutches I had previously bought in Tenerife into my suitcase and packed my bathing shorts in case I went swimming. The first time I used the crutches from the patio doors in our room to the beach I found the sand extremely hot so I hopped on them as quickly as I could using the crutches to get to the sea. It was lovely to swim in the sea but the tide and drag of the surf was difficult on one leg let alone two. The first day Brenda walked into the sea she got bowled over and rolled about four times in the surf. I thought she was playing around but then realised she was struggling. With the little help I could give her, she got out of the water and later found sand in every part of her bikini. We made our way back to the room and the sun had got up even more. I found the sand was burning the sole of my foot in just the short distance to the room, and when you only have one, it is most painful.

We paid a local guy, with his well-groomed dreadlocks, to take us on a tour of the island. He had an old Ford Escort car sprayed mauve, which he thought was the bee's knees and so we went visiting the island. Most memorably was the visit to the Main Ridge Forest Reserve, which was legally established in 1776 and is one of the oldest protected areas in the world. The English did a lot of bad things in the colonization around the world, but establishing this forest was an incredibly good thing to do. Bren walked into the forest with our guide for about an hour and a half whilst I just stayed on the edge of it looking, listening and admiring the wonders of Mother Nature there. When they returned, we got back into the car and travelled around the whole island, but what was quite noticeable to me were the names of the towns. Many had English-sounding names with the capital called Scarborough, but the poverty was there for everyone to see. I only counted four shops in the capital with many lean-to sheds selling their produce. With a population of only sixty thousand, tourism is a major factor in their economy.

When we were travelling around the island, I thought it would be a good idea to get a cheap pair of sandals to get from our room to the sea, avoiding the extremely hot sand and third degree burns to my foot. I did not need the right shoe, so I put it in the waste bin and off we went for a swim and sunbathing. It was magical lying down watching the frigate birds flying around five hundred feet up and looking almost prehistoric. We met a couple of locals there on the beach, one, a man who made sandals for you right there, and the other was a lady who did hair, nails and gave massages. There were the usual hawkers on the beach trying to sell everything from drinks to jewellery, but we mostly avoided them. We did both have a massage on the beach and Brenda had three pairs of sandals made for her, which were about a third of the UK made-to-measure price. The sandal maker asked where I came from and I said Portsmouth, Hampshire in England. From that day on we were called Mr. and Mrs. Hampshire. They were lovely, friendly people but so poor. The sandal maker used to go over to nearby Trinidad to buy his leather and dyes, so Brenda asked them for their address and promised to send them some things. When she returned home, she made up and sent a parcel of massage cream, makeup, dyes and a few other things to help them earn their living.

A strange thing happened every day when we returned to the room after a swim because the right sandal, that I had placed in the waste basket, was duly put by my other shoes. The maid was very reluctant to throw it away. This happened for four consecutive days until the fifth day when she finally took it away. I suppose not many throw away a brand new right footed sandal every day!

Besides a lovely lobster meal at a treehouse restaurant, one memorable occasion was booking a trip to Nylon Pool. It is a natural metre deep, crystal clear swimming pool with a sandy bottom in the middle of the sea created by an offshore sandbar and a still lagoon. We booked a glass bottomed boat and they travel along dropping anchor at a place called No Man's Land. I specifically asked the question about getting on the boat following my Turkey fiasco and was assured there was no problem. They said to get to this location by ten-thirty a.m. where someone would meet us and take us to the boat. In Tobago, like many Caribbean Islands they are very laid back and ten-thirty a.m. could be an hour later. The Bob Marley saying of 'don't worry, be happy' was a way of life there!

We looked around and could not see a pier to get on the boat. By eleven-fifteen a.m. we thought we had been seen off, but then we saw what can only be described as a native sumo wrestler with dreadlocks walking towards us. He asked our name, shook hands and said the boat was about seventy-five yards away where the water was a little deeper and we could just wade out to it. I looked at Brenda and said there was no way I could walk in the sea out there and explained to him I had an artificial leg, even though I had said this when booking. He just smiled at us and said, 'no worries, man', walked towards me and picked me up throwing me over his shoulders. Bren just took her shoes off, almost laughing hysterically and followed us. I would add this guy only had black shorts on, so I was over his shoulder staring straight down his back. Not being one to complain, I did notice that his shorts were torn at the crease of his backside. This was hard to avoid as I was only about twelve inches away from it. I cannot say I enjoyed the scenic beauty as we walked through the sea to the boat, but Brenda was highly amused, especially at my expression looking into this huge guy's torn shorts covering his backside.

I have been in some embarrassing situations, but it is one I will never forget because as we approached the boat there were about twenty people watching what was going on and cheering me into the boat. I thanked him for the lift (literally), looked around the boat and saw the glass bottom so you could clearly see the fish and seabed. We upped anchor, travelling about a mile and a half offshore and amazingly it was only about four feet deep that far out. The colours of the fish were amazing, and every passenger went in the water except me, but

I just enjoyed the views above and below. The seawater feels very silky there because of the minute amount of coral floating in it, the whole place was enchanting. As I sat there the slow realisation dawned on me that I had a return journey to make once the boat returned and dropped anchor. My sumo friend, with his torn shorts and my view into oblivion, would carry me once more to the shore. I just gulped and thought ‘don’t worry, be happy’.

Chapter 29:
Career Crossroads

As usual, I was busy at work and was asked to be the coordinator for a new Global Risk Dashboard, which had been developed in the company's headquarters in Oslo, Norway. This was a group-wide approach across all units around the globe, coordinating the training and problem-solving around risk management of projects. It enabled the CEO of the company to look on a risk dashboard in real-time, see all the projects we were working on and those which were high risk, showing their exposure. It was a good system and worked well, but like any system, if you put rubbish in, you get rubbish out, so training and an overview of this were imperative.

I had some training from a couple of the Risk Development Team in our local offices and could see the benefits it had to offer, which is important when you are basically selling a new system, as most people are reluctant to change. The way we made it happen was to get the CEO to issue a memo to all the group vice presidents around the world telling them they had to use this system, they then escalated this downward to oppose any opposition to it.

The senior vice president I now reported to was not a lot of help and wasn't well respected by the team who reported to him. He spent less than forty-five minutes giving me an overview of the system and his expectations, with absolutely no detail. I just had to manage it; in other words, sink or swim! I worked closely with the guys from Oslo and prepared the PowerPoint presentation material with appropriate screenshots. It was agreed I would give the presentation to the management teams at the various locations with one of the software developers giving detailed technical training on the computers set up in the same room. I planned firstly for the European countries and visited quite a few. The Scandinavian countries were interesting to visit as I had only been to Holland before.

One visit to Finland I remember well and flew from Heathrow to Helsinki. There was a lot of walking and I had to pace myself to avoid too many cuts and bruising. I remember seeing in the airport shops lots of reindeer skins with their thick fur for sale as I sought the next connecting flight to take me to the offices in Tampere. It was cold there and once I found the connecting flight it was only thirty-five minutes in the air. It was a small airport, but I got a taxi to the hotel and got ready for the next day's presentation. The offices were only about three hundred yards away and this was my dilemma. It was a long way for me to walk with my artificial leg, bearing in mind how far I had walked at the various airports, but too short for a taxi drive so I decided to walk it. The effort of walking for me is quite considerable and I have never felt the cold because of the exertion. I had my suit on and was carrying my briefcase and started walking. I thought, 'Thank goodness there's no snow or ice about or I'll be in trouble.' I thought I would not feel the cold but at -16C, I can assure anyone you do feel the cold. I made it quickly to the offices and thawed out and the presentation went well, with the bonus of the return journey being given a lift back to the hotel by one of the participants.

I remember getting a taxi back to the airport and passing the Nokia headquarters and looking at all the signage, which I just could not understand at all. I think being next door to Russia, the language is quite different to English and quite unlike some of the Latin-based European languages. I did not realise their headquarters was there in Espoo, so you can learn something with every trip you make. It was a successful trip, and the feedback was very positive.

My next trip was to Oslo, and we were in an office on the ninth floor, overlooking a scenic fjord. It was stunningly beautiful, and the ferries were periodically travelling in and out of the fjord. It was at this point, looking down into the water, I saw about fifty huge jellyfish about twenty feet down in the depths of the fjord. They are called helmet jellyfish and can be almost twelve inches in diameter. We started the presentation and eventually stopped for lunch, and I peered down to the water again only this time the jellyfish were now close to the surface. I guess the rise in temperature had lured them to the surface. It was a fascinating sight and most unusual but one to remember.

Norway is expensive, and I remember walking to a small restaurant alongside the harbour where the tourist boats were and having a simple meal of steak and chips with a beer. It was a good job I was on paid expenses, because the bill was over fifty pounds at that time, which, to put it in perspective to UK prices, was nearly three times more expensive.

The rollout of the new risk management system was going well and my colleague and I were asked to go to our company's main office in Texas, U.S.A., to present and implement the system there. It was a big building with over five thousand employees and it was hot. Like most things in America, the training room was large, and we presented to over fifty people, including their financial director. He was a charming and hospitable host, like most of the Americans I have met, and he invited us out for a meal to his Gentlemen's Club for an evening meal. In this part of the world, they eat early evening and go to bed quite early. They therefore rise early in the morning, mainly because of the outside temperature.

We were picked up from our hotel and driven some way to the club, where there were a lot of oil men and ranchers in their Stetsons, but not a woman to be seen. It was explained to us it was quite a select place and a lot of business was done over a meal. The menu was amazing with the usual steaks you would expect in Texas, but also some more exotic food like ostrich and crocodile. I decided to stick to a steak, but for starters I thought I would go native and have some Texan gumbo soup, mainly because I remember The Carpenters singing a song about crawfish pie and fillet gumbo. Gumbo originates from an African word meaning okra and is basically a soup thickened with okra pods and contains meat, seafood and vegetables. As I previously said, everything in America is large, but when my plate of soup arrived it was huge. It was so huge in fact, even one of the Americans said he thought he could do the backstroke in it. The steak was probably about thirty ounces and absolutely succulent, but I was pretty full after eating my gumbo soup so never did it justice, but it was a meal to remember.

Again, the feedback was positive and all the units we visited were inputting into the system, so the executives were happy. My boss at the time was getting all the accolades for a job well done, when in fact he had done virtually nothing. He was a poor man manager and was not well-liked. An example of this was four of his direct reports, including me, were asked to go over to Holland to work over the weekend. We left early Friday and returned Sunday afternoon. He invited all the wives over too, which was a nice gesture and he paid for a nice evening meal for all of us, in the Amsterdam hotel we stayed in. The memorable part being the chef preparing a lobster bisque for me, which wasn't on the menu, but was, to this day, the best I have had.

We went the next day into some offices and started working the whole day, whilst the wives, including his wife, went on a barge around Amsterdam sightseeing and doing a lot of shopping, as wives do. We came back to the hotel expecting to meet up in the evening for a meal, but he said, 'Let's do our own thing.' My colleagues and our wives all ate together, but he went somewhere else with his wife. We worked all Sunday morning and flew back in the afternoon. We all put our individual expenses in for approval, but for every one of us, he refused to pay for our wives' food on the Saturday evening. It was such a petty act that completely alienated him from myself and the rest of the team, destroying any goodwill he could expect from any of us. It was such a bad man management move and really the writing was on the wall as to where my future lay.

The good news at this time was Darren and Anita had their second child, a lovely boy they called Kyle. Both were over the moon because it was a boy, and I was too, not just because they had a healthy boy, but because Kyle also kept the family name going. We were so pleased for them and with the addition to their family they had decided to move to a larger house out of the city. They were happy and Darren was halfway through his exams to be a Chartered Accountant, enjoying his new job at IBM.

For the first time in twenty-seven years, working for the same company, I was unhappy. I realised from my experience of working for GlaxoSmithKline I knew more than I realised about project control. This, coupled with the poor line manager I was reporting to and having to endure, put me in a bad place until out of the blue I received a phone call from an old colleague called Steve. I had previously worked with Steve in helping to set up the Pharma Business Unit and got on well with him. He had recently left Aker Kvaerner, the company I worked for and was now the project director for a nine hundred million pound London Railway upgrade project of Main Line and Sub-Surface Line contracts, working for Westinghouse in Chippenham. He asked me if I would consider joining him to help with the control on the project. I said it was always good to talk about opportunities and arranged to meet him with his boss for an interview.

Westinghouse was, at the time, a large employer around the Chippenham area and on the day of the interview I was surprised to find buildings linked together which looked like factories, rather than offices. I went through a door from the car park and there were two flights of stairs and no lifts. The stairs were twice as many as you normally get between landings, but up I went, two steps at a time. There was a maze of offices and doors, but eventually I found my way to a reception area of sorts. There, I was directed to an interview room and eventually Steve and his boss arrived, and the questions started. I enjoyed interviews because I was normally the interviewer, not the interviewee, and I knew my subject matter so felt confident. The interview, I thought, went well and Steve's boss shook hands with me and left after half an hour. I then continued with Steve and agreed a daily rate as I would be a freelance. We shook hands and I set off on the eighty mile drive home.

Driving home, my mind was racing as I was thinking through the process of handing my notice in, the ramifications of that and the risks involved, especially if I were ill because I would receive no sick pay. I was travelling along the M4 motorway, lost in my thoughts, when I was suddenly brought immediately back to earth with a strange noise from the car, which needed me to pull over on the hard shoulder straight away. It was a nearside, rear flat tyre. It was an X-type Jaguar and I tried to undo the wheel nuts, but I just could not move them. I phoned for some break-down help and decided to wait outside of the car to be safe. Unfortunately, all I had on was a suit and no coat. It was freezing and it took nearly an hour before help arrived. It turned out the wheel nuts on that model almost fuse on and are extremely difficult to get off, but he had all the right tools plus a large hammer, so the spare wheel was soon put on.

With modern cars they supplied an emergency thin tyre, and you can do no more than fifty m.p.h. in them for safety reasons. It was a frustrating drive home because I was constantly being overtaken by large trucks and lorries, but at the time I did have a lot on my mind. I told Brenda when I arrived home and we talked about the work scenario for quite a while, but as usual she was always supportive of me, whatever choice I made. That evening, I wrote out my resignation from a company I thought I would never leave, and it was sad but exciting in many ways. It was a new chapter in my life, and after all, life is about change, so you need to embrace it.

I went to work and saw my line manager, Adrian, who was shocked at receiving my letter of resignation. Like me, he could understand the issues because he, at one stage, reported to the same senior vice president I did for the Global Risk System. He later moved his role, so he did not have to report to him. I had been at the company for such a long period of time, so I was on six months' notice. I was not particularly busy and requested to leave in two weeks, and Adrian said he would pass it on and upward. His line manager, who I did not like after the Amsterdam fiasco, came and saw me and typically said I would have to work my six months' notice, to which I said, 'Watch this space.' In many ways, I reluctantly left two weeks later, leaving behind many friends made over the years but I knew it was an exciting time of my career too. I was up for the challenge. The only daunting issues to me were my artificial leg with the associated problems of breakage and repairs which I constantly had, plus keeping good health. Since losing my leg at sixteen, I have been blessed with good health, so I took the plunge.

It was daunting, but I was confident I could do the work and so I became self-employed forming my own company. My first task, upon arriving at Westinghouse, was to do an audit and prepare a report with recommendations. In the project control team, there were some suspicions about my motives, but all I wanted to do was to improve the efficiency and accuracy of the work they were doing.

One of the first things I found was a ten-year project programme of thirty-six thousand activities. There was detail for every year, which was unnecessary because I knew it would change as the project progressed. I recommended a detailed programme for two years only, with reduced activities, then a summary only for the following eight years. There was also an element of research and development in the programme and that was not ring-fenced, so movement and slippage was happening all the time. I prepared the report on what I had looked at and gave ten recommendations for improvement. I firstly showed Jo the report as she had been running the team and was extremely knowledgeable. I needed to work with her, not alienate her, and she appreciated it. It was the start of a good working relationship with her and the team.

I presented the report to Steve, and we discussed each recommendation in detail, how they would be implemented and their impact. I was set the task of leading the team and implementing the changes. It was strange working in the rail industry environment when I had been used to an Oil and Gas industry, which had much more rigour and awareness of contractual implications. It did seem to me there was easier acceptance of slippage and a mindset of 'it will cost what it costs' especially as the technology was changing on the lengthy programme.

I also managed the project control team on a day-to-day basis introducing new, improved ways of working, particularly in Earned Value and Key Metrics reporting. I had found lodgings in Lacock, a beautiful small medieval village about four miles from where I worked. It had a self-contained ground floor flat, which was ideal for me with a lounge, bedroom and bathroom. I remember one evening going to bed and hearing the sound of little feet running above the ceiling. I told the people in the main house about it and they said they would sort it. All they did was buy three mousetraps and put them in the roof void. I remember in the early hours of the morning hearing the noise of the trap going off. The noises above me soon stopped but about two or three weeks later I arrived back one evening and went into the lounge to be greeted by a huge swarm of large flies and an awful smell. The owners had apparently just left the mice caught in the traps and flies had laid their eggs in the decomposing body, hence the awful smell. The fly maggots had eventually turned into flies when they hatched. It was quite gross.

The only downside for me working at Westinghouse was the stairs from the car park to the place where I worked. It was the equivalent of going up four flights of steps for me and it took its toll on my knee. I remember one day, leaving about six p.m. and going down the steps, which was a lot harder for me than going up, and stopping three steps from the bottom with the pain. It was an agonizing pain, and I was frozen on the spot hoping no-one would be coming down the steps and see me. I literally waited for about seven or eight minutes for the pain to ease and attempt the next three steps. It hurt but I made it down, then the thoughts about being self-employed and not being able to work came flooding back to me.

The next day I spoke with the company's personnel department, and they suggested using a goods lift from the car park. They said it needed to be used by someone who would be with me who had been trained to use it. This training entailed opening and closing the metal door and pressing a button because they considered this to be a safety issue. When I wanted to use it, I could never find anyone there, so I gave up on that task, but the stairs were continuing to cause me daily problems.

Brenda originally had her own hairdressing business but was forced to sell it around the time of the breakup of her marriage. She had continued as a mobile hairdresser, but I said she could stop doing it if she wanted. Like most hairdressers they form a bond with their long-term customers, which she did not want to stop, so she did continue. Gradually over the years it has decreased to a few long-term friends and some family members.

My mum took great pride in her hair, and she always looked lovely, ageing very well. Brenda and mum got on very well and every Saturday, Brenda would go to mum and dad's house to cut, blow-dry or perm her hair and cut dad's hair when needed it. Brenda's father had been a good piano player and even worked as the floor manager for Bentley's Piano's in Stroud. He could just listen to a tune and then play it by ear, something I have never been able to do. Brenda asked mum if she would teach her how to play and she was delighted to help. So, for a few years it was hair then piano lessons and during the football season mum always cooked a lovely roast dinner for us before dad and I went off to the Pompey match. Mum always made us a flask of milky coffee to take to the match. I know how lucky I was to have my parents for so many years, enjoying each other's company. Mum was the matriarch of the family and Saturdays were the hub of meeting up with them along with Arthur, Lyn, Margaret and Jeff calling in too. I miss those times a lot.

Chapter 30: The Years Roll By

The saying 'time waits for no man' is so true and before you know it life is speeding up the older you get. I have always used two words to remind me to enjoy my time on this planet, and those are 'if only'. I had an old aunt who lived opposite our family home, and she was always going to go to Scotland but never did and then she would say 'if only I had gone when I had my health'. It must have resonated with me at an early age because those two words are indelibly stained on my decision-making process through life's journey. In particular, the decision to go freelance was a major one for me, a crossroad in my life and what I did not want to do was to look back ten years later and think 'if only' I had.

Out of the blue, I had a call from Alan, a senior manager who I had worked with at John Brown Engineers. They say, 'what goes around, comes around'. He said he always remembered the help I gave him, and time spent explaining project controls to him when he first joined the company. Alan was now the operations director for a company called British Energy who had seven nuclear sites around the UK. After exchanging the usual pleasantries, he asked me if I would be interested in working for him to sort out the project controls across the sites in the UK. Although I had no nuclear experience, the fundamental principles of project control traverse across all industries, and I felt it was a challenge worth taking.

Again, it was one of those decision points where I could have stayed in the Railway Industry or tried something new. I went along for the interview and liked what I saw of the company, which was based at Cheltenham. I liked Alan, he had his hands full doing the job and the project control did need more structure and analysis to it. There were two people interviewing me with rapid fire questions, but interviews are not one-way but two-way processes and I have found it is important to ask searching questions of the company, their work and ethical approach, as well as the top issues they wanted improving, which I would be part of. At the end of the interview process they asked what my rate expectation would be, so I added fifty per cent. onto my current rate as a good place to start negotiating, but they just said 'Okay, when can you start?'

It was not a big decision to make because Steve had just left Westinghouse for new horizons, and I decided I wanted a different challenge. The downside was Cheltenham is not a commutable distance from Portsmouth, being one hundred and fifteen miles away, so I was away from Brenda and the family all week, yet again. I found some lodgings close by, which were self-contained, and they cooked a nice breakfast too.

One of the big advantages to me was to not face those stairs again, which were taking their toll on my one and only knee. At British Energy, I was on the top floor but there were lifts, which I used almost all the time. I met all the home office staff and, after a couple of months, got to grips with the issues and personnel. I was asked to project manage the corporate implementation of P3E, a planning software tool across British

Energy producing a Strategy Paper for its implementation. I also represented British Energy, project controls in the engagement and mobilisation of the selected prime contractors, Jacobs and AMEC. It was interesting work, which involved initially setting up and developing the projects control department, including managing a team of seventy personnel. I then assisted and mentored the British Energy programme and project controls manager in improving and developing the programme and project controls function by merging two divisions, which involved planning (P3E), cost control, estimating, progress measurement and risk.

I needed to meet the various teams that they had at the seven sites around the UK and ended up doing a tour enabling me to meet, greet and present to them. Having never worked on any nuclear establishment before, I had little knowledge of the industry only the haunting memories of what had happened at Chernobyl. What struck me first at each site was the high level of security required to even enter the establishment but most of all was the daily call down centred in Cheltenham.

Alan had asked me to attend, on his behalf, the daily call down, where about twenty or more key senior personnel were in attendance. Each of the seven sites were called and all safety, security or production issues were discussed. It was a meeting of minds, so the whole business could focus on helping or suggesting resolution of any issues raised. Sites would state the problem, the cause and effect, with the action being taken. Often this was fine, but sometimes suggestions or even moving key personnel for a short period of time to help would be actioned. Being an outsider, I was impressed with this and deep down pleased with the responsible approach being taken in the industry.

It was interesting being part of the approach being taken in the UK, but there was also the wider aspect of worldwide safety with well over four hundred reactors around the globe. It was explained to me there is a brotherhood of help for all sites because if one suffers a major catastrophe then there is a worldwide domino effect of confidence, so it really paid to help each other.

One morning as I got up to take a shower in my accommodation, I somehow slipped as I hopped in and fell onto the shower base edge. I did not know how it happened, but I did lay there for a couple of minutes trying to assess the damage. Sometimes when I fall, it is just a case of a few bruises or just being winded and you can get up quickly, especially if you are in an open public space, but this time as I moved just a little, it really hurt me. I found I was almost hyperventilating due to the pain as I moved, but eventually I did manage to slowly get up. I showered with great difficulty and towel dried myself. I tried to hop a few steps but that too hurt, and I realised I had done some damage to my ribcage. I then tried to put my leg on and as I pulled the straps in tightly to myself, I took a sharp intake of breath as the pain shot through me. I realised then, that I had cracked a few ribs and the healing time for this is around six weeks. I could barely walk with the leg strapped around me and it must have compromised the healing process somewhat because the top of the socket I sat in rested just underneath my ribcage.

If I had been staff, I would probably have taken time off sick, but apart from the time around Ann's death, when I took a total of six weeks off, I had not taken any sick leave for over twenty-odd years. It was a new era for me, and quite an in-joke amongst contractors, who rarely take time off sick, otherwise they lose money. If they do take time off sick, then they are invariably quite sick or going for an interview. Somehow, for the next few weeks, I just about managed to get to work. From where I parked, to where I sat was probably about one hundred and fifty yards, which, to begin with, was so, so painful and took me a while, slowly walking the short distance. Gradually, it improved until after eight weeks it was virtually gone, but I am always careful showering since then as I need to use a chair to sit down on to slide my leg over the threshold of the shower base to get in and out. At home, it is easy with a drop-down chair connected to the back of the shower wall, but most places never had that facility.

I needed to get more cost control experience into the team. It is a common misconception that accountants can do this function, but good cost control is about analysis and good forecasting. I phoned a colleague I had known for many years at John Brown called Courtenay. After getting his mechanical engineering degree he had started at John Brown in Paddington, London as an estimating engineer before converting about fourteen years later to cost control. He had a good pedigree of experience and although not the quickest, was very thorough, worked diligently and would never let you down. I interviewed him, offered him a job and he joined the team. He was a good addition, and he had a friendly disposition and immediately fitted into the team.

When you work away from home, the highlight of the day is often having a nice evening meal. On Mondays, having got up early to travel to work, then working the whole day, I was invariably quite tired so just a snack picked up from the local supermarket would suffice. Courtenay also lived in Portsmouth, so having known and worked with him for many years, we went out every week for a meal, normally on a Tuesday. I really enjoy Indian food having sampled chicken dhansak all over the UK and sometimes abroad, so my benchmark is high. I always tried to find a good local Indian restaurant to sample the culinary delights and Courtney would normally join me. We would just relax over a drink and the food, just chilling out, which was a routine we both enjoyed.

It was not the best way of starting married life by working away from home, but this is inevitably the life of a contractor. I had lost all the benefits of being staff from sick pay, paid holidays, free health care, company car and so on but I was earning three times more than my staff position, so it certainly softened the blow. In the back of my mind, however, was the thought of having an illness and being unable to work as I had not taken out any insurance for this, which I felt was a gamble worth taking.

It was difficult seeing everyone at weekends, so Brenda thought it would be good for the family to meet up at the end of every month at our house for a family meal. It worked well for a while, but as additions to the family arrived, it soon became impracticable for everyone to be there. It was a bit like Christmas time when we had the family over to us, but as they grew each year it was more and more a juggling game. We got to thirty-three in total, having two trestle tables in the lounge and a third going into the conservatory, but dishing up a hot Christmas dinner was quite difficult.

Lewis had met Victoria, or Vicky as I call her, and they were happy together. Vicky was doing her degree at Imperial College in London and Lewis was finishing his in Portsmouth and they both understood the importance of getting their qualifications. Eventually, they both got good degree passes and got engaged.

The family unit was certainly growing, and Jamie had met Carla and they too were besotted with each other, as young love flourishes. Darren was working hard to complete his numerous Chartered Accountancy modules and Russell had met Natalie in Bath. I thought Donna would not have any more family additions because she had two boys and a girl and suffered the loss of two baby girls, one of which had not gone full term. It was not the case, though, as she announced she was pregnant again. The pregnancy was not without its problems, and toward the end, she was told the baby had some brain damage, which was devastating news for all of us. It was further complicated when Donna was giving birth to Callum, with the umbilical cord becoming compressed against itself causing reduced oxygenated blood to the brain, resulting in further brain damage. It was such a sad time to see this poor baby entering the world, beset with so many problems. They did not think he would survive for long, but he was a fighter.

Both Donna and Andy were very pragmatic about the damage to their baby and took it in their stride, as parents, to care for Callum, no matter what problems he had. Andy had a disabled brother he was brought up with, so to some extent he was somewhat prepared for what lay ahead, in a lifetime of care required for Callum. Callum proved to be a sickly child who constantly had chest infections. I remember one year, he seemed to have an infection every month for a year and was constantly on antibiotics. He never developed any of the skills a baby does because of the brain damage and had impairment to both eyesight and hearing. Callum had cerebral palsy and suffered from epilepsy, so ambulances were frequently called and short stays in hospital were often required. He was fed through a gastrostomy tube directly into his stomach, so it was twenty-four / seven 24/7 care required for him. Callum is in his own little world and oblivious to those around him, although he seems to recognize the touch of all his closest family. I do admire their steadfastness, dedication and love in looking after Callum over the years, it is a credit to them both. Even watching Luke, Matt or Jo playing on the floor with him is lovely to see and they, too, love their little brother.

Brenda and I visited her sister, Mary, every few months and we always took her out for Sunday lunch. She really enjoyed her food, even though she was small in stature. It is such beautiful countryside around there and you know when you are getting close to your destination as the stonework on the houses gradually changes to a sandy white colour amongst some of the best English green and pleasant land. We had noticed Mary not remembering much for a while. She would write post-it notes to herself and was a creature of habit in many things. She would always catch the bus to the newsagent, buy two papers every morning, and every Saturday had a trip to the town centre to get her hair done.

On one visit, Brenda had taken her to the building society to pay some bills and move her money to a better savings account. Brenda was arranging this on behalf of her sister when Mary said to the assistant, 'She is only trying to get my money.' It was funny, but sad in many ways because Mary was starting to drift away from us with the early symptoms of dementia. I spoke with Mary and asked her if I could help her with her bills and any money matters, which she welcomed. It was a big weight off her mind, and I applied and got Power of Attorney over her estate. Mary did not have a lot of money, but it did need to be managed.

One Christmas, when we brought Mary down to us for a week's break, Brenda asked Mary to sit up at the table, which she did. Mary then asked, 'Where is my handbag?' so Brenda said, 'I will get it for you.' When Brenda lifted it, she could not believe how heavy it was. It must have weighed about ten pounds. To cut a long story short, it was full of coins. It turned out that every time Mary went to the shop; she couldn't work out the coins involved so gave them a note and put the change in her handbag. When it was counted out there was over eighty pounds worth of coins there. We went to the bank and exchanged the coins for banknotes and Mary was happy to get the money.

Mary had a lovely ground floor flat which she had lived in with her mother in sheltered accommodation. It was ideal until Mary could no longer look after herself, following a stroke. Between Brenda and her brother, Alan, they found a suitable nursing home for Mary, not too far from Stroud, in a village called Quedgeley. The stroke had changed Mary from someone who was quite reserved to someone who would talk and make friends with almost everyone. It was a strange transformation, but welcome as it made her stay there much better than it might otherwise had been. Bren and I went to Nailsworth, a village close by, and bought her some bedroom furniture and a lovely armchair for her new room out of her savings. We filled it with a few personal belongings she treasured in her own way to make it feel like home. She had taken a liking to a small toy cat she called 'Bengy'. Everywhere Mary went she took her 'Bengy'.

Mary was happy being there for about nine months and even celebrated her seventy-fourth birthday but sadly another stroke took her from us. It was sad for the family, especially for the six remaining siblings, as this was the first one to be lost and as always, is a reminder of one's own mortality. We arranged the funeral, and she was cremated and buried alongside her mum and dad in the grounds surrounding Rodborough Church. The church is so lovely, dating back to 1384 and you can almost feel the history when you are walking around the grounds. If we had asked Mary, I could think there would be no better place than this for her to be at peace, lying with her dearly loved mum and dad.

In 2006, a work colleague called Angie at British Energy had gone on holiday with her partner to The Emirates Palace Hotel in Abu Dhabi and said how fabulous it was, so I decided to book it for our third wedding anniversary. At the time it was the third most expensive hotel in the world and cost three billion dollars to build in 2005. In June it is their low season because temperatures are as high as fifty degrees celsius, being in the desert. It was just as well because it was expensive to go there and three times more expensive in high season. Neither of us had been to Abu Dhabi before so there was a novelty factor for both of us.

When we arrived at Abu Dhabi Airport, I had booked a Seven Series BMW to pick us up and take us to the hotel. I could have paid three times more and got a Rolls Royce but thought better of it. The chauffeur greeted us and when we got into the air-conditioned car, we were passed bottles of cold water and cold towels, which were welcomed as temperatures were in the forties.

We arrived at the hotel, and it was spectacular having everything a top five-star hotel has to offer. We never touched our suitcases again and were greeted and escorted to the reception area, where we were shown to some seats and asked for our passports. These were taken to the reception desk and the room keys collected whilst we had a cool drink. We were then escorted by two people to our room, one being our butler, where we were introduced to the maid for our room. Apparently, you could hire a maid and a butler for twenty-four hours a day, who are there on a twenty-four hour beck and call basis. They asked if we were celebrating anything or just visiting the area, so we told them it was our third wedding anniversary. We also had welcome drinks, flowers and fruit in the room.

A few days later was our anniversary day and we found a lovely, decorated cake in our room with our names on wishing us a 'Happy Anniversary'. There were lots of special things there like bath robes and slippers. The bed was turned down every night and a chocolate box placed on your pillow, but the really nice thing was having rose petals sprinkled on and around the bed, which was a lovely romantic touch.

We had arranged to be shown on a guided tour of the hotel, which was huge. I used one of the hotel's wheelchairs because of the distances you must travel. During the tour we learned there were six tonnes of twenty-two-carat gold leaf painted in the central atrium dome about two hundred feet in the ceiling. One room they showed was used for functions like weddings and could hold two thousand five hundred people. This room had folding doors down one side, which opened into another room capable of holding a further two, thousand, five hundred people; this also had another room alongside to hold a further two thousand, five hundred people so seven thousand, five hundred in all. It is so impressive even the President of Abu Dhabi lives on the top floor Presidential suite and has his own driveway to his palatial suite. Dignitaries and famous people from around the world have visited here and the fourth and fifth floor rooms are reserved for them accordingly.

There is so much to write about the hotel, which then had six restaurants and delicious food in each one. We stayed for five nights and we both enjoyed the lazy river they had, which I even went swimming in every day. The workers outside the hotel even used two-wheeled motorized Segway's to get around because the floor size is eight hundred and fifty thousand square metres. Bren even tried a Segway. As we sat close to the lazy river the ground staff brought us, every couple of hours, cold flannels and cold fruit on sticks.

On our first evening, we went to their Lebanese restaurant, having never eaten their food before. Both of us really had no idea what to order but noticed there was a set menu with many dishes on. We spoke with the waiter, and he enthused over this choice, so we went for it. After about twenty minutes the dishes were brought to the table, then more and more dishes appeared. There were over sixteen different dishes and the waiter explained what was in each one, with Brenda listening intently. We tucked into the food but there was too much for both of us. It was lovely food with some spicy and minty dishes, but I found a tasty dish of rolled meat in balls, I believe it was lamb. I was tucking in to my second portion, really enjoying this when Bren said, 'I didn't think you would like that particular dish.' 'Why would you think that?' I asked. 'Didn't you listen to what was in all those dishes?' she added. Well, I had not because after the eighth or ninth dish I had switched off. Bren then said, with a beaming smile, 'It's finely chopped raw lamb.' I immediately pushed the plate away and felt queasy, much to the merriment of Bren. I just wished I had listened a bit more intently to the waiter explaining the contents of each dish!

During our stay, we decided on our second night to go to 'The Mediterranean Restaurant' within the hotel as we had only booked a bed and breakfast stay. We made a reservation and found our way along marbled corridors with Bren pushing me in a wheelchair. As we moved along the corridors, we noticed a lot of jewellery in display cabinets, but no prices. We both assumed if you needed to ask the price you probably could not afford it. At the restaurant we left the wheelchair outside and were greeted by the maître d' or head waiter who showed us to the table. We were asked if we wanted an aperitif and given the food menu, then a wine menu. The food prices are what you would expect of a top dining restaurant and after some deliberation we decided what to have. I looked at the wine menu and bottles of wine ranged from thirty pounds to five thousand pounds, so it did not take too long for me to decide on the wine. The décor, ambience and background music were special, and we soaked it up, drinking our aperitif.

The waiters were all attentive, always watching to make sure everything was perfect. The waiter took our food order and then the wine waiter appeared and asked if I had decided on the wine. I said yes, I would like a bottle of this and pointed to what I had chosen in the wine menu. He said, 'Thank you, Sir, may I say what a good choice of wine too.' I just smiled back, not really understanding his comment and said to Bren as he left the table, 'Why would he thank me for ordering a bottle of wine which is only thirty-five pounds a bottle?' We both shrugged but within about twenty seconds the wine waiter had returned and said, 'Excuse me, Sir, but it was this bottle of wine you ordered wasn't it?' showing me the wine menu. He had pointed to a two hundred and eighty-five pounds bottle, so

I said, 'No, it's the thirty-five pounds bottle'. 'Oh, I see, thank you,' and his whole demeanour seemed to change. I guess you get a lot of riffraff at these places occasionally! We laughed afterwards and we both enjoyed our thirty-five pound bottle of wine as well.

The breakfasts, being part of the package were excellent. They had three chefs there cooking eggs however you wanted them, as well as fillet steak, which I guess is an American type of breakfast. It was an incredibly good five-day holiday and when I went to settle the account, my food and drinks bill was well over one thousand pounds but you pay for what you get.

It was a holiday to remember, and we did return there seven years later for our tenth wedding anniversary, but it was not the same. The lazy river was closed for maintenance, and it was Ramadan, so there were rules to abide by. You could not eat or drink outside of the hotel building and it was a scorching fifty degrees Celsius. We were sunbathing around one of the pools, but if you wanted a drink you had to go back into the hotel and not drink by the pool. Bren also got sunstroke over there and was quite poorly on the last day and on the return air journey. Bren often reminds me of this because she was being quite sick on the plane, and I suppose it did not help that I ordered a fish biryani curry on the plane whilst she felt so unwell, which apparently made her feel worse. It was a lovely curry though!

We have always kept in touch with Lorraine because she will always be part of our family. She was now the mother of two children (with another two to follow) and had a completely different lifestyle to what she previously had. Steve, her husband, with his parents owned two large nursing homes in Norfolk and they were planning to build a third.

Steve had his own plane and regularly flew but as well as this he had a fifty-foot long 'Sunseeker' motor yacht. We had a call from Lorraine asking if we would like to join them on a trip to Cowes on the Isle of Wight and we could bring some of the family too. It was the annual Cowes week, so we knew it would be busy but jumped at the chance.

Steve had moored at the Port Solent Marina, about three miles from where we lived so we took Darren, Jamie and Lewis with us. It was a unique experience and being a complete novice to this was excited by the thought of travelling across The Solent to the Isle of Wight in something different to a ferry. We all met up and got on board where Steve slowly manoeuvred from the docking position, through the marina lock gates and toward the main channel in the harbour toward The Solent.

It was really exhilarating sitting with Brenda, high up on the top level, next to Steve driving the boat and the boys were really enjoying it too. As we were about three hundred meters from the harbour entrance, Steve turned to me and said, 'I just need to spend a penny so can you drive this for me?' I said, 'Okay', and he was gone. I suddenly realised as I was approaching the harbour entrance toward the open sea, I did not know whether I should be on the right or left side of the channel through the entrance otherwise known to us sailors as the port or starboard side. I slowed down a bit, looked around at other boats leaving and just followed them hoping no large vessel was suddenly going to appear.

Steve returned and took over, much to my relief, and once away from the harbour entrance he opened it up to around twenty-three knots. I did have another go at driving the boat at speed, which was really thrilling. What amazed me during the trip was looking at the bottom sounder and realising how shallow The Solent is in places. I saw the boat registering only five metres at one point and another ninety-three metres, but the average depth was only in the mid-twenty metre range.

It seemed to take no time at all before we approached Cowes and Steve slowly manoeuvred the boat upstream as far as he could go, to find the mooring he had booked. We got out and saw the pub along the river's edge not far away, but I thought, 'How will we get there?' when, out of the blue appeared what they call a 'water taxi'. This is basically a boat about twelve feet long, on which you sit around the sides and off you go. We all somehow squeezed into the boat and it took us a few hundred metres to the pub's jetty, where we got off. I paid for the water taxi, but to me it was expensive, but I guess the locals make their money at Cowes Week every year and it's a necessity to get from ship to shore.

We had a lovely meal and thoroughly enjoyed the day with Steve, Lorraine and the family. It was one to remember and I had always wanted a boat but never this big. The realities of owning a large boat like this were recalled when, several months later, Lorraine said the boat was travelling through the harbour when it had an engine fire on board causing thousands of pounds worth of damage to it and they had to evacuate it. I believe after the repairs were carried out Steve sold it.

In October 2007, we had a call from Bren's brother Rob and his wife Rose, asking if we would like to re-home a cat. The cat was called Spikey and we had met him before, when we had previously visited them. Bren had always loved her cats and we had just lost Fat Lucy with only Suki at home now. Spikey was a Devon Rex and quite a character, looking somewhat like Yoda from the Star Wars Film, 'The Empire Strikes Back', with his long scrawny neck. He had a sad life because he was on a farm in Devon that bred long-horned cows, with another cat and two aggressive dogs. The farmer's marriage had broken up and the cats were just left to fend for themselves. Rob was doing some electrical work there and saw both bedraggled cats and asked the farmer if he still wanted them. The farmer said just take them. One cat was so emaciated it had died but Spikey just about made it. Rob took it to a vet to give it the once over and learnt that part of his tail had been bitten off by one of the dogs when he got too close to their cage in the kitchen.

Rob offered Spikey to his next-door neighbour who was over the moon and he had a loving home there. Unfortunately, the poor woman died two years later from cancer and so Spikey was homeless again. We had arranged to meet Rob and Rose at a pub halfway between Portsmouth and Paignton, where they lived, and we would pick him up, having a nice Sunday lunch at the same time. When we got home and let Spikey out of the cage in the garden, he immediately climbed up the garden wall and went on walkabouts. I tracked him down about twenty yards away and managed to get hold of him. I then realised, for such a small cat he was extraordinarily strong, and those claws of his went through my coat into my back. We kept him in for a week and gradually he found his territory, which was centred on our house. Suki did not really like the intrusion, but she just about put up with it. He strolled around his territory like the mini-Lion King he was, daring any other cat to enter at its peril. Indoors he was so affectionate and melted our hearts, but outdoors he was the leader, afraid of nothing and a mean fighter. Although he was nearly eight years old by now, he would go on to give us another eight years of real pleasure having him in our lives. A wonderful cat indeed.

Chapter 31: Global Financial Crisis

I had worked at British Energy for over three years and there were many things to take into consideration. Firstly, as a contractor, you had to be aware of a tax implication called IR35. Basically, if you have been with a company longer than two or three years, you could be considered for tax purposes, an employee of your end client and therefore subject to PAYE. One individual there had to pay thirty-five thousand pounds back in taxes, so many contractors were wary of this. The second consideration was British Energy was in the process of being bought out by a French Company called EDF. To cap it all there was a severe worldwide economic crisis happening so times were very uncertain.

Alan, who I worked for, called me over one day and gave me three months' notice due to so many things happening with the company and its uncertain future. I was more than pleased with getting three months because it is normally one weeks' notice for contractors. It was therefore decided for me to move on, so I used agents and my contacts to see what the market was like. With the markets in turmoil, I was not too hopeful.

Having put my C.V. in the marketplace I was getting calls, but out of the blue I had a call from a colleague I had worked closely with at Aker Kvaerner who was now the engineering director of an oil and gas company in Northampton. He invited me for an interview. On the day of the interview, I left Cheltenham for Northampton and was allowed three hours to get there. There had been torrential rain for many days before this and rivers were swollen with some low-lying land flooded but I set off in the rain. After two hours, I had only travelled about fifteen miles as the traffic was chaotic because rivers were overflowing. I tried for another hour and decided to give up and drive home to Portsmouth. I phoned the company, explained my predicament, and rearranged the interview for another day. I used my sat nav to get the quickest route home, which somehow took me down a country lane. I should have stopped and stayed on the main roads, but this would save me half an hour, so I continued. The road turned to a single-car track and in the distance, I could see the road I needed. The problem though was the one hundred-foot flooded river in front of me, making it impassable! I had to reverse back for nearly half a mile to be able to turn the car around and join the traffic jam I had left. The moral of the story is never to be completely trusting of your sat nav! It took me six more hours to drive back to Portsmouth and I was not offered the job in my follow-up interview.

I did talk to another colleague who mentioned a role in AWE (Atomic Weapons Establishment) at Aldermaston, so I went there for an interview. It was a good interview and at the end, he said with a wry smile that he did not have anything suitable for me there with my experience, apart from his job, but there was a role I might be interested in at a large American company called Jacobs, in Reading, as head of project services. I always think it is good to go for interviews, so said I was willing to talk to them.

I was still having to go regularly, every two or three

months, to get my leg repaired. I really disliked it when they condemned your leg because it really is an extension of your body and such an important part of your mobility, however limited it is. I understand you can only repair a leg so many times or the parts you require are no longer made, but nevertheless it is a traumatic time for an amputee changing legs. My spare leg has never been one which I can just put on and think that it is fine, so this results in more fine tuning and other visits. It normally takes me three weeks to adjust to a new leg so in the interim it is always a painful adjustment but that is just the way it is.

I have spent, and continue to spend, many hours at the Disablement Centre getting repairs carried out. You do meet some colourful characters along the way and on this day, I had met a South African and got talking to him. His name was George Richard Mawson, otherwise known as Dick Mawson. He lost his right leg as an eleven-year-old on a farm in South Africa. A few years later, when he was on a speedboat in Victoria Falls, travelling at one hundred m.p.h. in his boat he had an accident and irreparably damaged his left leg. He apparently came back, undaunted, with a zest for speed a few years later to speed boating and was a local champion there even marrying a Junior Miss Rhodesia; fascinating tales.

Dick wrote a book called The Gods Who Fell From The Sky, in which his precept is 'A soul that is afraid of dying has never learned to live'. He told me about his life and adventures. He turned to motor racing and not only won races in South Africa but also in Europe too. His first win at twelve years old, where he became powerboat champion in Rhodesia, at thirteen he represented his country and became an international champion. At sixteen he won the International

Gold Cup Regatta at Victoria Falls, where he badly crashed, despite which, he then took up motor racing. All this wonderful story from just going to get my leg repaired one morning. Life is full of surprises.

The most surprising discussion I had was with two men in their late thirties, I would say. Both admitted to being drug addicts in the past and were talking to each other about methadone after heroin. It was a whole different vocabulary to me of types of drugs that were helping them wean themselves off the hard stuff. The conversation slowly got round to one asking the other how he lost his leg, to which he said, 'I had a motorbike accident but didn't lose it because of that'. He said 'My leg was badly mangled, they tried for a year to save it, but the pain was incredible and part of the reason I got hooked on drugs. There seemed to be no end to it, and I asked them to amputate it below the knee, but they just would not. I was desperate with the pain, so I went to the railway line and put my leg on the line and waited for the next train to come.' The other guy said, 'You must have been desperate', to which he replied, 'I really was.' I was listening in and half included in the conversation, and he said to me, 'Do you believe me?' Before I could think of the right answer he said, 'This is my name, just put it in Google Search and you will see.' I did and there the story was in black and white.

I was quite taken aback, he was not spinning yarn but then he said to the other guy, 'So how did you lose your leg?' You normally expect motorbike or car accidents or some medical condition, but not this time. He said he was heavily into drugs at the time and went to a squat he knew, to go on a bender. Then he said, 'unfortunately I took a huge dose and just sat cross-legged in the corner of a room. I was found four days later and where one of my legs had rested on the other, it had cut the circulation off and they had to amputate it. I guess we all have tales to tell but that day stuck with me as one of those lodged in my brain.'

I always tried to make sure my artificial leg was safe when I was going abroad on business or holiday so often just went for a maintenance check-up. There was normally something smallish to sort out but sometimes something more important can be discovered. I have, in the past, had a simple clicking noise investigated and they found metal fatigue on a key component, which could have let me down at any moment. What I have never done is to take my spare leg with me as luggage! It is just impractical, besides which it weighs around fourteen pounds, so is quite heavy.

I travelled abroad quite frequently for holidays and business trips. For my holidays I had to accept, if I wanted to enjoy it and not be in pain, then I needed to use a wheelchair at the airports. Previously, I had used some of the airport buggies they have there but sometimes on the return journeys, you would request them, they never showed up. It is much better nowadays but there were problems to begin with. Some of the walks from check-in to the boarding gate can be quite a distance for me and if I tried to walk them, I would be hurting from day one of the holiday. We went abroad for many years with Mum, Dad, Margaret, Jeff, Arthur and Lyn. It was a good family time, and we laughed a lot, mainly at Mum and Dad's expense but we all treasure those memories.

One of our holidays left from Gatwick Airport, where you can bypass a lot of queuing in a wheelchair. Brenda was pushing me, and we said we would meet the others near the boarding gate. We went to the security check-in and as I was in a wheelchair, they just patted me down and of course felt the belt around my waist. It is usually a formality as I explain I have a higher amputation than most. They were fine and over the past few years the security there had been taking swab samples from my shoes and leg. This time they put the swab in the machine, and I expected to be waved on as I normally was, but no, not this time. The alarm sounded, all eyes turned to me and I was suddenly surrounded by security guards. They told Bren to stay where she was and pushed me in the wheelchair to a discrete room. Two stayed inside and two outside the room and they explained to me the swab had shown traces of nitro-glycerine, a high explosive. They asked me to lift my shirt to ensure I really had an artificial leg and after some questioning called Brenda into the room. It turned out Brenda had cleaned the wheelchair with some cleaning agent which had minute traces of nitro-glycerine in it. Phew! I wasn't a terrorist, but it showed how sensitive the machines were to detect it, and in many ways, it is reassuring for everyone's safety when flying.

I received a letter from Jacobs inviting me for an interview in Reading for the head of project services role. It was not ideal from a location point of view as it was over sixty miles from Portsmouth, however I was, by now, used to working away from home but thought I might be able to commute this distance. I arrived and was greeted by the vice president of operations and taken upstairs to a large corner office. He asked me if I wanted a tea or coffee so, I said yes to a coffee and he disappeared. After a couple of minutes, two guys walked in and introduced themselves then sat down in the room, closely followed by another two, then another three. The VP came in with my coffee and introduced me to everyone. It turned out they were the senior management team and if successful I would be working with them.

I had never had an interview before with eight interviewers firing, what seemed like, non-stop questions at me. I suppose too, they were trying to look good with their questions in front of their line manager, the VP. It did not faze me because I knew my subject, but for others, I can imagine it being quite daunting. The interview lasted two hours, with the last half an hour one-to-one with the VP.

I had learnt early on it is a small world in the industry and the VP, as I did for my interviewing, had taken up references, speaking to several people about me. I learned later one of those was our previous MD who had pushed me in the wheelchair he had acquired at Schiphol Airport when I could not walk any further. He had apparently left Aker Kvaerner and joined Jacobs as a vice president in the Indian office. I would have liked to have stayed freelance, but the VP explained this was not possible in this senior management role, which I could understand. We shook hands and he said he would be in touch.

Within a week, I had an offer of a job as head of project services, a six-figure salary, car allowance, medical cover and a bonus scheme. Very few people go back to a staff role from a contracting one because of the drawback of earning less, but this must be balanced with better job security, pension and sickness benefits. I pondered the offer amidst the time of crisis in the world with the banks and not too many other job opportunities around. I phoned the VP and said if they could increase their offer by a further ten thousand pounds then I would accept. He came back two days later and said yes, so I accepted the job.

I started within a couple of weeks and decided to travel

home to Portsmouth each night. They were long days, travelling for ninety minutes after a full day to get home, then to leave at six a.m. and it took its toll. After a fortnight, I spoke to the VP and said I found the travelling to and from Portsmouth too much. I needed to find local accommodation and asked if they would pay my expenses. He kindly agreed and I booked into a four-star hotel close by, fully expensed. Jacobs was, at the time, a good company to work for and their ethos was 'people are our greatest asset'.

Now I did not have all the travelling I could spend longer at work, so I would arrive at seven a.m. and leave at seven p.m. every day apart from Fridays when I left at one p.m. . There was a lot to do, a lot to sort out, and with any new company it takes at least six months to get to know the procedures, systems and people with their strengths and weaknesses. Jacobs were keen for new employees in management roles to get to understand the core values of the business, so after just a couple of months I was nominated to attend a five-day induction course of their ways of doing business at their headquarters in Los Angeles. It was a great way to start networking and meet some of the executives of the business. I was there for the week and what impressed me was at one session the CEO gave us a lecture about the business and its core values. He then said after the hour, anyone could ask him any question they liked for another half an hour, along with the financial director. It was impressive and made quite an impact early on, on my views about the company.

The only downside working in the Reading office was the stairs, which I had to use because it was an old building with no lift, but there was only one floor to climb so it was manageable. The other aspect was attending numerous meetings and spending many hours just sat there because the impact to my leg was more pain. I had a lifetime of knowledge now, as to how to best manage the pain, but sometimes there was no reasoning why the pain suddenly happened. I managed it when the pain occurred mainly with ibuprofen and paracetamol, having tried most other types of pain relief. If it was bad, I used co-proxamol, but I was careful how much I used because you do feel spaced out at times with them. The worst part is having the pain throughout the night, getting little sleep and then having to do a full day's work. I did pride myself in not taking any time off sick but maybe in hindsight there were a few times I would have benefited from it.

After nearly two years, we moved to a brand-new building in Winnersh. We were based on the top floor and the lifts there were very efficient as you would expect in a modern building. The parking was in the basement, so everyone was pleased with the move.

Just before moving to the new offices, we experienced a winter where the snow came unexpectedly. There were a lot of weather warnings about it coming and on the day of the snow's arrival, people were told they could leave work at midday. I finished a few jobs to wrap up some outstanding issues and left a little later. This was a mistake because it took two hours to get from our carpark to the main roundabout about one hundred yards away. Reading was gridlocked and the snow was falling. I had a Mercedes 350E Coupe, which was great fun to drive but its traction on snow was abysmal. As I tried to leave the roundabout, I had been on for two hours, the car just couldn't find any traction to climb the inclined road to the main motorway route out. Fortunately, two good souls were there pushing cars up the road and eventually, with their help,

I made it.

The journey home was uneventful but as more snow was shortly forecast, I thought I would go cross country to get home quicker rather than get snarled up on the motorway. It was going well until I arrived close to Petersfield, which is about seventeen miles north of Portsmouth. It is a dual carriageway so I thought the roads would be good, although there is a gradual incline over a mile to get over Butser Hill just to the south of Petersfield. I wrongly thought the snow would come from the north and I knew I was ahead of it, but not this time. The snow arrived from a north westerly direction, and as it got heavier and heavier, the cars on the road got slower and slower until everything ground to a halt. It was around four p.m., the light was fading, the snow getting heavier by the minute and I was stuck just a few miles from home. I recalled thinking about the Gene Pitney song, 'Twenty-four hours from Tulsa' because I was just 'Seventeen miles from Portsmouth'.

Several people just left their cars and walked through the snow to Petersfield, which was impossible for me. I phoned home, told them my predicament and the jungle drums must have been working because I kept getting phone calls from all my relatives with some humour involved. I started to get cold but knew I could not get out of the car to my boot to get my coat because the compacted ice on the road was treacherous for me. Fortunately, I asked this kind-hearted guy, who walked by the car, and after explaining my problem, asked if he could open my boot and get my coat out for me, which he did, thank goodness. He even gave me his mobile number if I needed any further help. In times of crisis, I have always found people rally round to help each other.

After three or four hours of just sitting in the car, not knowing how long I would be there for, I was getting a bit thirsty. By this time, the snow had laid about four inches deep on the top of the car so I thought I would scoop a handful of snow and put it in my mouth to quench my thirst. I did this and it tasted awful and to this day I still believe a seagull must have deposited something in the mouthful of snow I scooped into my mouth. It was yuck!

I was getting mobile calls during the evening and slowly drifted off to sleep about eleven-thirty p.m. but at one-thirty a.m. my phone went. It was Kerry, my niece, phoning to make sure I was alright. We joked about it, as you do but it was nice of her to phone after my welfare. There was some activity about five a.m. and I hoped something was happening because I had been in the car about fifteen hours by this time. A policeman appeared and said to the car in front, the road should be passable now and off it went. The biggest problem was the abandoned vehicles where people had just left their cars where they stopped and walked off to Petersfield, never to be seen again. After some manoeuvring, I did manage to pull away and drive slowly home, arriving about an hour later. It was some journey but memorable and thank goodness for my heated seats.

Being away from the family during the week had become the norm for me now so it was important to cram as much time in over the weekends to see family and have some fun with Brenda, whilst recharging the batteries for the next week's challenges or opportunities as we called them. We always saw Mum and Dad on Saturdays and when Pompey were at home, we always went there for dinner and Brenda would then take

Dad and me to Fratton Park. It was a good year for Pompey in 2008 as we got to the FA Cup Final and Dad, Darren, Kyle and Jamie all went to Wembley to watch it.

We were all excited on the day of the Final, none more so than my dad who had even been to the Manchester City Final with Pompey in 1934, where we lost 4-1. As we parked the car at Wembley car park there was a television crew doing supporter interviews, so Darren had an idea. He went over to them and said there was a story for them with his grandad, who by this time was ninety-three, with his previous Wembley outing in 1934. They came over and interviewed him for ten minutes and Dad thought he was famous at last, a real celebrity! It appeared on the local TV channel that evening, and many people recognized Dad. He lapped up the star status he thought he had. The day was even more special as we beat Cardiff to lift the cup and we all celebrated together. I have a lovely photograph of Dad, Darren and me all smiling together on the day, which takes pride of place on my study shelf at home. Treasured memories indeed.

Lewis had finished his degree, getting a two: one and we went to Portsmouth Guildhall for the awards ceremony and photographs. He has always been very much focused on his work projects and we were proud of his achievement, particularly as he suffers from dyslexia. By now he had met Victoria at a party in the New Year celebrations and they were both smitten. They were sensible in ensuring Vicky finished her degree at Imperial College, London but it was nice to see love blossoming. Vicky plays the piano and is one exam away from being a concert pianist. When she plays, I am awestruck because it seems so easy and effortless to produce such beautiful melodies. I can just sit down and listen to her playing any time, wishing I had just a little bit of her talent.

Russell had made Bath his home place and was working in a coffee shop there, whilst doing his degree. He could not settle into the degree course so opted out after a couple of years. We went to visit him quite a few times and met his girlfriend Natalie. She was a ballet dancer, had a beautiful voice and could play the violin and piano beautifully too. Unfortunately, Natalie had ME, otherwise known as Chronic Fatigue Syndrome, which causes extreme tiredness and a range of other symptoms. Russ spent a lot of time looking after her. Both were heavily involved in the Freedom Church in Bath and did a lot of work with them. Bren and I went to one of their services one Sunday and were surprised as the average age of the congregation was so young, but I think being a university city there were a lot of transient students there too.

Bren is a bit of a worrier and was concerned about this being a cult organisation as Betsy and Andrew de Thierry only moved to Bath in 2000 to found the new church. We were made welcome, but we did not feel any pressure or misgivings about the place. They just seemed genuine Christian folk who were doing their own thing. Bren made some enquiries at a local Southsea church and they were very understanding even making their own internal enquiries about the Freedom Church. A week later, Bren had the feedback all was fine with the church and it was not a cult organisation just another offshoot from the more traditional type of church. I guess a mother never stops worrying about their children, no matter what age they are.

Darren was gradually knocking off the exam modules to become a Chartered Accountant, but he chose the hard way to do it. Having a demanding job, a young family and then moving to a new house again, where Des, Anita's father was helping to build an extension, meant there was little time for studying. Anita was also suffering from ME, so life was proving difficult all round for them. None of us knows what life will throw at us but the calibre of your inner strengths will hopefully shine through as you rise to the challenges you face.

Jamie had, by now, finished with his girlfriend Hayley, whom he had been seeing for over three years and had just met Carla. Carla was attractive, very bubbly, had a good sense of humour and brought the best out in Jamie. They seemed to be made for each other.

Donna and Andy had four children with Callum quite disabled and permanently in a wheelchair. Andy no longer worked, being a full-time carer for Callum and they had a council house with some conversion there to suit Callum's needs. His chest infections were getting less now but there was no speech or other communication from him. The whole family loved him, and it was good to see the children on the floor playing and cuddling him. Although they never had a lot, the children were all well behaved and good mannered. Life for their family was difficult at times but we all have a path we have chosen, and choices along the way.

Work at Jacobs was demanding, and I was constantly interviewing to try and improve the workforce under me. I needed to get more experience in the Cost Control Department so decided to ask Courtenay if he was interested in moving from EDF in Cheltenham to join me in Reading. He agreed to join us and brought some stability, knowledge and professionalism to the team. Not only that, but I had a friend who could join me once a week for a nice curry after work just like before. We have certainly had a few curries together over the years and put the world to rights too.

As time moved on and I got to know the management team I was part of, I formed some good friendships with some of the other directors there like Pete, Shashi and Fred. The number of people in the offices approached five hundred and the job was sold to me to help grow it threefold. We had some experienced personnel there but whether it was a global downturn in the marketplace or lack of a clear sales focus for the Reading office I am unsure, but the new work was not coming in as any of us thought it would.

The Jacobs company at the time I joined was in excess of fifty thousand employees throughout the world and grew quickly by acquisition and growth. If there was a problem project, people would be brought in from other offices to help sort issues out. About eighteen months after I joined, I was invited to be part of a five-man audit team to review a project in Holland. I was wary of this trip because of the snow and ice there. For me with my artificial leg, walking on ice is a major problem. Fresh snow is just about manageable but ice, for me, is a fall waiting to happen.

We left Gatwick Airport for Holland and it was a cold November day but on arrival there was a coating of snow everywhere. We got through passport control and picked our luggage up from the carousel before heading for the taxi rank to the hotel. Once out of the main airport I walked slowly to the taxi avoiding any ice. We arrived at the hotel, checked in, and arranged to meet at the bar before having a meal that evening. All was well until after the morning breakfast, when we had to make our way to the offices. The office was literally three hundred meters away, and you could physically see it, but for me it was a big problem. Overnight there had been more snow on compacted ice and I just could not risk walking on it. I explained to my colleagues who were very understanding, and we got the shortest taxi ride ever to go three hundred yards. What amazed me on the short journey was the whole place is geared up for bikes, who often have the right of way and there they were riding bikes on snow and ice.

The audit went well and only took three days. We interviewed key personnel, after which we presented our findings and recommendations before formally writing up the report. I enjoyed doing audits, but I certainly did not enjoy walking on ice and was something to consider when travelling in the future.

I remember travelling to Zoetermeer in Holland many times in the past but one visit I recall sticks in my memory. We had worked hard during the day and were staying in the local Tulip Hotel. It was geared up for businessmen and our team were propping the bar up, as you do. I was with Kevin and a few others, drinking gin and tonics and I must have had about ten of these, which was unusual for me. It was a late, late night and eventually I made my way to the room and crashed out. In the early hours of the morning, I needed to use the loo, so hopped to the bathroom and then it happened. I think with my inebriation I did not take note of the bathroom threshold. Sometimes there is one, other times there isn't. There was certainly one this time and I stubbed my toe so hard on it. With only one leg you cannot just hop around, and I fell heavily on the bathroom floor, laying there in real pain for about ten minutes. It taught me a lesson to look at this every time I went to a new hotel.

A few months later in the summer, I was again asked to be part of a small audit team for a lump sum project being undertaken in the Milan offices, worth over three hundred million Euro. I had only ever driven through Milan on a family trip years earlier to Varazze and not stopped for any sightseeing so was looking forward to this trip. On a business trip you rarely get the chance to see the place you visit, so we only had one spare evening to have a look around. The audit started with the whole team meeting up and the most senior manager presenting the team with an overview of the project. He was making statements of progress and out of the corner of my eye I saw the head of process have a wry smile and shake his head. It is little signals like that which raise the alarm bells, so afterwards I told the team, and we decided we needed some time alone with this guy. It proved fruitful because all sorts of issues came wriggling to the surface and the project was less healthy than was being reported.

Midway through the audit we decided one evening to go and see the Milan Cathedral and have a drink in the Piazzo del Duomo or Cathedral Square. It is a beautifully stunning and eye-catching building built in 1865. This place has always been the central point of the city of Milan and the meeting point for the inhabitants to celebrate the most important events. We found a nice café overlooking the square with outdoor seating and ordered five bottles of beer. It was awfully expensive, but it was a prime location. We sat there talking about the day's events and just watching life go by.

Milan is known for its chic sense of fashion and there were some stunningly beautiful women walking by that caught the eye, most enjoyable. One sight worth mentioning, which also caught the eye, was an Italian guy who passed right in front of us. He was a least six feet three inches tall, very slim and was wearing lederhosen with an Alpine Tyrolean hat. To complement his attire, he had very pointed shoes and rainbow-coloured socks up to his knees. As he effeminately swayed in front of us, he must have enjoyed soaking up the admiring glances he was receiving or thought he was receiving. We all looked at each other, astounded, trying not to laugh, and waited until he was long gone before one colleague said he thought I would look good dressed like that! I will not repeat my response.

There was never a dull moment on those trips, and I made some good friendships along the way. The Milan trip had opened a can of worms on the project status, but audits were meant to give a project health check and with appropriate recommendations to follow.

In April 2010, we had the incredibly sad news of Basil passing away. Since Margaret had married Jeff in the early 1980s I had known Basil for nearly thirty years. He was Jeff's son from his former marriage and a really nice guy, with a keen sense of humour, very polite and always keen to help. His job was in the police force and he was a motorbike rider there. He had met Melanie and they were just made for each other, being so happy together. They got married and later had two girls, Gabriel and Rosanna. They lived close to London, and when visiting over the years, would often come to us to celebrate Christmas or join us for family barbecues or celebrations.

Basil had kidney problems, and the eventual diagnosis of cancer, which had spread, was a real shock to everyone. Basil was only forty-eight years old when he died, and we all miss him a lot. The police force did him proud for his funeral and there were many policemen there. I vividly remember as the coffin was being taken into the church, which was lined either side by policemen, there were two police helicopters flying above that both dipped their noses as the coffin was carried from the hearse to the church. There were senior police officers there and a lovely eulogy given. The police certainly know how to say goodbye to one of their own. It was so sad to see Melanie, Gabriel and Rosanna in their raw grief. We all miss Bas a lot.

There was a lot happening in 2011 for both us and the family. Lewis and Vicky got married and had a lovely wedding in an old Norman church in Catherington, about ten miles north of Portsmouth, which is steeped in history. It was nice to meet a lot of Vicky's friends and family at the reception, as we had only really met Phyllis and Rees, her mum and dad previously. They had bought a house in Woking as they both worked in London and the location was easy for the commute.

Darren had finally passed his CIMA exam and was now a Chartered Accountant. We were immensely proud of his achievement and I know Ann would have been too. With the tireless help of Des, their house had been extended and looked good. Tayla and Kyle were growing up fast and, in many ways, it mirrored my early days where it was busy times with the family, work and doing things to the house.

Jamie and Carla were happy together and had rented a house. Carla was working for PETA Training and Consultancy as a training manager, which delivered business apprenticeship training. I had managed to get Carla an interview where I worked. A colleague and friend, Pete, who was the engineering director there, was looking for an engineering coordinator and I had mentioned I might know someone. She went along for the interview, which went well and was offered a role there in Reading at a significant increase in salary. Jamie was happy working for double glazing installers but was self-employed, as many are in the industry. The downside is the wages are not always paid on time and they often treat their employees poorly, but unfortunately this was the industry he had chosen.

It was around this time Courtenay and his wife, Chris, had separated and he was deeply upset about this. He mentioned this one evening when we were having our weekly curry in Reading and I could see the pain he was going through. He had moved out of the family home, staying in a Travel Lodge hotel at the weekends and in lodgings at Reading during the week. When I heard this, I invited him to come to our house at weekends until things settled as I knew he was hoping to get back to Chris. Brenda was fine with this arrangement to help him out and said she was amazed at how clean he left the bathroom after using it. It may have been a subtle dig at me, but I ignored it. This arrangement went on for several years, but he was a good friend who we were happy to help.

Chapter 32: Cruising

I have never been on a cruise because I do suffer from sea sickness, in fact, I feel seasick having a bath. This all stems from our early Sunday school trips on coaches smelling heavily of diesel and constantly having to use sick bags. Arthur and Margaret both suffer to some extent from this, so it must be hereditary.

Once when I was getting my leg repaired, I remember talking to someone in the waiting room who also had a high amputation, and he was extolling how good cruises were. He had been on many and never had a problem. Two of Bren's brothers said they were going on a cruise and asked if we would like to join them. Bren was very keen, as, like me, she had never been on one. It was the Azura operated from the P&O Cruise Line. I looked up the details and at the time it was only one year old, and what they term a Grand-class ship. It was impressive being nine hundred and fifty-one feet long and one hundred and eighteen feet wide. In total, the ship had eleven restaurants and eating areas, twelve bars and places to drink, four pools, a gym, two spas, an outdoor cinema, a theatre and two show lounges. The trip started in Southampton, just twenty-three miles west of Portsmouth and went to Madeira before cruising around several islands around the Caribbean.

It was an opportunity to go on a cruise with Bren's relatives, who we all got on well with and with all the business travelling I had done, my travel sickness had all but disappeared, or so I thought. Bren is always encouraging me to try new things as she is quite adventurous and persuaded me to go for it. We booked an outdoor cabin so we could see the sea and just relax on the veranda. I had some trepidation about my disability and balance, but I was assured the stability of these boats was good nowadays. It would be interesting to say the least, but I had no idea what lay ahead.

We met up with Chris, Barbara, Rob and Rose in the boarding area of Southampton Docks and it was lovely to see them all again. It was well organised and soon we were in our room with the suitcases there too. We had agreed to meet up on the top deck, which was 'Deck 19' so you can get an idea of the size of the ship. There was a band playing as we departed and a waiter with a tray of champagne came by so naturally, I asked for two glasses. He then asked for my cabin number to charge it to. I did think it would be free as it was a good advert for the cruise ship, where everybody was waving and having a good time, but that is business for you. There is no money exchanged on board as it is all done via your cabin number key card. It is very quick and easy with shore excursions paid this way too. We got underway and soon had the safety induction on board as they are very safety conscious.

We had booked some trips in the Caribbean so had a lot to look forward to on this voyage. We headed from Southampton through the Bay of Biscay, which is known for its rough seas and violent storms and much of this is thanks to its exposure to the Atlantic Ocean. It was not too bad, but I did feel the need to take some sea sickness tablets to be sure and walking was not easy for me in the swell of the waves. I had the assurances from many saying it would be fine as modern ships have stabilisers, which are fins or rotors mounted beneath the waterline and emerging laterally from the hull to reduce a ship's roll due to wind or waves.

I had been reading about a storm, a few days before, in the Caribbean and thought thank goodness, we never encountered that. We continued sailing toward Madeira and the temperature was rising and spirits were lifted as the island appeared on the horizon. The food on board was incredibly good and we were on a table with ten others whom we got to know well on the trip. When we finally docked at the harbour of Madeira everyone was keen to explore it. Bren and I decided to stay on board as the previous year we had visited Madeira for a week and gone on various island excursions so felt there was nothing to gain in visiting it again. Besides which, we had everything on board you could wish for with the sun shining and a quiet time as most of the three thousand passengers had departed.

The shows on board were excellent and virtually as good as those of the West End in London we had seen. The only downside for me was the amount of walking required. We were on the fifth deck, about two thirds of the way along the ship toward the bow. The dining area was towards the aft, about six hundred feet away but up one floor. This meant either waiting for a lift to go up one floor or just use the stairs, which I did most times, but doing this three times a day was for me taking its toll. It is always difficult for me to walk on a full stomach too because of the straps around my waist securing the socket of my artificial leg. Added to this was going to the shows of an evening, where the location was right at the bow, plus steps to get to your seat. Small things for most but significant for me.

I get used to these problems daily and have to decide what I can reasonably do.

We soon set sail from Madeira for the Caribbean, heading west, and I thought with those trade winds it would be a smooth crossing. It started out calm but then we hit the tail end of the hurricane I had read about earlier. I took more sea sickness tablets but must admit it was exhilarating seeing the size of the waves and realising how small you are in such a powerful sea. The waves were almost hitting us side on but not quite, which only served to create quite a roll in the swell. I am sure it would have been much worse without the stabilisers, but it was proving exceedingly difficult for me to walk.

Bren with her 'free spirit' mindset encouraged me to try and walk around the ship. She held onto me tightly but not as tightly as I gripped the railings as we walked. It was a thrilling experience and one I will always remember, especially at the aft of the boat where you could look up at the peak of the waves about thirty feet above you. We had this rolling motion for over a day and that evening was to be a dinner jacket affair. I got dressed up, really struggling to keep my balance and felt quite unwell. Bren was more resilient and coping well with it. I just felt I could not walk to the evening meal or even face eating, although I was dressed for the occasion, I decided to stay put in the cabin, insisting Brenda went and met up with her brothers. I got out of the clothes, laid down on the bed and just wished I could stop the ship's motion. Anyone who has suffered sea sickness will know you just want to die, well not literally, but you do feel rough.

After those eventful couple of days on board, the rest were literally plain sailing. It was warm, the sun was shining, and we approached the Caribbean eager to see the various islands.

Having seen several plantations and the conditions the slaves lived in you really have to hang your head in shame, but they were different times then with different views from an uneducated society. How dreadful for those poor people to be taken from Africa to a land they did not know and work until they dropped, with no human rights at all. Nearly thirteen million of these souls departed their country over four hundred years, never to return, and around two million died on the journey, which are truly shocking statistics.

We stopped at one island, then during the night travelled to the next and so on. One highlight of the various island hopping tours was visiting Nelson's Dockyard, which is a cultural heritage site and marina in English Harbour, located in Saint Paul Parish on the island of Antigua. You could almost feel the history around you, and it was a fascinating insight to how life was like on that idyllic island.

I believe Brenda will remember the island of St. Martin's stop-off well for a couple of reasons. On the ship they had a grand sale of jewellery and we waited three days to see what bargains they had. I had been wary of these so-called bargains as I had previously bought Bren an eternity ring from a bespoke jeweller from Tenerife on one of our first holidays abroad to the Canaries. It had been two thousand pounds and was in a sale. I negotiated a bit and got it for just under one thousand pounds but six years later I had it valued for insurance purposes whereupon they said it was worth only five hundred and thirty pounds. Bren kindly said the sentimental value of the ring was priceless anyway. The moral of the story is never to buy rings or stones which must be imported hence I was wary of the ship's bargains.

The deep blue Tanzanite ring had caught Bren's eye on

board and was reduced from three thousand, two hundred pounds to two thousand, four hundred pounds. What a bargain, or so we were led to believe. I held off buying it because we had arrived in St. Martin's and were going ashore. Maybe there was a bargain to be had there I thought. We left the ship and walked through the port gates, along a lovely promenade towards all the jewellery shops in this prime location overlooking the bay. A large chunk of the island's income is from tourism and they were very hospitable. I could not walk far so I said to Bren let us find a jewellery shop a road or two back from the main promenade. I thought their overheads would be less and they might be more accommodating on price.

Eventually we found a lovely shop and by the time we entered we were sweating heavily in the tropical sun. They immediately made us welcome, brought out chairs and made us a coffee. They asked what we were interested in and I mentioned the Tanzanite ring on board the ship we liked. Out came the tanzanite rings and there was a much better selection to choose from. Eventually after nearly an hour of looking and Bren in seventh heaven trying various rings on, I bought a larger stoned ring than on board but for only one thousand eight hundred and fifty pounds. The shop now had a sale and they asked if we would like another drink, maybe something a little stronger. We had a couple of gin and tonics and he mentioned he had some lovely diamond rings, which we might like to look at. Bren's eyes lit up like diamonds too as we looked at their wares. They are after all 'a girl's best friends'.

We had been at the jewellers over two hours now, had three drinks and Max, the shop owner had teased out of me what I was prepared to pay for a diamond ring. He craftily started showing me a twenty thousand dollar ring, then fifteen thousand dollars until I agreed I was interested in the ten thousand dollar rings. We haggled, he smiled, we had another drink, haggled again and eventually I bought a one and half carat diamond ring for just over seven thousand, five hundred dollars or five thousand pounds at the time. I was happy, the jewellers were happy, and Bren was even happier with two rings, not one. It had been a marathon shopping visit but worth it and as we walked back to the ship along the promenade, I took a photograph of Bren holding her hands in the air with the two new rings on and the biggest smile you could ever imagine. That smile was priceless.

The holiday was soon over, and we were back to our normal way of living with some lovely memories to treasure because it is those memories together which make up our lives. Those moments in time indelibly etched in your mind to remind us of those special occasions we can recall from time to time. This reminds me of one of my first dates with Bren when I said to her, 'We do not have a lot of history between us to talk about', but we certainly do now and some amazing memories.

One of the perks of the job I now had was medical insurance and the ravages of time were catching up with both Bren and I. Bren had problems with her lower back and my one and only knee was painful so we both knew it was time for some professional guidance. Within a few weeks of each other, we got referrals from our local doctor to see a consultant for each of our issues. I was fortunate to have this facility to go private, but I would say from my experience with Ann, the National Health Service was excellent once a serious or life-threatening event was diagnosed. As with Ann, I always went with Bren to the orthopaedic consultant appointments, not just for support but to ask any questions not already covered in the consultation. Bren was examined and after some X-rays and an MRI scan the problem was found. Between each of the bones in your spine (the vertebrae) is a disc. These discs act as shock absorbers and help cushion your bones. It was diagnosed as a herniated disc, which extends beyond the capsule containing it and pushes into the spinal canal. You might develop a herniated disc from lifting something the wrong way or from suddenly twisting your spine. This is exactly what happened with Bren lifting a large tub of hot water and twisting slightly, when she worked in the local hospital.

The fascinating part of the consultation to both of us was the clarity of the 3D MRI image and the way the consultant could move the image around to see where the problem was. It was amazing technology, and it was good to get a diagnosis. Bren had been having physiotherapy on her back for quite a while without any success and this one picture would have avoided all those appointments because it clearly showed she needed surgery. The consultant recommended a discectomy, which is the most common surgery used for a herniated disc in the lumbar region. In this procedure, the portion of the disc that is causing the pressure on the nerve root is removed or trimmed, as he called it. An operation was booked for just two weeks later and this proved successful, alleviating a lot of the pain Bren had been getting for so many years.

Shortly after Bren's recovery from her surgery, I was referred to a consultant about my knee and he said I needed a knee arthroscopy. This is a surgical technique that can diagnose and treat problems in the knee joint. During the procedure they make an exceedingly small incision and insert a tiny camera, called an arthroscope, into your knee. This allows them to view the inside of the joint on a screen. During my surgery, the surgeon used this to investigate the problem with the knee and using small instruments within the arthroscope corrected the problem. I even had six small photographs taken of before and after the scrape, which he likened to a lunar landscape with craters, to then be somewhat flattened.

I did wonder how long it would take before I would be walking on my one and only knee again, but surprisingly to me, I did not find it too painful. In fact, I only stayed in overnight and even managed to walk with crutches the next day to the car. I soon recovered after the micro-surgery, which is much less invasive than normal open surgery, with the pain in my knee soon subsiding.

It was around this time I had a new prosthetist allocated to me at the Disabled Services Centre, called Steve. He was in his mid-thirties and was technically very able, always listening to you and explaining what he thought was the best approach and why. What I liked about him was he always listened to me, and between us we agreed the way forward. He would explain the dynamics and what was needed but he always kept an eye on any current innovative ways or new components to use. During one regular visit, my leg was being condemned, as they called it, because it was beyond reasonable repair. As an amputee you dread those words because they can never make two legs alike and you know there is pain and frustration ahead of you in changing over. What he suggested though, to cushion the blow, was a new technique in making the socket I sat in using a 3D laser scanner. He left the room and appeared with a laptop and a wand-like stick which he placed around all the nooks and crevices of my existing comfortable socket. These images were then transferred to the computer screen and my new socket miraculously appeared for a reverse cast to be made.

About six weeks later, I was called in for a first fitting of my new leg and, with the usual trepidation, put it on. I immediately felt how comfortable it was compared to the many other times when the socket had been handmade. It was an amazing improvement and saved hours of trial and error, which I had unfortunately become resigned to experiencing. It was one of the best innovations to happen for me, apart from the use of carbon fibre in the leg construction. I had never had a fitting go so well and feel so good after a visit. There were still lots of other things to sort out on the leg before it would be ready to take home because it is bespoke, but it was a giant step for me, if you pardon the pun.

From a health perspective, I have been fortunate apart from the cancer when I was sixteen, but the ravages of time take their toll on all of us. One day, I was in the garden sawing up some old fencing I had replaced, to enable me to burn it. I was really exerting myself doing this as it was a form of exercise because walking was so painful. The next day, I suddenly found my shoulder really aching and wondered what I had done. I went to the doctors and he prescribed a course of physiotherapy. I was able to go private and Rachel, the physiotherapist, was good, knew the body and its movements within its structure well. I initially made some good early progress through physiotherapy, with the pain reducing and my range of movement improving but then found the remaining symptoms had failed to respond further to treatment. I continued to struggle to sleep on my left side and lift heavy objects.

The resulting diagnosis was shoulder impingement syndrome, following referral to an orthopaedic consultant for further investigation. This syndrome involves tendonitis (inflammation of tendons) of the rotator cuff muscles as they pass through the sub acromial space, the passage beneath the acromion, if you want the formal medical analyses. Apparently, shoulder impingement is a quite common cause of shoulder pain, where a tendon inside your shoulder rubs or catches on nearby tissue and bone as you lift your arm. It happens through over exercise or just the ageing process, so I guess in my case it was both.

An operation proved necessary and it was booked in at the same local private hospital I had my knee scraped. It is amazing what they can do nowadays using keyhole surgery, otherwise known as arthroscopy. The operation is done using small surgical instruments passed through small cuts in the shoulder. I had three small cuts, no more than half an inch long, under general anaesthetic and was soon home being able to use my shoulder the next day.

Bren also needed another operation on her back to trim another disc and it coincided with me having an operation two weeks after hers. For some reason, she always reminds me her recuperation period was only two weeks as she needed to look after me. All I can ever say to her was what her mum used to say to her when she was a young girl helping her wash and clear up after a Sunday dinner, with all her brothers suddenly disappearing. Bren told her mum it just was not fair, all those boys just disappearing, and she was having to do the dishes. Her mum just said, and I quote, 'That's just the way it is.' So, I am sorry Bren about your recuperation period but 'that's just the way it is.'

Chapter 33:
Life and Death

Having both families combined means we have many grandchildren, which keeps getting added to with Lewis and Vicky assisting this with Lily. I knew how they felt having their first child and I knew how important it was for Brenda and Vicky's parents too, being their first granddaughter. A new life is so lovely to welcome into the family circle.

At the same time there is, within any family, the circle of life, and for my parents they were approaching the end of their lives. Nothing is forever and I suppose having faced the horrors of the World War they were both happy they had lived more than their three score and ten years. Their health was starting to gradually fail with Dad now using a walking stick. He was finding it so difficult climbing the stairs of Fratton Park to watch Pompey play football, a real struggle at times and we would wait until the crowds left before we made our way out of the ground. He eventually conceded he could no longer manage the stairs and would not be able to join me going to football, which we had done for fifty-two years. It was an incredibly sad day for both of us, I miss it tremendously, but I do treasure all those wonderful memories together.

In January of 2014 we celebrated Brenda's sixtieth birthday. Almost every woman loves surprises and Brenda is no exception. I decided to make this birthday fun, memorable and full of surprises. I told her I was taking her away somewhere for two nights and she should pack for both smart and casual wear. When she asked whether she needed her passport, I just said 'maybe', such was the build up to it. She hated not knowing but loved the intrigue and suspense of it all.

On Bren's birthday, I gave her a bracelet and five hundred pounds to spend on herself, knowing where she was going. I booked a taxi, which took us to the local train station, and we headed for London. Bren still did not know where she was going and this continued when we arrived at Waterloo because I got to the taxi rank before Brenda could hear where I wanted to go.

If you do not go to London very often, it is fascinating to see places you normally only view on the television, like the London Eye or Buckingham Palace, so Bren was really taking it all in. We arrived at number one Hyde Park in Mayfair where the five-star InterContinental London Park Lane Hotel was. It was a stunning hotel and Bren's beaming face said it all. We walked into the lobby going over to reception, where I said my name and the receptionist mentioned the name Davis. Bren asked, 'Why Davis?' and with a straight face, I said it was recommended by Joy. She seemed to believe this and just took in all the ambiance as we made our way up to the room on the tenth floor. We had been upgraded thanks to Joy, who worked for a large company involved in business travel and hotel bookings, amongst other things. Joy had done us proud as they say. The room was excellent and at six hundred pounds a night you would expect it to be. We had a corner view right over the 40-acre Serpentine Lake in Hyde Park and a perfect position for Horse Guards Parade. We unpacked and I suggested going to the seventh floor where the Club InterContinental bar area is exclusive for guests.

When we arrived, there were free drinks and we sat down looking over the superb view of the Serpentine. Suddenly, there was the singing of 'Happy Birthday to you' from behind us and Bren thought maybe the waiters were being nice as it was her special birthday. She turned round to see Keith and Joy there and we all laughed and hugged. What a wonderful surprise, and it had only just started!

In the evening, we hailed a taxi and went to a renowned steak restaurant called Gauchos. Keith and Joy are a very generous couple and insisted on paying for the meal, where the steaks alone started at fifty pounds each, without any side dishes. It was delicious but what was amazing to all of us was the place was full, even at those prices. It was a great start to the short break, and we made our way back to the hotel for a nightcap at the bar before the next day of surprises.

It was quite a whirlwind day of visiting I had planned, starting at Madame Tussauds in the morning, which I was really impressed with. There was the usual walk through, seeing the waxworks of the famous and infamous characters. Of course, we all posed for photos as we slowly moved through the rooms and got to a London cab ride through time. We got into a cab and slowly went through the history of London from the Roman beginnings of Londinium to the present day. It was such a unique way of seeing how London had changed through the ages, but it was over too quickly and now we had the torture rooms and dungeons to face.

The lights were dimmed and one of the guides to the dungeon entrance made sure there was nobody entering who had a dodgy heart, which meant to me there were frights ahead.

Keith was not daft, and he made Joy go first into the darkness, whereupon the shrieks started. You were being touched by someone or something jumping out of the shadows without seeing them, and out of the blackness things were dangled on you too. It was hilarious with both Bren and Joy screaming away and Keith and I glad we were behind them.

Bren had always wanted to go to the Tower of London where the crown jewels are kept, and I had previously booked tickets for the four of us to visit. We caught a taxi and made our way there. Unfortunately, I misread what I had booked because it turned out to be tickets for Tower Bridge not the Tower of London. It was interesting walking across the bridge and reading about the history of it, but I guess for Bren it wasn't quite the same as looking at the crown jewels, but we did laugh about my faux pas! She understands I am only a man!

To celebrate Bren's birthday in style we went to Claridge's for a champagne afternoon tea. Bren was really pleased to go here because she had previously been to The Savoy Hotel with her friends for tea a few years back. As we entered the lobby leading into the restaurant, we could not fail to be impressed by the floral display of red roses from the floor to the ceiling. It was magnificent and the service was everything you would expect of a five-star hotel. No sooner had you finished a sandwich or cake, they were replenished, and the choice of different teas was amazing. We toasted Bren's birthday in style with champagne and soaked in the ambience.

From Claridge's we caught a taxi to Victoria Palace Theatre to see Billy Elliott. After the show, we found a nice Italian restaurant just near to the theatre and with a couple of bottles of good red wine, we had a lovely meal reminiscing over all the things we had done during the day. I had one last surprise for Bren the next and final day.

After breakfast, we checked out of the hotel and said our goodbyes to Keith and Joy. They were great company and had really helped to make it a special occasion for both Bren and me. They were going shopping somewhere different to our final destination, and then catching the train to the West Country. We hailed a taxi and Bren gave me a look when I said, 'Harrod's please!'

Harrod's sells so many things, some of which are quite bizarre, but they do cater for all tastes. Bren had her birthday money to spend but after looking around for an hour or so we decided to get a coffee. The restaurant was just by the fresh fruit section and I could not help but notice just one pomegranate from Israel was seven pounds but it was all good quality food there. After we had finished, I got the bill and was amazed to find they charged twelve and a half per cent. service charge for two coffees, but I suppose it was Harrods! Although we looked around, we did not see anything to purchase and before we knew it the time had come to get a taxi to Waterloo, then a train back to Portsmouth. It was a memorable sixtieth birthday treat for Bren and one we will always remember.

This was also a good year for our granddaughter, Tayla. We had been watching her sing and dance since she was only four or five years old and always did very well in competitions. Anita was a good dancer, and she encouraged her daughter to do well all through those early formative years, improving year on year. In 2014, through all the family's hard work and of course Tayla's, she was in the team representing England in the Dance World Cup. This was in Portugal and she was

England's mascot. The competition from around the world was fierce but she won a silver and two bronze medals. Tayla performed even better the following year, in Romania, where she won a gold in tap dancing. This put her through to the Gala, where all gold medal contestants perform against each other, winning a gold there for the tap dancing. She is incredibly talented and the whole family are proud of her.

On Saturdays, we always went to Mum and Dad's house to see them, and as Dad could no longer go to football, we always played three games of crib together. Dad and his dad, my grandfather, had both taught me crib and I have always enjoyed playing the game. Dad and I were both evenly matched and we enjoyed playing together. Dad was getting frail but had done so well as he approached his ninety-ninth birthday. He struggled to lift his left arm and found it difficult to play crib; even feeding himself was proving difficult. It was a sad time to see him struggle like that and we had to stop playing crib. Mum was not well either, so we used to go to their house on a Sunday and cook a Sunday roast, which they enjoyed.

Mum was poorly with a water infection, needing hospitalisation and treatment to stabilise it and was in hospital for Dad's birthday. As a family, it was decided to have a family breakfast together on Dad's ninety-ninth birthday. Lots of us turned up and had a lovely breakfast with Dad. It was a great time recalling so many things done as a family together, through all those years, as we had so many wonderful memories to recall. It was a moment in time where everyone was really celebrating and recalling their memories together with Dad, and he loved it because of the importance of the family to him. Later, Donna even took Dad to the hospital, as a surprise, to visit Mum in hospital. Unfortunately, the infection Mum had confused her, and she did not recognise him, which disappointed Dad. The get together was over too soon and Dad's health continued to deteriorate throughout April. Mum was stabilised and allowed home from hospital, so they were together again.

Dad knew he would not have much longer on this Earth and spoke with all his children individually. He said some lovely personal things to me, and I thanked him for all the help and support he had given me over the years. 'I could not have asked for a better father', I told him, so it was a very emotional moment for both of us, heart-wrenching, knowing the end was near.

A few weeks later, on 5th May 2014 all the family met up again, it was unplanned and on a Saturday. It was like most Saturdays, where we were laughing and talking, when Dad started to cough and really struggle for breath. Margaret and I held him so he could sit up to breathe easier, but we knew it was serious and called the ambulance, which arrived within minutes. They helped stabilise him, and then got a portable wheelchair from the ambulance. He was carried into the ambulance, which was parked in the middle of the road outside, and taken to the local hospital, with Margaret travelling in her car to be with him. When he got to the hospital ward, Margaret recalled the conversation where he said to the nurse, 'My name is Alfred George Paffett, and I want to die.' He knew his time had come to an end and did not want a lingering end of life scenario. The next morning, and within twenty-four hours of the conversation with the nurse, Dad had passed away, with Margaret close by. It was the end of an era in which love, self-sacrifice and appreciation of the many small things in life played an enormous part for him. He loved and cherished his wife and family throughout his life as we, in turn, loved our dear Dad. Be at rest and know from all your children, you were a good man, a great father, the best we could wish for. We miss you every day.

Dad would have been so proud to have gotten his letter from the Queen to celebrate his one hundredth birthday but it was not to be, and life for the family would never be the same. He had a lovely service celebrating his life and the many good things he did in his life, filled with fun, laughter and love. The most difficult moment for me was waiting outside the crematorium chapel, where the undertakers had drawn up in their limousine, getting out and watching them lift his coffin onto their shoulders. I struggled to breathe, and my emotions were so raw, just looking at all that remained of my dear old Dad. Bren could see the state I was in and gripped me hard saying a few supportive words, bringing me back from the brink. She was marvellous and I do not know how I would have managed the day without her.

Mum was now, of course, on her own, with Margaret visiting her every day and carers were seeing her four times a day. The whole family was visiting regularly and Mum, being the old stalwart she was, never complained, but her condition was deteriorating with several medical conditions. She also had slight dementia, which I had noticed had started a few years earlier. The only comfort from this was her full realisation of Dad's passing, which otherwise might have been even more difficult. We were all trying to help Mum in those difficult times as she gamely struggled on with the beautiful smile she always had.

Both Arthur and Margaret had retired by now, and I was

fast approaching the decision to do the same. It was different for me because women used to retire at sixty and men at sixty-five, but a change in the law meant there was no retirement age now. I had always intended to retire at sixty, especially remembering Frank, my prosthetist, all those years ago telling me I would be lucky to make sixty because of the strain the artificial leg would place on my heart. It was just something I had never considered too much because I did enjoy my work, but then I knew I would be limited later in life with my leg and associated mobility, more so than if I was able-bodied.

Bren and I had been at our 'new' house for over fourteen years and I had produced some planned elevations to extend the property around three sides of the building. We decided to look around for another property but could not find anything we liked until one day we saw a property had just come on the market we both thought would be ideal. It was on a newish estate, in the north of Hayling Island just a few miles from Portsmouth and it had sea views too. I arranged a viewing with the estate agent who said there was a first viewing for someone just before us. We were just about to go and visit the house when a call from the estate agent said the other viewing couple had made an offer of the full asking price, which was accepted. We were quite disappointed, and so decided rather than move we would stay and have the extension. It was a big building project, and I had the plans formally drawn up and approved by the local council to enable quotes to be obtained.

I had been scarred by a builder on my very first house, so wanted to make sure I picked the right one for this job. I had four builders lined up to give me quotes, but only three turned up, and only two quoted. At the last minute, we had someone doing some internal work indoors, who had said to Brenda he knew a good builder called Gary and gave us his number. I phoned him and he said he would come around to look at the job. First impressions are always important and this builder we both liked, and I thought I could work with him. He had photos of his work and I asked him to quote. A week later, I had a quote from him on a single A4 sheet of paper and a value approaching six figures to do the work, which was comparable to one of the other quotes.

Bren and I talked and talked about the pros and cons of each builder and, with a leap of faith, we chose Gary to do the work. It took seven months to do and we had a lot of extras too, but it was a great decision to use him. He did a really good job, taking pride in what he did, and he only used good tradesmen too. We were really pleased, as it almost doubled our downstairs space. Bren did a superb job of the go-between and decision-maker between Gary and me whilst I worked away. She also had to put up with a lot of discomfort and mess during the building process, but never complained. I had it easy as I was in a hotel all week in Reading, enjoying their comforts and food.

I got up at five-fifteen a.m. , one Monday, to drive to Jacobs in Reading but the strangest thing happened to me as I got out of bed; I just fell on the floor. I had lost all sense of balance and felt quite sick. Bren was quite worried and helped me back into bed. I thought I would soon feel better, but it stayed with me. I really dislike staying in bed, so it was difficult just lying there. Bren had called the doctor in to see me, something I had never done before, and he came later in the day, diagnosing me with severe vertigo. He wrote me a sick note for two weeks as he said it may take some time to clear up, but if I felt better before then, I could return sooner. I got out of bed the next day but continuously felt nauseous and giddy, which is bad enough with two legs, but with one it is a nightmare. After two weeks of the symptoms persisting, I was given another two-week sick note and some tablets, which helped a little, but there was no way I could drive or return to work. It would take almost seven weeks before I was able to return to work and I had not had any personal sick time off work for over thirty years!

When I returned to work, I took a long hard look at my job as head of project services and who was replacing me when I retired. Our previous vice president, Conor, had been side stepped and in five years there had been four other VP's, much less able, in my opinion, than Conor, to lead us. The future work had not been forthcoming, and I no longer enjoyed working there. Companies, or rather the people in the companies who really reflect its values and direction, were changing, and certainly not in a positive way for me. I was not alone in my thinking as most of the senior management team felt the same way.

I had previously spent a morning at Jacobs in Reading with Iain, a senior manager working at the Heathrow airport expansion. He was moving onto a role in AWE at Aldermaston and I gave him a three-hour presentation on project controls. He thanked me after the meeting, and I went back to work. A few weeks later, I had a call from him asking if I would consider working for him on a freelance basis. It was decision time, and I thought a nice swan song to finish my career because the hourly rate negotiated was exceptionally good. I liked Iain and our individual skills complemented each other as part of a team. It felt good, so I accepted the offer and handed in my notice. I just needed to get a higher-level security clearance sorted, which would not take long as I had a lower-level clearance at British Energy.

It is a strange feeling when you hand your notice in because in most instances you are leaving for a reason or have been offered something better that cannot be matched by your current employer. It can also be very uplifting, having decided because you have not been too happy for some while. The time was right, so I looked forward to my new and final role in my working life, which was a strange thought as I moved on. In many ways, I miss the friends I have made in many places and many jobs, but I am sure I am not alone in this sentiment because it happens in every working life. At Jacobs, I will miss Jack, who was head of quality at the time. She was quite a character and we enjoyed each other's sense of humour. I remember one day at a high-level review meeting on projects she suddenly produced pastries and cold sausages she had got from the hotel she where was staying. Jack placed them on the table during the review and just calmly said, 'Help yourself'. There were some very funny times I will always remember.

When I started work at AWE it was nice to meet up with several people I had worked with in the past, especially Fred who was the manager of projects at Jacobs. He was following a similar freelance route to me, from there to AWE. One thing I usually have some trepidation about is the amount of walking from where I park the car to my place of work. We moved offices within the huge AWE complex quite a bit, so I was always mindful to get as close as I could to avoid these walking issues. The site at Aldermaston is huge and you are securely fenced in and surrounded by armed guards. If a meeting is called, it can be a long walk to get there so there is a site bus system to use. I used to take my car and park as near as I could to where I was going but parking and the amount of walking for me was an issue which I had to manage.

Iain soon got his team together and we were pulling together a way forward to change the business, which would benefit all the projects, both in managing and reporting. It was a major business change programme we were working on and it was novel for me. We spent many hours pulling this together and often went to the office complex at the Madejski Stadium of Reading Football Club to work and brainstorm the issues. One day, Iain had a phone call, and everything was thrown up in the air. The powers that be had decided to bring in Ernst and Young to streamline the systems and reporting. What we had done was not going to be used. It was devastating news to the team, and we were all demoralised from the call, Iain included. I think it was from that moment in time I started to think about retirement, having just had the rug pulled from beneath our feet. I decided to keep my head down for a few more months and just take the money!

At one stage after the planning manager left, I was asked to look after the planning department, amongst other things, and this was quite a task as there were around one hundred and thirty planning engineers there. I was also looking after all the project control managers too, so it was a busy time. I needed to improve the cost control expertise, so I invited Courtenay to join me there, which he did. His divorce was now going through as he moved on in his life and he also returned to his old house. He had been living with us most weekends for about five or six years and we got to know each other well. He knew our family too and was often there at family barbecues or other celebrations. He even took Dad to watch Pompey play when I was away on business. Courtenay will always be a good friend.

Since working away from home, I always had a curry (chicken dhansak) at least once a week. When Courtenay joined me at British Energy we would go for a curry on a Tuesday, and this continued when we worked together at Jacobs. There we were often joined by the Manager of Projects, Fred, and good friendships were borne. All three of us ended up working at AWE so the weekly visit to the restaurants to have a delicious curry continued. I miss those times when we put the world to rights.

Several senior Ernst and Young staff were integrated into the AWE team to understand the methodology of working so they could map the whole site process and propose improvements. There were more and more meetings, and we were going over a lot of old ground, which we, as a team, had already done, but I was just counting the months now. I spoke to one old employee who was not fazed by all the new changes taking place. He said laconically this was the sixth major change in the last twenty-one years. Every three years, they throw it all up in the air, rename things and 'shuffle the pack', as he put it. When it does not quite work, they start all over again and this major reorganisation was no different to the previous changes occurring. I know I could never have worked in a place like that for as long as he had.

At home, the extension was finally finished, and we were very pleased with the increased floor space it gave us. Bren and I enjoyed furnishing the whole of the downstairs and it was like a new house again. I had a new patio laid with raised beds put into the garden to make life easier for me to manage the flowers and vegetables I grew. I enjoy gardening and some of the physical effort required if I pace myself.

My dear Mum was not doing too well but always had that

lovely twinkle in her eye, along with a good sense of humour, which I think I inherited from her. She had some medical issues with her kidneys and life was becoming difficult for her. Mum was the stalwart matriarch of the family and we loved her for it, but it was so sad seeing the deterioration, especially after just losing Dad. Mum had carers in daily and with Margaret going there daily, she was able to spend those last days in her home. Margaret visited Mum and Dad almost daily throughout their lives and toward the end it really enabled them to live in their home rather than a nursing home. Margaret was exceptional in looking after them.

Mum did not have the love she gave us as a child from her mother. She was a twin, and her brother was always favoured by her mother. Mum joined the ATS (Auxiliary Territorial Service) during the war, working in an ordinance depot in Stevenage. It was dangerous work, but it was wartime and Mum told me she never felt more alive than when she worked there. We were all loved as children by our parents and Mum only had to give us one of her looks for us to stop in our tracks any mischievous deed we were doing. Mum joined the Salvation Army when she was only eighteen and stayed for another seventy-six years, during which she played the piano and organ, as well as leading the junior and senior choirs there. She did so many kind deeds during her lifetime, not just in the Salvation Army but including things like separately fostering the young girls, Beverley, Nora and Debbie.

Mum often went without her own dinner to feed her family as the early post war years were hard. As a growing rebellious teenager, I remember having this thing about onions and if I saw some in any meat, I would refuse to eat the dinner. We spoke and laughed about it later in life, which then must have been upsetting for her, but a mother's love is unconditional.

All the family knew how lucky we were to have such loving parents for so long in our lives, but time catches up with us all and it was our mum's time. She had been unwell and now needed a nursing home to safely look after her. The family had found a lovely place on the slopes of Portsdown Hill, just to the north of Portsmouth and only two or three miles from all her children. Her room was made homely with photos she treasured and there were lots of visits from friends and family. Within just a couple of weeks of being there, her condition worsened and in the early hours of 30th March 2015 she passed away from this life. All the family went to her bedside as soon as we heard to say their final goodbyes to a special lady, our mum, who we loved dearly and will miss for the rest of our lives.

Both Mum and Dad were ready to leave this life and had little fear of death as I spoke to them both about it. They were good people, good parents who lived good lives and what better epitaph can you give them. For all of us, it was the end of an era, not just losing our parents but also selling the family home we had grown up in and been visiting for over sixty years, but those wonderful memories filled with love will always live with us. Life will never be quite the same, but we recognise life is about change and how we adjust to it.

Chapter 34:
Retiree Apprentice

I had been planning my retirement for some time, originally planning to retire at sixty, however, as events transpired it was to be just after I reached sixty-five, at the end of July 2015. It is difficult to prepare for, but I had several things planned for my time, yet for me it was still the stepping off the cliff edge, as I likened it to. One day, you have all this experience of nearly fifty years at work and are at the top of your game only to never use the years of acquired knowledge again in a working environment. It takes some adjustment and although I had a few calls from contacts and agents to consider other roles, I knew it would have to be something special I really wanted to do.

There was of course Bren to consider in all this because it is also a major change for your partner too. She had, however, decided I was now a 'retiree apprentice', but unfortunately the number of years for this apprenticeship was indeterminate, she told me! Just as I thought I was in line for a credit pass or maybe a distinction, I was told I was in danger of not passing. Bren thought it highly amusing as she was the only assessor, and her decision was final! I did find giving her regular flowers helped a lot but there had to be action on my part to score high, which was the downside. I think she will send me a telegram when I reach one hundred years old to say I have just passed!

It was a new learning curve, this domesticity side of life, but I felt it only fair to now part share the workload, but I could never compete with Bren's energy and cleaning regime. I also remembered Dad's comment to me when I first married, he said, 'If you do a job well, you will do it for the rest of your life!' Marvellous insight from someone who was married for nearly seventy years.

It was a wonderful feeling, somewhat surreal, leaving Aldermaston on the last day of my working life but also quite uplifting for what lay ahead. I was financially secure and could now look forward to a relaxing time with Bren. I was also expecting to not get so much pain from my leg as I had been experiencing with all the walking and sitting down at meetings, but this was not to be.

Life for me at this time was unfolding in so many ways. My grandson, Luke, was now with Sharnice and they were celebrating their first baby, Oscar, my first great grandson. It really is amazing looking into the eyes of a new-born baby, wondering what life has in store for them, but as a first great grandchild it reminds you too of your own mortality and the circle of life and death, we are all in.

It was also a time to celebrate Keith's fiftieth birthday and he and Joy invited us to join them on a short break over to Vilamoura in Portugal. It was a lovely break being with them, and the hotel Joy had chosen was right by a marina full of restaurants. There is something about eating abroad at lunchtime which makes it so enjoyable, whether it be the continental food, the company you are with, the drink or beautiful weather I am not sure, but it was just the tonic.

We never ate at the hotel but went out and sampled the delights of the local restaurants. Being Keith's fiftieth, we all wanted it to be special and memorable, so a superb restaurant called 'Willie's', just a couple of miles from the hotel, was booked. The place is described as a bastion of discreet fine dining, serving international gourmet cuisine in an elegant atmosphere. It was a marvellous place where we enjoyed exquisite food and champagne to celebrate. It was one of those meals you will always remember, and it was lovely to celebrate with Keith and Joy.

The house was now finished inside and out, but I did want one more thing inside, which was a piano. Mum always wanted me to have her piano, but instead we gave it to the Salvation Army with a small plaque on it in memory of Mum. I bought a new one locally and have spent some time improving my playing skills, which, even now, are not brilliant but it's a nice hobby to have. What I like about playing is you can pick it up at any time interval from when you last played, whether it is days, weeks or months. I know Mum would have been thrilled that I bought one and it is a shame I will never play four hands piano duets with her again, but I will cherish the times we did, including her patience with me.

I had also planned to study certain cuts of diamonds. How many of us know what we are buying in a jeweller's shop? It is a leap of faith when you can part with thousands of pounds, so I thought, with a little knowledge, I could buy and sell diamond rings at auctions. We went to our first auction and I liked a particular catalogued ring, as did Bren. Two people were bidding for it and as one dropped out, I joined in, eventually buying the ring. I now needed to resell it but Bren took such a liking to it and asked if she could keep it. I thought, 'If this is going to happen every time, I am going to lose, not make money', so that was the end of that hobby!

Since losing both Mum and Dad, the Christmas get-togethers are not quite the same because it seemed an integral part of the celebrations being with them. It was about this time Margaret and Jeff were talking about a cruise trip to Norway, in March of 2016. Neither Margaret nor I travel on boats very well, but with the help of seasickness tablets we decided to go.

The cruise line went from Tilbury Docks in North London to Bergen in Norway and the weather could have been worse but there was quite a swell on that necessitated the tablets. Once there, we took lovely trips at various locations, but in Bergen itself the weather on the day we arrived was sunny. This was an opportunity not to be missed because it is a fact it rains on average two hundred and forty days a year there! I was pushed in a wheelchair and we headed for the funicular, which is basically two train carriages that have transported people up the mountain for over one hundred years. Being in a wheelchair, you go straight to the front of the queue, where it was only a short journey to the top, but the acute angle of the track makes it a unique experience. When we arrived at the top, the view over Bergen and the surrounding area was breath-taking on such a clear day. We were truly fortunate as there was no snow up there for me to slip on, and with the restaurant being open, we just sat outside enjoying the view with coffee and cake.

Some of the other trips were also quite spectacular, with one trip by train up a mountain, which passed a huge frozen waterfall which did not look real but was stunningly beautiful. At the end of the line, most people got to walk on the snow and ice to enjoy the views, but with my leg, snow and particularly ice are a real no-no, so I stayed on the train. The cruise was only for a week and soon over, but we were lucky with the weather to enjoy the scenic beauty of Norway. The trip back through the North Sea was a little rough and whilst Jeff, being an ex-mariner, said there was a slight swell, both Margaret and I took more sea sickness tablets. Bren is rarely troubled with sea sickness so helped me move around the boat as it navigated back home to Tilbury.

When I got back home, I needed once again to go the Enablement Centre, having been renamed from the Disablement Centre, for some repairs. This time I met a double amputee who was also a Paralympian competitor in running. He was getting some adjustments to his running blades, which are made from a special carbon fibre reinforced polymer. Having seen the latest design he was wearing, it made me cast my mind back about forty years ago when I saw someone with a wooden peg leg, just like Long John Silver used to wear. The fitter at the time said they were made of willow, but they were not making any more just maintaining it for the existing users. I have never seen one since but wondered what that person would have made of the running blade.

A similar experience occurred when I saw the first articulated artificial leg once belonging to Henry Paget, the 1st Marquess of Anglesey in 1830. He led the charge of the heavy cavalry at Waterloo and lost his right leg in one of the last cannon shots of the battle. It was made from lime wood and vegetable-tanned leather with a buff leather flap at the top of the thigh. The reason for mentioning it was the technology has hardly changed and when I saw it, I was quite amazed with the similarity of the current day legs.

The family continued to expand, with Lewis and Vicky having a son called Ryan, so Lily now had a brother, and we were so pleased for them. The grandchildren count was now eight, with one great-grandchild. The house they had in Woking was ideal for commuting to London but size-wise was quite small for a growing family and thoughts about moving to get a bigger house were in the air.

Unfortunately, I was still going quite regularly to the Enablement Centre and Steve, my prosthetist, was always keeping track of new, innovative designs for his patients. I believe he liked dealing with my leg because it is challenging and there are few about. He and the team were gradually making inroads to making it more robust, but it was taking ages to do and get right because there was an element of trial and error in the build. One day, he mentioned, that it may be worth considering a 'bikini-style socket' he had been reading about, which was one of the latest innovations to come out of the USA. He said someone who had a hip disarticulation had been trying it out in Manchester for the past six months with some success. The net result of this new limb was it was lighter, easier to put on and take off, but the big thing was you could walk for longer in more comfort. Hearing those words, I immediately said 'Yes, I'll try it.'

I have often thought about myself and how other people who have lost a limb would feel if they suddenly had their limb back. How euphoric it would be, how marvellous to do all those things you cannot do or are so restricted in doing. Just recently, I read of a person who had lost both hands five years ago and they did a double hand transplant with great success. It brought tears to my eyes when I thought of how exhilarated that person must be, and I felt their excitement at this new lease of life. I do believe in less than one hundred years from now, people like me will also have this, but it will be a lot sooner for those with lower leg amputations.

Steve had given me some literature and contact details for the man, called Damian, from Manchester who was trying out the new socket and working on improvements with the team up there. He had mentioned a more than ten per cent. improvement in walking capability but I thought even a few per cent. would be an improvement. I was keen and contacted Damian. We exchanged details and he wrote candidly about his hip disarticulation and the initial problems, refinements and improvements in his walking capability. He mentioned how minimal the socket is, which makes it much lighter to wear. It is also a lot more comfortable than the conventional socket as you are not as enclosed, so sweating is lessened. The straps were ratchet buckles tightening over the hips rather than across the abdomen, which means on the swing phase, when the leg is suspended, the drop-off of the leg is negligible, so control and gait are much improved. He also mentioned they would be casting me using a different technique which makes the socket fit a lot closer with minimal gaps. This prevents you from sliding around in the socket with less friction rub, again improving control and as a bonus the socket is much smaller.

There were many positives Damian went on to describe, like reducing his trouser size from a thirty-eight to a thirty-four simply due to a much smaller socket. He also said, in terms of his walking gait, it had improved massively and a large reduction in effort, which was music to my ears. It was amazing to me when he said he can walk a mile in twenty minutes, which is three miles per hour, something I only dreamed about. It was a life-changing improvement for him and a difficult transition from a bucket socket requiring a lot of determination and effort to adapt. Damian gave me encouragement to be open-minded and persistent and try to give as much feedback as I could to my prosthetist during the dynamic fitting process, as they will be learning too.

I went back to Steve and said I would really like to try this. It was an exciting, promising time for me, and I was thinking of the potential walking I could do by myself and with Bren. Within a couple of months, I had an appointment for my first fitting. The leg itself was about two-thirds of the weight of my existing artificial leg and the fitting around my waist was a ratchet system, different from the Velcro straps. It had to be pulled extremely tight into your body so there was no movement between your socket and the skin. My existing strap just went around my waist, but the new leg had straps or supports from the back of the leg over each hip which were ratcheted very tight. It was so tight I could hardly breathe, and when I took my first few steps in the rails it was not the improvement I had expected.

Together, over a few months, we tried various ways to improve the leg to suit me but, in the end, I had to concede it just was not suitable for me. I believe it is a great improvement for those with hip disarticulation, but it is not suitable for those, like myself, with a hemipelvectomy. The reason being on the bikini style leg, the straps secured from the back of the leg fits over both hips and are ratcheted into a very tight secure position. Part of my right hip bone was removed in my amputation and so I do not have the same support a hip disarticulation amputation has. Steve and I were disappointed with the outcome but, as they say, it is better to have tried and lost than never to have tried at all.

Chapter 35: New Challenges

The year 2017 was a busy year, in many ways, because there were some life-changing decisions made. When I say life changing, I really mean decisions which gave us a completely different direction for spending quality time together.

Having lost our cat 'Spikey' and having no pets around us, life seemed rather quiet indoors. Bren will tell you she is a 'free spirit' and loves nothing more than an open road or forest to walk in, something I would really love to join her in but is impossible for me. We had seen the motorhome her brother, Chris, and his wife, Barbara, had down in Paignton, Devon, and the thought of having one herself had obviously lodged itself in her mind, for the freedom of the road she craved. We thought it would be good to go to the Motorhome and Caravan Exhibition at the NEC in Birmingham to look at what was on the market. We had a list of imperatives for the motorhome, such as an automatic transmission, not too wide to go up the driveway and so on.

An exhibition in the previous November resulted in us identifying the type of motorhome and finish we wanted. When visiting those places, there is so much to see you can easily get spoilt for choice with the huge selection and not end up deciding. We knew what we wanted and were actively looking for the right one to come on the market. The model we chose was a Lunar Landstar EWS on a Mercedes chassis. The finish was head and shoulders above the competition, but you had to pay for this. I thought I would try and get one that was one or two years old but there weren't too many on the market and when they appeared, they were snapped up very quickly. It was frustrating but we continued to look.

Bren and I had some discussions about a new pet, be it a cat or even a dog. Bren was wary about having a dog and understandably so as she had been bitten by an Alsatian when she was only eight years old that left a scar on her hip. I had previously had dogs and really missed them because they are so affectionate, giving you unconditional love. I knew Bren would love a dog, but it had to be the right breed and the right size. We started off looking at cats, thinking about another Devon Rex like Spike but then moved onto dogs. Again, you are spoilt for choice with so many breeds, but it had to be a smallish dog for Bren. We thought of small breeds and a sausage dog came to mind, so we looked at the available images. They are so cute and of course there are different varieties such as smooth haired, wire haired, miniatures, standards and so on. Bren seemed to focus on a wire-haired dachshund and liked the miniature type. I looked at the Kennel Club for breeders but there were not many close by and one, forty miles away was not breeding for another six months. It was frustrating because there were few reputable breeders with the dog we wanted in the whole of England.

Bren had a family friend, called Susan, who had a couple of rescue dogs and Bren did get on well with those dogs. Susan suggested there was a Dachshund Rescue Centre, and it may be worth phoning them. I soon found the number and phoned them. Having a dog from the rescue centre requires you pass a certain criterion to prove you are, or will be, a responsible owner. Following an initial conversation, there was a form to be filled in for final approval. Questions like your garden size, whether it is enclosed, if you had dogs before and so on. I fully understood the reason for the questions because they did want the dog to go to a good home after the poor thing's initial owner experience. After a short time, we were accepted but disappointingly told the waiting list was two years long and they would be in touch later!

We resigned ourselves to a long wait, however, a week later we had a call from the rescue centre to say someone had been in touch to say they had two wire-haired dachshunds that were needing to be re-homed. One dog was a major decision for us but two! We were told, though, we could decide which one we liked and go from there.

We were given contact details of the owner and phoned them. Conversations like this are two-way because we wanted to be sure the dog was right for us and conversely, they wanted to make sure we were going to be responsible owners, providing a loving, safe home for their dogs. Angela, the owner, was a lovely person and explained she had over-indulged in her love of dogs because she now had nine. There were six pugs, which she had previously bred from, a golden retriever and two wire-hair dachshunds. She said she was seventy now and had to think about the future and decided the two dachshunds had to go to a loving home. We arranged to go and see them, which turned out was about ninety miles north of Portsmouth in Oxfordshire. Apparently, she had a rented cottage on the Blenheim Estate and just opened her back gates where the dogs all ran out for their walks. They could use five hundred and fifty acres of the two thousand acres of the estate to exercise in, such an idyllic setting compared with someone like me born and bred in a town environment.

We arrived in late January to see the dogs and from the road we entered a track for about three-quarters of a mile to a farm with two cottages, one of which was Angela's. As we drove up toward the cottages there was a cacophony of sound with nine dogs barking away at rarely seen strangers. Angela greeted us at the fenced frontage and after smoothing and petting nine dogs, we made our way into the cottage. Angela separated the other dogs so just the two dachshunds were there to greet us and we could fuss over them. One was a bitch called Erica and the other a dog called Gerald, brother and sister from the same litter. They had impeccable Kennel Club lineage and looked such attractive dogs, so full of character. Angela mentioned an older man had previously come to look at the dogs, but she was not comfortable in him giving them sufficient exercise, so she decided against him having one.

We were at a crossroads of a decision being made. Angela talked about us and how we would be looking after the dog. We were trying to decide which dog, if any, to have. We had a nice cup of tea, fussed over the dogs, and spoke a lot with Angela, who was happy for us to have a dog. Then she said, 'You could always have both if you wanted.' We looked at each other and thought, 'Wow! There is a decision to be made here'.

We drove home and our minds were in turmoil to make a major decision we would both be happy with. We could not decide and agreed we would sleep on it to decide the next day. That night was one of the longest I had experienced in a while, as it was for Bren too. All the scenarios of either none, one or two dogs were played out in my mind time and again that night. In the cold light of morning, I said we should just have one dog, but which one was the question and surprisingly Bren agreed. I went downstairs and ten minutes later when Bren came down, she said, 'I cannot separate them, and I think we should have two.' I said, "I agree' and the decision was made just like that.

We contacted the Dachshund Rescue Centre and part of the agreement was the bitch had to be spayed as the other dog had already been neutered. They said they would pay for it, but we said we would pay for the operation and give them a donation too. The market price for each of them with their pedigree would have been well in excess of one thousand, five hundred pounds each so it was only right to do this.

We made arrangements with Angela to collect them, and she was delighted we were having both, so they weren't separated. We were so happy to collect them, but it must have been hard for Angela seeing them go. It was a long journey for them in the car, but they travelled well and once home, they ran around and around the garden, sniffing everywhere.

The first night they whined a little due to the strange environment and a completely different bedding arrangement in our kitchen. They must have missed their seven other dog companions too, but soon adjusted to the new way of living. They were now part of our family and we had adventures to have.

An additional grandchild, called Piper, was born to Jamie and Carla in March of 2017. Everyone was so happy for them because they had been trying for many years to have a baby without success and now the IVF had worked. Having a baby and being there for the birth is right up there for me as one of the highlights of my life. For Jamie and Carla, it was the same because they had been trying for so long and it was marvellous to see their happy faces when we went to the hospital to cuddle the newly-born baby. Piper was grandchild number nine and a beauty.

Vicky and Lewis had decided on an area to move to, between Vicky's parents' house and ours with good schooling. They found a new build site and were amazed at what you could get for your money compared to Woking house prices. They ended up buying a new five-bedroom detached house with so much more space than the Woking house. In fact, they said they were lost in it for many months as they adjusted to the size, but it was ideal for the new children's school and being close to their grandparents.

We had made the bold decision to buy a motorhome and the model we were after suddenly appeared in an outlet in Eastbourne, about seventy miles east of Portsmouth. I phoned them and they said it had only arrived five days earlier, so I made an appointment to view it. When we arrived, we viewed it and went for a test drive. I had never driven anything this size before. It weighed three and a half tonnes and was over seven metres long, but I managed it. What amazed me most was how comfortable the driver's seat was with its armrests, it was just like sitting in an armchair at home. We negotiated a price, but I was not happy with it, so we had the brinkmanship period during which we left the salesroom and got into our car. The salesman came running out and said he could meet me halfway between his final offer and my best offer. We shook hands and agreed a price. Life was going to change for both of us and the dogs with the new motorhome.

I had another new challenge to face, which to some is not

a challenge, although I am sure many will understand the dilemma. It was whether to buy a mobility scooter or not. I try not to think of myself as disabled as I have tried to do the absolute best I can with the limitations I have. My innermost thoughts said for me, to be seen on a mobility scooter was like having a sign saying, 'Look at me, I am disabled'. I really had to think about why I thought like this as it has been a lifetime of trying, as best I could, to hide my disability.

The dogs had no leash training as they were so used to running with the pack on the Blenheim Estate so they could not run freely and exercise themselves. All their walking was being on a leash and I just could not walk far at all, so it fell on Bren's shoulders to do this, not that she minded. If I had a scooter, I could go with her on some of the walks and she really encouraged me to buy one. This made sense so, somewhat reluctantly, I bought one, which I could break down into five pieces enabling me to put it in the boot of the car if needed.

The dogs seemed happy in their new environment, and Bren's initial concerns about meeting other larger dogs with them was getting easier. We decided to rename the dogs, Alfy and Peggy, instead of Erica and Gerald, after my dear mum and dad. I am sure they would have approved and laughed at the idea. When you are outside and calling your dogs, we found Alfy and Peggy rolled off the tongue much easier than Erica and Gerald.

Both dogs loved the motorhome and our adventures started with our first visit to Norman's Bay in Pevensey about sixty-seven miles east of Portsmouth. Every site we went to had to accommodate dogs and be good for dog walks. In fact, every site we have ever visited I have logged in a book to give a rating out of ten. This rating covered things for and against the site, including observations and price. Although we had a shower and toilet on board, I did use the disabled facilities on most sites every day. These were mostly of a high standard but where there weren't these facilities, it proved quite difficult for me to take my leg off and put it on afterwards.

Alfy and Peggy, being wired-haired dachshunds, were bred originally in Germany for badger hunting, so they loved the countryside and sniffed everything as they walked. In fact, rather than call it a walk with the dogs, we called it a 'sniffari'. One of the early trips was to go to a campsite on the Isle of Wight, which is only five miles south of Portsmouth across the Solent. The dogs stayed in the motorhome as we travelled across the sea for the short forty-minute journey. The island is quite small, measuring twenty-three miles by thirteen miles and we soon arrived at the Adgestone Club Site. There are often narrow roads leading to the campsites hence the timing of not arriving before midday or thereabouts was essential because this enables those leaving the site easier access to drive out. I must admit to scraping the side of the motorhome with the odd hedge here and there, mainly because the roads are so narrow when you meet large oncoming vehicles. Occasionally, I did lapse into thinking I was driving my car and forgetting the width of the motorhome. To this end, I asked Bren to occasionally remind me if I was seen to drift towards the nearside too much.

We travelled around the country quite a bit the first year we had the motorhome, visiting several sites and learning an awful lot about site etiquette and the motorhome itself. It seemed every time we used the motorhome, we would learn something new about it or additional storage areas hidden away. It was quite a learning curve as we were novices to camping but it was an adventure for sure.

Bren had never been to Scotland, so we planned a two-week visit around Loch Lomond, Loch Ness, up to Aberdeen then back to the Lake District and back home. We decided it best to go in October to avoid the midges and we arranged to meet up with Fred and his wife, a good colleague I worked with at Jacobs, who lived in Glasgow. We had a lovely lunch at a beautiful hotel overlooking Loch Lomond in an idyllic setting, which was a great start to our Scottish adventure. Scotland is a beautiful part of the UK, but it does rain a lot and we did experience some during the holiday. The dogs just loved their walks, three times a day and all the different scents around. At every campsite, there seemed to be rabbits everywhere, so the dogs were always excited by them, with, of course, the occasional duck waddling by.

The journey and the many stopovers we had were tremendous experiences. There was a campsite we stayed at on the shores of Loch Ness and although the dogs kept watch they never had sight of the legendary 'Nessie'. One memory though was staying on the grounds of a pub called the Harbour Bar in Aberdeenshire. The view from the car park where we parked looked directly onto a shoreline of craggy outcrops of stone in a wild sea full of foam. The rise and fall of the tides were something to behold and there was a wild beauty to it. We had a drink in the pub and asked for some hot food, but they did not have any and recommended a place just across the road, which sold fish and chips downstairs and had a restaurant upstairs. We went upstairs to the restaurant, which was quite busy, and looked at the menu full of different fish dishes. I noticed they were serving lobster so we both agreed to have that with a good bottle of white wine. It was delicious, and we thoroughly enjoyed it. One of the real benefits of a motorhome is you can just crash out when you want. We were now rather inebriated and decided to get the bed out and have a nap overlooking the crashing waves all around us. It was a very memorable stopover in many ways.

In the evening, after Bren had walked the dogs along the beach, we went and got some good fish and chips, eating them in the motorhome. We never expected the food to be so good, which was a real bonus. In the morning, we headed south, past Edinburgh on the east coast to Beadnell Bay Club Site, where we stayed for one night, before heading west across to Crook in the Lake District. We stayed on the grounds of the Sun Inn pub and had another excellent meal with some delightful pink gins. The only downside, literally, was the car park, which was on a slope, so sleeping on a slight incline is somewhat odd, but the gins helped us to get to sleep.

We travelled the next day, back to another site south of Worcester before driving home the next day. We had travelled nearly two thousand miles in just over two weeks and Bren, Alfy, Peggy and I had a completely different holiday with many things to remember.

Chapter 36: Dogged Adventures

By now, the dogs were an integral part of our family and most days we went out together, unless it was raining, every morning with me using my mobility scooter, walking the dogs. The Three Lakes in Milton is a lovely place to walk the dogs and is just a few hundred yards from where we live. There is a tremendous array of wildlife there and the mud flats are a site of special scientific interest for the wading birds. Dark-bellied Brent Geese are winter visitors from Siberia and when they fly around the feeding grounds it is a wonderful sight.

Keith and Joy were visiting us from Somerset one day and walked with us around the Three Lakes with the dogs. The dogs were off their leads when Peggy got the scent of something and went headfirst into a huge area of brambles. It is almost impenetrable for a human but for smaller dogs it is a possibility. The problem is, it is so dense in there, a dog cannot always turn around so has to walk backwards to get out. This bramble patch was a least fifty metres square and we could hear her distressed bark somewhere in the middle of this. Bren had shorts on, and the brambles are full of thorns, so she was getting cut to ribbons. Keith and Joy were in there too, trying to find a way through to Peggy. It took forty-five minutes to locate her and get her out, so this marked the beginning of Peggy's adventure here and there.

Peggy and Alfy love their walks but their recall is not good, in fact sometimes it is non-existent. Alfy is slightly better than Peggy, but it still leaves a lot to be desired. Peggy seems to have the desire to catch a seagull and will chase them, even in the mud. Thank goodness she has never been successful; this, however, has not deterred her in any way. We let them off their leads in certain locations to give them a little freedom, but on this day, Peggy decided she wanted seagull pie. Off she went chasing them, completely oblivious to our calls and whistles. Alfy stayed with us and seemed bemused by all the intensity of our calling. The reason being she had gone out in the mud, it being low tide, to chase a seagull. When she got within about twenty feet of the said seagull it just flew another fifty yards along the shoreline. This, Peggy must have thought, was a challenge, which she readily accepted and so the chase continued.

The pathway along the shoreline ran parallel to where Peggy now was, about two hundred and fifty yards away from us in the mud. We followed her for about four hundred yards, but no amount of calling distracted her from the seagull she so wanted to catch. The shoreline has a pub overlooking the harbour and Peggy continued past this into an inlet. She had gone well over half a mile in the mud with Bren trying all sorts of things now as desperation set in, from calling, whistling, even barking like a dog to get her attention. Finally, another dog appeared on the shoreline, barking away, and this distraction caught Peggy's attention as she headed towards the other dog, which was near Brenda. Fortunately, a neighbour, Ethel, who was walking her dog, had a spare lead and Bren was able to put this over her bedraggled, muddy head. We got her home and bathed her because the smell of Langstone harbour was well entrenched in her coat. She slept well that day, but little did we realise this adventure was nothing compared to what was to come.

In January of 2017, Arthur reached the ripe old age of seventy and the close family were invited to a pub in Whiteley, which is about eleven miles west of Portsmouth. It was nice catching up and celebrating all together, and it almost felt as if Mum and Dad were there enjoying the evening, as we had done so many times before over the years. This evening of celebration reminded me of a time when I was around thirteen and a neighbour across the road was having his seventeenth birthday. I thought then how old seventeen was, and here we were having Arthur's seventieth , but it is all relative, with time waiting for no man.

Later in the year, Lyn and Arthur celebrated their golden wedding anniversary and they hired a large dining room at a lovely hotel in Whiteley. To make it a little special he requested we all wore dinner jackets or lounge suits. It was fun dressing up because it was only at Christmas company functions, we wore our dinner jackets and attire. It was a super evening with around thirty or forty friends and family seated around several tables for a sit-down meal. There was a lot of talking, catching up and of course laughter. I enjoyed seeing Christy, Dave, Kerry and Stewart and their children. My two nieces had both done well academically. Christy was a teacher and Kerry, who had continued her education after getting her degree, had got her MSc. and was a social worker. They both had their families too so there was a lot to catch up on and it was a celebration to remember.

In February of 2018, we wanted to get some sun, as did Arthur and Margaret, so all six of us went away to a resort in

Spain, not far from Benidorm. It was good to have a break and spend time with the family because we always have fun together. We were lucky because only three months earlier we had got back from a week's break in Tenerife. At times, retiring seems to be one holiday after another, but I remember when I was working, I would always be checking the phone for emails and toward the end of the holiday my mind would be getting ready for work mode. With retirement, you just continue to relax knowing those days are well and truly behind you.

In May 2018, we went to our favourite Canary Island destination, Lanzarote for another week's break and started to plan an adventure in the motorhome to France later in September. I really like France with their quality food, drink and laid-back lifestyle. In fact, I did think about buying a holiday property there but that does tie you down to one place.

In the July of this particular year, we went on a river cruise from Budapest to Strasbourg with Arthur, Lyn, Margaret, and Jeff. There was no seasickness on a river cruise just miles and miles of smooth water with the occasional loch, historic town, and castle to admire. It was a great holiday but not so good for me going on the occasional trips to the local riverside towns. Most of these towns are old and steeped in history, having existed for hundreds if not thousands of years, along the meandering Danube River, which was once the long-standing frontier of the Roman Empire. The roads built during medieval times were invariably made from cobbled stones, which for someone like me with an artificial leg is difficult to walk on. Not that I could walk far anyway, so we took the wheelchair and believe you me it is a most uncomfortable journey in a wheelchair over cobbled stones. In some instances, it is impossible to push someone in a wheelchair so that was disappointing. I also must consider those pushing me as it does take some effort, especially on an incline, and the years are taking their toll on all of us with different ailments. In fact, with Bren having her second back operation, and then having to push me in a wheelchair, on the odd occasion it was another reason for me getting a mobility scooter.

The one visit I really enjoyed was going on a coach trip to see the baroque palace at Wurzburg in Germany. It is a magnificent building, built in the mid-eighteenth century, with stunning architecture but there are also beautiful gardens to see too. We all enjoyed the visit, but I am always reminded, when visiting these opulent buildings, of the hardship endured by the peasants or poor of the time. They were often starving, and I just wonder about their thoughts of inequality and acceptance of their station in life.

We were soon home, having had a memorable river cruise along the Danube, but those cobbles have put me off river cruises for a little anyway. We now had our planned French trip in the motorhome to get ready for in September. The amazing thing about France is their 'low season' starts at the end of August when the children return to school so it is cheaper to go then and still get magnificent, almost guaranteed good weather. The cost of the campsites for sixteen days was half the cost of transporting the motorhome on the ferry from Portsmouth to Le Havre and return. It was quite a cheap, memorable holiday.

The French have a good motorway system but invariably they are tolled but it is so quick to use them, providing stress free driving. When we landed at Le Havre, we headed west to a site called Les Sept Îles at Trelevern, where our pitch had a magnificent view overlooking the whole bay. We stayed there for seven nights, exploring the local area and the dogs sniffed and sniffed. Bren is a good cook, so we had some super meals al fresco.

The only problem, if you want to call it that, is me being somewhat static at the sites because I cannot walk with Bren when exercising the dogs, so it is limiting for me. The motorhome was not big enough to carry my mobility scooter and the only way would be to have a trailer to carry it in but for me driving the motorhome is sufficiently challenging without a trailer.

We set off for our next destination at La Cote de Beaute, which is due south and about three hundred miles away, so quite a journey. There were plenty of places and picnic areas to stop and walk the dogs, who travel very well. It was a nice, shaded site with large trees and only one road to cross for the sandy beach. We went out touring most days in the motorhome and the weather was excellent. Locally, there was a fish restaurant which all the locals used and was recommended to us, so we decided to try it one lunchtime. It was a long walk for me, but I knew we would be there for a couple of hours before the return journey, and it was nice to walk along the promenade with Bren.

My French is not good, and it came into play when we got to the restaurant because you had to queue up in front of the counters with fresh fish and shellfish on display, then when your turn came, to order your food. The place was full and what you order is weighed, you pay, then make your way out back to a table in a large, seated area. I ordered four large langoustines each and a nice bottle of chardonnay. We were bathed in glorious sunshine; the wine was superb and with no worries we enjoyed this exquisitely French meal with the locals. When the meal arrived, it was just the langoustine on ice and nothing else, no salad or side dishes, just some plain bread. I wished my French were better, but we just laughed, drank some more wine, and indulged ourselves. It was so French and so memorable.

After the meal, we took a slow stroll back to the campsite and although I suffered for a few days from this exertion it was well worth it. There were some lovely places to visit but we both like to go to the local supermarkets or hypermarchés, as they call them. I find it interesting to see the prices of things compared to back home but what the French do well is the way they prepare and show their meat. We bought some excellent fillet of lamb and there was no fat to be seen on it. We then bought some cutlery, pots, pans and some wine. The wine was in a wooden case and for less than twenty euro you got six bottles. When we went to pay for everything, I asked how much the wine was, and it turned out the bottles were twenty euro each. I decided not to take them!

When you return to England, having taken a dog abroad to France, you had to, by law, get them seen by a vet. He examines them, gives you some ringworm tablets, stamps a form and charges you forty-five euro each for the service. Without this, you cannot bring them back to England as they strictly apply the rules. This must be done between one and five days of your return. We asked at the campsite if they could recommend a vet and eventually in a built-up area, we found his practice. We were lucky to be able to park outside because the long motorhome is not always easy to park in a residential area.

We were coming to the end of our French excursion and had one last site to get to. I planned it so it was only about fifty or so miles from Le Havre for our journey back to England. The site was called Domain du Logis at La Chappelle aux Filtzmeens and was rated five stars. We were booked in for just the one night, but I wished we had booked longer as it was an excellent site. There was lots of space, a large outdoor swimming pool, free Wi-Fi, tremendous dog walks, but above all else a superb restaurant, where we once again indulged in the delights of French cuisine and wine.

The return ferry journey was overnight, and I booked a dog-friendly cabin. The dogs, when not in the motorhome, had to be muzzled, which they did not take too kindly to, but we eventually found our way to the cabin, passing a few dog owners along the way. Some of the dogs never had muzzles on board so they did not enforce the rule very well, which was annoying. The dogs did not like the journey, the noise on board, the swaying of the boat or the room we had, and never settled very well, but it was a small price to pay for our French adventure. The joy of living in Portsmouth is once the ferry docks it is literally a ten-minute drive to get home.

In December of 2018, we travelled to Lanzarote for a week's break in the sunshine. Not only was it nice to catch some sun, but it also gave Bren a rest from walking the dogs three times a day, every day. I decided not to get some airport assistance at Bournemouth Airport because it is quite small and not too far to walk. I did request assistance at Lanzarote because as the airport has expanded over the years so has the amount of walking from the plane to the carousel.

I do find walking in hot temperatures difficult compared to cold because the body sweats more and the socket of the leg seems to further rub, causing problems. We did not take the wheelchair this time as I had made some enquiries about hiring a mobility scooter. I only hired it for three days as a way of seeing more than I would normally, and to be with Bren rather than just be inside the hotel complex. It worked out well as they brought the scooter to the hotel and I could charge the battery in the hotel foyer or our room.

Bren has always encouraged me to hire a scooter in the past, but I have been reluctant to. Now I can be with her on her shopping expeditions so maybe there was always a subtle ulterior motive. It is, however, a nice break from the hotel as we have been on many of the coach trips they recommend before to see the island and its culture. It was a good break before Christmas and looking back, it had been a busy and eventful year so was useful to recharge the batteries for whatever 2020 brought.

Even though I was now retired, we still have a routine and after the holiday we soon fell into ours. The dogs have always been exercised by Bren three times a day and it has certainly made her a lot healthier, she readily admits. Before we got the dogs, she had been a size twelve/fourteen, but she is now size eight/ten and admits to feeling so much better. It was a lovely sunny August 2019 day and we again ventured over to the Three Lakes to exercise them. I had, by now, acquired another mobility scooter with pneumatic tyres and it was faster than my other one, so it helped make it a more comfortable drive. We were walking the dogs without their leads on assuming Peggy's past misdemeanours were a thing of the past and she had learnt her muddy lesson. This turned out to be a false assumption.

On this day, we had Lily and Ryan, our grandchildren, who had an overnight stay with us, so they were having fun. As we all passed Swan Lake and turned the corner, Peggy always got excited to see the sea and perhaps chase a seagull. We fatefully decided not to put her lead on and both dogs were happy running along the shoreline path. We saw a few other dog walkers, many of whom you got to know and talk to, and suddenly, after a brief chat to another couple, we could only see Alfy. We looked around, then heard a bark as Peggy raced across the mud flats chasing seagulls. You could not fault her determination in chasing them, only her recall capability was very questionable. She just would not come back and totally ignored us because of her seagull mindset.

We called out 'treats', to no avail, tried whistling, to no avail, shouting at her, to no avail. She moved further and further away from the shore as the tide was low and we noticed she was sinking a little in the mud. It was a good job she only had little legs because she was able to slither across the mud. Her determination to get a seagull knew no bounds as she continued running and sliding, even swimming in some of the little channels which had formed far in the distance as the tide had receded.

A couple of ladies who we knew well were jogging by and as they always made a fuss of the dogs, they stopped to see if they could help. They called and said they would wade in to try to get her. We said not to as the mud can be dangerous there, but they insisted. They waded in and got about five metres out whereupon the thick, oozing mud was making them sink up to their knees. They had to come back and by this time Peggy was a pin prick in the distance about four hundred and fifty meters away toward the main channel in the harbour. Bren made the decision, unbeknown to me, to call the coastguard, and to their credit they were there within thirty minutes.

While we were waiting for the coastguard's arrival,

several other dog-walkers had seen what was going on and the predicament we were in. A lot of them knew Peggy and at one point there were eleven dog-walkers watching, and many were calling her name. It was somewhat surreal I must admit.

Eventually, the coastguard vehicles arrived at the point of the war memorial area. There were three in total and about eight guys, which was surprising. By this time, Peggy was floundering because her whole coat and face were covered in mud, but she was still several hundred yards offshore. They caught glimpses of her with their binoculars, between the mud gullies and they said they were concerned how far they could go out in the mud because they only had four hundred metres of rope. This memorial area has several benches, which, by this time, were full up with spectators and dog-walkers watching the proceedings unfold. It was such a spectacle, and it was our dog causing it!

Bren had decided to take Alfy home, and I was trying to also look after the grandchildren and assist the coastguards. Out of the blue, Carla appeared with Piper, asking what was going on as Bren had briefly passed her and explained what was happening. She was able to help with the grandchildren, which was great and made things much easier.

The coastguards had a loudspeaker on the top of their vehicle, and they suggested using this to call her. I started the first calling and looking around I found the audience of around forty people laughing and cheering me on. Some days you just want to forget! My calling fell on deaf ears and when Bren tried, that too failed. They asked if we had some dog treats as they had decided two of them in full gear may be able to reach the dog with ropes attached. The treats were there to tempt Peggy to them, who, by this time, had headed back towards us, but we all thought she was totally disoriented.

They set off with full audience support and about one hundred metres out, enticed Peggy to come to them for a treat. One grabbed hold of her in their arms and carried her to shore whilst the audience gave thanks with a round of applause to show their appreciation of a good show and first-class entertainment. We were so relieved to get her back and Carla, with the help of the memorial area keeper, helped bathe Peggy and get some of the mud off her face and body.

The crowd were now dispersing as the entertainment was over, I had profusely thanked the coastguards for all their help and Bren had just returned. What a morning and to cap it all, the next day there were photos and a narrative on the coastguard's Twitter account with a piece on page six of the local Portsmouth News about Peggy. Such was Peggy's claim to fame and she still never got her seagull.

Our friends, Mano and Gita had sent us a wedding invitation for Sunil, who was marrying Lindsey in August of 2019, which was lovely to receive, having known him and his younger brother Sanjay from a young age. Both are doctors and associate professors and were well educated at Oxford and Cambridge University, respectively. Their wedding service was going to be at Trinity College Chapel, Cambridge with the speeches and dinner at the main hall of King's College. We accepted the invitation and were both excited to not just be part of the family celebrations but to see Cambridge University and its grounds too.

Gita had booked several rooms at the Stephen Hawking building, where the students stay, for her guests and offered us one of these. We booked in for two nights because the day after the wedding, there was to be another ceremony at the Hilton

Hotel alongside the banks of the River Cam. I could park close to this building so it was ideal, and Gita had arranged transport for those guests staying there so I didn't need to worry about parking near the university, which would have been difficult.

The journey to Cambridge took a little longer than anticipated with the usual M25 traffic jams to get through but we made it eventually. The next morning, we had breakfast then changed into our wedding attire and made our way to the reception area, where we got to know everyone as we waited for the seven-seater taxi to take us to the university. Neither Bren nor I had been to Cambridge before, which is steeped in history, beautifully maintained and has that medieval air about it. It was packed with tourists as we drew up to the old gates at the university and made our way through the grounds toward Trinity College Chapel.

Just walking through the hallowed grounds was awe inspiring and something I will never forget. The history is just oozing out of every brick and flagstone you walk on, knowing all the names of past scholars who have long since left their mark on our lives and humanity's history. Names like Charles Darwin, Isaac Newton and of course Stephen Hawking immediately spring to mind. It is the second oldest university in the English-speaking world and the fourth oldest in the world. It was founded in 1209 and granted a royal charter in 1231 by Henry III. It was a beautiful sunny, cloudless sky and we took photos along the way, with Bren looking stunning in the outfit she wore. I am her number one fan, by the way.

As we entered Trinity College Chapel, there is a waiting area before entering the chapel itself and there are large marble statues of previous Cambridge University incumbents like Isaac Newton with many inscriptions to read. I particularly like weddings because everyone is happy, friendly and looking forward to the ritual hand ceremony where they hold hands, appreciating how they will change, grow and mature over the life of their marriage through the actions they take with their hands. We met and said hello to many people before slowly making our way into the chapel. It was a marvellous place for a wedding and there is so much to see but above all the ambience is amazing, almost breath-taking.

We sat and watched as all the guests appeared and walked into the chapel. I think it is a woman's thing where they find it interesting to see the different choices of apparel worn on the day, whereas for men, most wear suits so the range is not so great. Gita arrived and looked a little apprehensive, whereas Mano looked as though he was taking it all in his stride. Sunil, too, seemed to have his father's trait and looked quite relaxed, smiling and joking with his best man. The wedding music started, and the bride appeared, and all eyes focused on Lyndsey who looked a gorgeous bride walking down the aisle with her father at her side.

The ceremony went well and lots of photos were taken. Upon leaving the chapel, all the guests followed and were told to make their way to the grounds of King's College. Being alongside the river, several guests decided to take a punt along the river to the grounds. We approached the place to get a punt but there were about one hundred people looking at the proceedings going on and a few trying to get into the punts. I looked and decided there was no way I could easily get into the punt and sit comfortably coupled with a large audience so decided to walk around to King's College. It was quite a walk for me along the cobbled streets, bustling with tourists but eventually we got there. There was a large, grassed frontage to our next venue, going right down to the river and we found a few seats, then along came drinks and canopies. It was well organised and a lovely summer's day to have a wedding on.

We waited some time there, as guests mingled and walked closer in the grounds to the river, then there was a flurry of excitement because the bride and groom suddenly appeared on the river in their own punt, which made super photos. Slowly, everyone made their way into King's College halls to a beautiful room so well dressed for the occasion, and we were on a large table seating ten guests. We introduced ourselves to those seated by us. I sat next to a charming lady, who it turned out was Mano's sister, so we had quite a chat.

The speeches followed, with joviality and some secrets shared, then the food came with an abundance of wine. Music and mingling followed afterwards, and a good time was had by all. We had thoroughly enjoyed the day and eventually made our way back to the Stephen Hawking building by taxi, where we slept well.

The next day after breakfast, we drove down to the Hilton Hotel on the riverbank and had drinks under the shade of a huge oak tree. It was a relaxing time watching people punt by some with more skill than others judging by the near misses encountered. A large room was hired in the hotel and all the guests joined Sunil and Lindsey for a traditional Tamil Christian blessing ceremony, with Lindsey in her sari. More food and drink followed, with some singing too. It was a wedding to remember, which we will always be grateful for with all those wonderful memories and especially being able to share Sunil and Lindsey's special day.

Chapter 37:
Motorhome Travels

We were using the motorhome quite a lot now and were becoming seasoned campers. There really is quite a lot to learn about camping, locations, and the motorhome itself. The friendliness of most people on sites is tremendous and, of course, you invariably talk when you see fellow campers with their dogs as well.

We were looking after Piper every Friday now to help Jamie and Carla. She is a bright girl and quite funny with a good sense of humour for someone so young, with a beautiful smile. We were slowly being introduced to all the places children of those early years go to in keeping them entertained. One of these is called 'Pirate Pete's' and is a building with a large framework activity centre inside. I do not know how she does it but Bren, being quite flexible and young at heart, keeps pace with Piper in manic running around, up and down levels, through hoops and down slides for over an hour there. I get worn out just watching her and the noise level when many youngsters are all screaming is deafening. The challenge is to keep finding somewhere new to go but this is just what grandparents do.

The motorhome was good fun, which took us on new adventures to places we would otherwise never see or visit and meet some nice people along the way. We had the motorhome nearly two and a half years and we were coming to a decision crossroad. Do we just continue with what we have, do we sell it or buy a new one? The driver for change was the need to make up the bed every night, which only takes about ten minutes, if that, but only Bren can do it. She was struggling a bit due to the ravages of time on her body with her back and some arthritis in her thumb. We tossed the idea around a lot but were undecided. A visit to the Birmingham NEC Camping Exhibition was needed to help us see what was new in the market and perhaps help decide.

Life quickly goes by, so we were trying to pack many things into it. There were many things happening in our family circle, some exciting things and some tragic, but this is what life is about. The good news was Luke and Sharnice had a second boy, called Olly, who was also our second great grandson too with Oakley arriving in 2021 too. Russell had met Jeanette and was head over heels in love, even moving to Hertfordshire to live together so we were happy for them both. The sad and quite tragic events unfolded this year with Phyllis, Vicky's mum.

Phyllis came to see us in July, and Bren was out shopping so we just talked about everyday things for about an hour before Bren came back. She said she had not felt too well and struggled to find food she could eat. The doctors had done tests but had not found anything wrong, but she looked well and was her usual jovial self. She was always a generous person and had brought down to us two kilos of redcurrants she had picked from her garden. When Bren arrived back from shopping, they had a nice chat where she talked about Ryan and Lily before leaving.

About five or six weeks later we had a call to say Phyllis

was in a hospice and the eventual diagnosis was pancreatic cancer, known as the 'silent killer'. The prognosis was days not weeks, so it was shocking news for everyone. We visited her in the hospice where Vicky, Lewis and Rees were, and the site of poor Phyllis compared to six weeks ago was so apparent you knew she was close to leaving this world. Phyllis was a smart woman and knew all too well what was happening to her so the poignant goodbyes as we left her that day were so painful. Phyllis died a couple of days later and we all miss her flamboyant style, her generosity, her joie de vivre and radiant smile. Rest in peace, Phyllis.

Life continues, and I needed to go for repair to my leg at the Enablement Centre. Steve had been my prosthetist for nearly five years and if you pardon the pun, had made great strides in sorting many things out for me. He always listened to me and then we would talk about the dynamics and what he was proposing. It worked well sorting the problems out together. It therefore came as a surprise when he told me he had just handed his notice in, and whilst disappointing for me, I could not help but be happy for him in his new position. The new role was at Ringwood about thirty-five miles west of Portsmouth, where there is a company that deals privately for prosthetic limbs and repairs. Steve was doubling his salary by moving there and I think he had the potential to go far, which would have been impaired if he had stayed at Portsmouth.

When you lose your prosthetist, you lose all the inherent knowledge the person has built up over many years regarding the nuances of your limb. Finding someone new and willing to replace them is quite a challenge. There are few hemipelvectomy patients and the associated issues are often more complex than say, below the knee patients, and not everyone is up for this challenge. Fortunately, the new prosthetist, also called John, is someone I have known for some time and he had drawn the short straw. He is a few years older than me but still working and has a fantastic knowledge of artificial limbs as he was previously a manager at another centre.

John has already looked at things for my leg in a different way, suggesting and implanting some new designs. It is not any more comfortable, but it seems much more durable and for the first time in fifty years I did not need to get my leg repaired every two or three months. In fact, I now have a spare leg at last, which is also quite good to walk on, if ever my favoured leg breaks and I feel quietly confident about that too, which again is a first. I guess you cannot beat all those years of experience and when John, who is already part-time, retires it will be a sad loss for the Enablement Centre and all his many patients, myself included. It is a bit like mindfulness, you must enjoy the moment.

Darren and Anita decided it was time to move home so they had previously built on the side of their house an extension that could later be converted to a separate home. They completed the conversion and had to sell both homes as well as find the house they wanted to move to. It was a stressful time for them but eventually it all came together, and they have moved to a house not far from where they were but backing onto a golf course. The house had a lot of potential and with the help of Anita's dad, Des, they have done some major expansion work, even building a huge cabin at the end of their large garden.

Tayla had done well at school, getting some excellent exam results, and is now in her final year of a Criminology and

Forensic Studies course at Portsmouth University. She is very dedicated and will do well in the future. Kyle had decided to go down the electrician route and hopes to work and combine college with his studies. He has recently had a change of mind and has gone back to college for his A levels to be like his father and get an accountancy degree. An excellent decision, I believe.

The planned trip to the Birmingham NEC camping and caravan exhibition we attended was to prove fruitful. We had done our homework and spent some time looking at the criteria of the motorhome we wanted. If we could not find what we wanted, then we would just sell our motorhome eventually, as there was no rush.

It really is a huge convention, and you are spoilt for choice, but being focused on the make and type of motorhome we wanted made the visit much easier. We still ended up looking over many potential buys, but you know almost immediately if it suits you. I needed an automatic with a rear bed made up and straight away we saw a conversion motorhome that fitted the bill. After some time carefully looking over it with a discerning eye, we were happy with the finish and layout. The salesman could see our interest and was hovering all the while we were looking before pouncing on us. He took our details and said he would ring me in the next hour with a part exchange value for my motorhome.

We moved on to another motorhome made by Adria and straight away it pushed all the buttons, as they say. It was light and airy, had the layout we wanted, was an automatic and although the price was high, we thought, let us see if a deal could be done. Straightaway, they made a reasonably good offer in part exchange and he gave me all the details. We were quite excited by this model and the phone rang from the other salesman we had previously visited, who offered ten thousand pounds less in part exchange than we had just been furnished with for the Adria. They were being greedy, and I told them there was no way I could do business with that offer.

After about four or five hours we both had had enough of looking and made our way back to the car. We had a one hundred and sixty-mile journey to get home but there was a lot to discuss on the way back. Bren was really excited about the Adria and spent ages reading the magazine, browsing over the specification. On the way back, I thought there was more wiggle room to do a deal and get a better part exchange offer. The next day I sent an email expressing our interest and asking for an improved offer on our motorhome to finalise a deal.

It was a long wait to get a reply because they were busy at the exhibition all week, then had to return to their premises and deal with the all the other enquiries. About a week later I had an email making a final offer of another two thousand pounds on the part exchange value. Both parties were happy, and a deal was agreed, subject to them seeing the condition of our motorhome.

We arranged a meeting at the end of February 2020 and travelled to the showrooms near Hereford. We had spent time cleaning the motorhome to sell it, and it was pristine when we arrived for them to view it. It had, after all, only travelled just over six thousand miles. In many ways, like a house, you get attached to the motorhome because of all the happy, funny, sometimes scary moments you have experienced with it, but the thought of a new one was exhilarating too. The salesman made us a drink and then disappeared to look over the motorhome. He was only gone about ten minutes and said he could see how good the condition was so there was no need to look any further. We shook hands on the deal and agreed a delivery of mid-April.

We had taken the dogs with us in the motorhome, which I drove, with Bren driving our other car. We said our goodbyes to the salesman and to the motorhome for the long journey back. Bren was gushing with excitement, but I was thinking, will the new motorhome, which was nearly twelve inches wider than the last one, fit down the driveway with the overhang from the recent side extension to the house. I may need to move the driveway gates and widen the driveway, but these were not insurmountable problems. The only insurmountable problem was the pandemic caused by Covid-19 because it delayed delivery a further five months for our new motorhome!

Chapter 38: Coronavirus

What a wakeup call, the Coronavirus, or Covid-19 was to the world, which affected so many people globally. It changed people's priorities in many things, which perhaps they took for granted and were previously the norm in their lives, but the norm changed. It will go down in history, like the Spanish Flu of 1918 because like then the world was again not very well-prepared for a pandemic of this intensity.

Although official statements by the Chinese government to the World Health Organisation reported that the first confirmed case had been diagnosed on 8 December, the doctors who tried to raise the alarm there with colleagues about a new disease in late December were reprimanded. Authorities did not publicly concede there was human-to-human transmission until 21st January 2020. The spread had therefore started earlier around the world without anyone, but a few in China, knowing.

It was a unique crisis for many countries around the world and those who did track and trace early with the virus performed well in controlling the spread. This worldwide pandemic has claimed the lives of millions globally. Here in the UK, with the measures we took, we could have done better but that is always easy to say in hindsight. The lockdown measures started on 23rd March and a worldwide race for the vaccine began. Companies were helped by the Government to furlough their staff as an option to keep them on their payroll, but this cannot go on forever and there will be widespread redundancies, I fear. The self-employed were also helped but there were a lot of people wondering what the future held for them.

In the current climate, Bren and I are still self-isolating nearly a year later. When allowed, we see the family and try hard to maintain the recommended two-metre distancing rule when meeting outside. It is so strange especially for the grandchildren who just want a hug and to play. There is a whole array of vulnerable people whom the Government have told to self-isolate and those over seventy years old fall into the category too. I have hardly gone out except on the odd occasion to take Bren somewhere to walk the dogs and then I have stayed in the car. Bren has been walking the dogs, visited the odd shop but she is very mindful and careful when venturing out. She sanitises her hands in the car and washes them thoroughly indoors when returning from a trip outside. We have been through the range of levels through to total lockdown and were pleased, almost relieved, for me to have my first Covid vaccine injection in January with Bren in February 2021

We have the usual 'Covidiots' as they now call them, who seem to think they are immortal and many do not have a clue whether they may or may not catch the virus, spreading it to their loved ones. The new norm is in a stage of metamorphosis where nobody knows what the future will hold. As the vaccinations increase, the pandemic will ease, and we will find people have short memories. They will want things to return quickly back as they were, but this thinking caused a second wave of infections, as the strain mutated. Both of us would like to think the pandemic has given many, not all, a new perspective on what is important in life. I know when I was faced with dying at sixteen, you afterwards appreciate so much you have previously taken for granted. Your health is a priority, followed closely by family because you need your health to support your family. Other material things just fall by the wayside and maybe some will step back and think more rationally and be more appreciative of life and their loved ones.

One of the good things to emerge from the pandemic was the ecological improvement. Very few cars on the road, very few planes in the sky, no cruise liners and so on meant the atmosphere was a lot cleaner, the seas a lot clearer and the whole world a lot quieter. Living in a city, there is always a background hum of noise from people or traffic but going out to the garden at night was somewhat surreal. It was so quiet, unlike I had experienced in the city before, where you seemed to be in the middle of the countryside. It was lovely for a short while, until cars and people began moving again. With the second spike of the virus and shutdown, the amount of traffic on the road certainly increased from the previous shutdown. I believe there was an element of complacency by many.

From a family perspective, the pandemic shutdown meant many were working from home, not everyone though, because there were a few scares to begin with. Luke, my eldest grandson works at a large supermarket and was on nightshift at the very start of the Coronavirus outbreak. In the early hours of the morning he was coughing, had a high temperature and difficulty breathing. An ambulance was called, and they managed to stabilise him and said he had all the symptoms of the virus and should go home and self-isolate for fourteen days. It affected his whole family because Sharnice could not work and their son, Oscar, was taken out of school to avoid infecting anyone else. We were all concerned because none of us knew, in those early days, enough to understand the full implications. Fortunately, within a week he recovered but it did have quite an impact on him. It was a shame too for Matthew, his brother, who had the offer of a job and was just about to start when the lockdown happened.

As the number of those infected or dying decreases, the Government is slowly loosening the reins of lockdown but for some it is never quick enough. Now the reins are tightened as the second wave takes hold and infections and deaths are higher than the first wave. Time will tell when all the analysis is done around the world on this virus, and the real truth filters through. I do not believe what is currently being reported globally and how bad things have been. There is a lot of information suppressed by certain governments to make them look more in control than they may otherwise be shown to be.

We had a holiday booked in April 2020 to go to Lanzarote with Arthur, Lyn, Margaret, and Jeff but the virus put paid to that. I was trying to get a refund from the holiday company, but they made it so difficult to get and so protracted. I paid by credit card through my bank and raised a dispute with them to recover the money, which is several thousand pounds and now have been paid back. Again, the impact is catastrophic on holiday companies and they are trying to protect their cash flow, which is 'king' in the current climate. It is just the customer who suffers in this instance and many are in the same boat as me.

Life was still going on even in these dark days and Russell

and Jeanette had visited us in November of 2020 and announced they had become engaged, with a wedding planned for June 2021. We were pleased to see them so happy but unfortunately only two months later we had a call to say they were splitting up. The only consolation to be drawn from this is that it is better to find out they were not compatible before marrying, and thank goodness there were no children involved. Russell decided to move back home with us temporarily to take stock and evaluate the future path he will travel. After nearly a year with us Russell has met Hilary, a lovely girl you easily get to like, and she has given back to Russell the joie de vivre.

One blessing for me has been the good work John did on my artificial leg because I did not have a problem with my leg for a year. In the fifty-three years of having repairs on my leg, I have never gone this long, so it demonstrates a big improvement for me and the great work John and Danny, who is the workshop manager, have done. I recently met with John and requested a new leg be made, as my 'spare' leg is not quite right. The reason being, I want to use John's expertise in making the new one as his knowledge and ability is second to none.

Jamie phoned me in February 2021 to say he felt unwell and was going to the doctors. He never went because he felt so unwell and it was decided he should take a Covid test, which proved positive. He and his family had to self-isolate for ten days. Difficult time especially with our latest grandson Otis, who was born in December 2020. A much-welcomed addition for Jamie, Carla and Piper making their family complete. Fortunately, Jamie recovered very quickly but it is a stark reminder of how quickly the impact of Covid can happen.

A year later than Jamie I along with Brenda caught Covid too as I guess most people will soon. It's the new flu which will probably evolve each year. Nothing stays still for long and with Russia invading Ukraine we face a cold war yet again. Peace, it seems is a fragile commodity in the world nowadays.

What legacy Coronavirus leaves behind for everyone will be written in history with analysis going on for many years to come. If any good can come out of all the deaths from this dreadful virus it will hopefully make people more appreciative of their family, their home and their surroundings. I hope they enjoy these simple pleasures and see how wonderful the world can be. We all take things for granted but in better times, how often do we stop, step back and take a moment to think just how lucky we are to have our health and family to enjoy. So many people have lost their loved ones and I hope the lessons learned from this pandemic will help us be better prepared and universally more open throughout the world when the next one strikes, which is somberly inevitable.

Chapter 39:
A Long Walk Through Life

As I look back on more than fifty years of walking with an artificial leg, I always think of the Yin and Yang, the good and the bad side of it because there are many of both. Throughout everyone's life there are many crossroads or decision points which dictate the path you follow. We all know the path we have chosen because we are living it, but if we chose something different, at those points in time, we all wonder where life would have taken us. Good decisions, not so good decisions and bad decisions make up life because it is all about the choices we make.

In many ways I have been quite fortunate and remained positive about life's cards I have been dealt. I was brought up in a loving family who gave me a good upbringing with a social conscience. I, like my siblings, had a close relationship with my parents for well over sixty years where they gave us so much love, fun and laughter even though there was not a lot of money, and at times they struggled bringing up a post-war young family. They had good values, being both kind and helpful to many throughout their lives. There were many simple acts I noticed and recall, which I believe over the formative years helped all their children to live good, meaningful lives and be respectful of others.

During those early days when both of my parents had

suffered the hardships of the war, I recall some of my dad's kind deeds, like always inviting the milkman in for a cup of tea on a Sunday morning. On cold winter days, I am sure he was incredibly grateful. I remember Dad having an allotment and smiling away he would give neighbours some vegetables he had grown as he arrived home from there on his bike. A friend of his had a flat near Fratton Park, where Portsmouth Football Club played, and he said we could use his allotted parking space on match days. I remember Dad knocking his door on the way to the match with a dozen runner beans wrapped up in newspaper. His friend was so grateful for the simple act of kindness it really struck a chord with me too. Small, simple acts of kindness can have a huge impact.

Mum gave so much time to the Salvation Army too. She played the piano and organ there and at various times of her life also looked after the Songsters and Singing Company. When the Sale of Work came around, there was Mum, always baking cakes and pies for the occasion. At the Army, her apple pies were legendary, always selling out quickly.

Mum and Dad also fostered three girls at different times from troubled backgrounds during my childhood, giving them stability and love, which was somewhat missing in their lives. All these things help you as an individual to build your own character knowing right from wrong and helping people along life's road. Arthur and Margaret both have the same ethos on life, and we have our parents to thank for that.

I did some things I regret when I was young, nothing too outrageous, just a bit anti-social but boys will be boys. I did always have a conscience about it though but looking back it was part of growing up in that era. I mentioned earlier about crossroads in your life, some of which you control by decisions you make, but some by events you cannot control. The one major life-changing event for me, which I had no control over, was having my leg amputated as a sixteen-year-old. In many ways, it has curtailed me and affected the decisions taken throughout my life, reflecting the impact and the limitations it has given me.

Having a good sense of humour, sometimes dark, has really helped throughout my life but some people do not realise their humour can still hurt depending on how you tell it. I have heard many jokes about my leg with some being quite funny. A few people think it is the first time I have heard it as I politely laugh but in reality, I have not heard a novel joke about my leg for about twenty or so years. I have always said I have one foot in the grave and when asked how much a prosthetic leg would cost, I of course reply 'an arm and a leg'. A recent one I heard was 'why are prosthetic limbs so in fashion… because anyone can pull them off.'

One aspect that continues to be a problem and is getting worse is the control of pain. Walking for me is painful and the further I walk, the more pain I get, which may be immediate or deferred pain a few hours or days later. Walking in a hot climate proves to be problematical because of the sweating and rubbing from wearing the artificial leg so it is always a measure I must make at the time what I can or think I can do. If I walk too far, I get a thumping headache caused by blood pressure. When I was young, I tried to continue walking through the headache, but it was a bad mistake never to be repeated.

After walking, and in most cases, once the pain starts, I have to decide what pain relief tablets to take. If it is not too bad then a couple of paracetamols will suffice, if it is more painful, I add an ibuprofen. This works about fifty per cent. of the time and when it does not ease the pain, I need to decide on alternatives. The pain itself can just be through soreness but what can really hurt are the phantom pains. These nerve pains can be horrendous and come in waves of about a minute at a time, lasting for just a few seconds, but they are bad and relentless. These can last anywhere between six hours to five days and affect your sleep pattern, which is quite debilitating. In these cases, I take co-proxamol, but you can only take a maximum of eight a day. This does not always get rid of the pain but works about seventy per cent. of the time. When you are in constantly bad pain, you do get desperate, and I have recently been prescribed some liquid morphine, but surprisingly enough this has not been too effective either so maybe I need to up the dosage I take. It is a judgement call every time and I really dislike taking tablets regularly so sometimes I get it wrong in taking the tablets too late. Pain management is just difficult.

I have creams to apply to my skin when it gets cut and a few years ago one of the prosthetists, called Steve, gave me a tube of gel that he uses for cycling. You apply this over the affected area to form a thin film to ease the friction of rubbing. It did not work for me, but I will always try anything new on the market if it can possibly help. As a last resort I do not wear my leg to allow some healing to happen, but I really do not like doing that because I cannot sit comfortably in a chair and it's embarrassing for me when unexpected visitors arrive. It is challenging at times but eventually, the pain starts to go, and the sleep afterwards is blissful because you are shattered from sleep deprivation.

I have throughout my life taken personal pride in my

appearance and tried hard to fully accept how my disability looks to others. I do not like seeing my reflection in a window, seeing myself walking or being pushed in a wheelchair, seeing myself riding my mobility scooter and do not particularly like going up or down stairs around people. I cringed somewhat when I saw my wedding video of Bren and myself walking down the church aisle as all these things remind me too much of my disability. Although I accept that I am disabled, I can honestly say after fifty-odd years I would rather it was not visible. Is it a hang up? 'Yes!' Is it not fully embracing your disability? 'Yes!' This is me though being honest and sharing my intimate thoughts and something not often written about.

From a health perspective. I have been quite fortunate throughout my life with just the one major blip at sixteen. One of the problems with ageing is your skin thins out and your recovery powers reduce so the aches and pains take longer to go. With some arthritis in my hands and hip, the pain does not always go but remains. My knee has been scraped once and bears the brunt of my walking or hopping so I hope I do not need a knee or even a hip replacement later. My back aches quite a bit nowadays from wearing the leg and hurts if I walk a distance or stand for longer than twenty minutes or so but this is a small price to pay for all those extra years in my life span. I have been most fortunate indeed.

When I look at my life and the inherent prejudices around those early years of losing my leg, the lack of emotional and financial support in living a meaningful life compared with now, there have been great strides moving forward. This is a good thing and the Paralympics have really helped educate people on all kinds of disabilities as well as see how individuals are still performing to their absolute best, despite their limitations.

For me, there have been many lessons learned and as I live my life, I continue to learn with my glass always half full not half empty. Through my experiences, I do have empathy for many where fate has perhaps dealt them consequences less fair than others. I have tried to help other amputees or those having to face it through counselling over the years whenever asked. I also did some time at the Samaritans and I hope I have helped a few people along the way.

I always remembered when I was working, to have people around me with the right 'can do' attitude. It is too easy to say 'I cannot do this or that' but finding a way through issues, either at work or throughout your life, can be quite a rewarding thing.

I have been fortunate in having two loves in my life, firstly Ann then Brenda. Despite marrying Ann so young and learning much about each other as you are still growing up, we were blessed with three children. All of them different but all of them loved, and the sadness of losing Ann, a wife and mother so young still hurts all of us to this day. I never thought I would marry again but when I first set eyes on Brenda, I had something to look forward to rather than looking back on all the sadness. Bren has brought so much love, fun and laughter into my life, it must have been heaven-sent. She is a special, special lady and I have been fortunate to have her in my life for almost the same time I knew Ann.

Looking back, there are many things I would change, like not getting married at twenty, but life is about choices and I made mine, had a good life and did the best I could. I have never felt self-pity or asked for sympathy because I just did the best with what I had. Lessons in life continue for the whole of it and if I could do anything different about my disability, it would be to fully embrace it because it is with you forever.

Acceptance is an easy word to say but the disabling realities for me have not been easy, and I wish I could have accepted my disability one hundred percent. I do though have inner satisfaction knowing I have given my best. I can reconcile that because each of us is an individual and no one knows how any of us will react to a major upheaval in one's life. I would say, 'Do not worry how you are judged, just know deep down you did your best and embrace every day you have left because none of us knows how many we have left.'

A life in the biblical sense is three scores and ten, which I have now passed. Life does ebb quickly, but it is the same for everyone, which is why you sometimes need to get out of your comfort zone occasionally to push yourself into doing something different. It is quite ironic because most people do not like change and enjoy the comfort they are in, but if life is about change then perhaps, we should embrace it to get a more fulfilled life.

I look forward to my years ahead with Bren, the motorhome, the dogs, and the new places and people to discover. It is lovely to see the family grow, taking their different paths in life, sharing their achievements, their happiness and being there when needed. I have Bren to thank so much for the love she has given me, the fun, laughter and exciting times we have had, and of course, for all those things to come. As we both grow older, the toll on the body becomes ever apparent but with the right attitude, we will do what we can together, knowing how precious every single day is.

Bren and I often remind each other about the Cherokee Prayer read out at our wedding, the last sentence being 'With all the forces of the universe you created, we pray for harmony and true happiness as we forever grow young together. Amen'.

John was born and bred in Portsmouth, the city he loves and apart from four years living ten miles away, has lived all his life within its boundaries, where his ancestry goes back hundreds of years.

He has spoken openly about how his disability has not been fully embraced by him during his life and has written honestly about the difficulties of acceptance. Whether it was the young age of losing his leg, when you are more concerned about what your peers think, or just a part of him which will not change, he cannot fathom out. It may have been sampling life able-bodied rather than being born with a disability. He has not just written about some of his achievements but has been incredibly open with his emotions, which are rarely mentioned, much less written about. He would like to think it may help others in similar situations as his or give food for thought.

He was educated at the Portsmouth Northern Grammar School for Boys during which time the progressive problems he had endured for around five years resulted in him having the whole of his right leg amputated at the age of sixteen because of cancer.

Returning to work after nearly ten months as a draughtsman, he continued his education on a day release and evening course basis for the next eight years. Changing his job after four years he built up a general knowledge of electronic circuit design, heating, ventilating and air conditioning and a manufacturing environment getting 'Engineer' status. It was with this background he started work for John Brown Engineering as a planning engineer working on international construction projects for the pharmaceutical and chemical industries.

John married Ann in 1970 at the age of twenty after a whirlwind romance lasting fifteen months. Six years later they had their first child Donna, followed by Darren then Jamie. It was a busy time in his life balancing the demands of three young children with the demands of a job, which required some time to be spent away from home as his career progressed.

There were many times, because of his own experiences, when he was asked by the Enablement Centre to give counselling to others who had or were about to experience similar difficulties through losing a leg as high as John had. Later he would also use these skills he developed to work for the Samaritans.

In 1987, Ann was diagnosed with breast cancer and the awful journey of its progression has given him empathy for those on similar paths, not just those associated with amputation of a limb. Eventually losing Ann in 1995, with three children trying to be both a mum and dad, he went through a dark time in his life until he met Brenda whom he married six years later. Brenda has been incredibly supportive and their strong love for each other endures to this day.

John's career continued with the same company for twenty-seven years, rising to general manager project controls, after which he went freelance. He formed his own company and started working in the railway industry for Westinghouse before moving to the nuclear industry working for British Energy, heading up their project controls department.

The next career move was joining Jacobs Engineering in a staff position as head of project services in Reading. This job entailed some travel internally in the UK and overseas before his final freelance position as project controls consultant at

AWE in Aldermaston, after which he retired.

There have been numerous incidents over the past fifty-odd years since losing his leg, which have given rise to some merriment, some difficult times, some funny and sad times but throughout his life John has always remained positive with a 'can do' attitude.

John still lives in Portsmouth, close to his family, close to the Enablement Centre and of course close to Portsmouth Football Club at Fratton Park.

He looks forward to what lies ahead, the adventures to come with what life throws his way and the experiences still awaiting him with his beloved Brenda as they grow young together.

Finally, if he has missed anyone who has travelled along his life's journey, influenced, or helped him and he has not included you then he can only apologise and thank you for your contribution to his full and enjoyable life.

Printed in Great Britain
by Amazon